ASVAB

ARMED SERVICES VOCATIONAL APTITUDE BATTERY STUDY GUIDE

By: Sharon Wynne, M.S.

XAMonline, INC.
Boston

To obtain permission(s) to use the material from this work for any purpose including workshops or seminars, please submit a written request to:

XAMonline, Inc.
25 First Street, Suite 106
Cambridge, MA 02141
Toll Free 1-800-509-4128
Email: ASVABinfo@xamonline.com
Web: www.ASVABexamStudyGuide.com
Fax: 1-617-583-5552

Library of Congress Cataloging-in-Publication Data

Wynne, Sharon A.
    ASVAB Armed Services Vocational Aptitude Battery Study Guide /
    Sharon A. Wynne. – 1st
    ISBN 978-1-60787-107-1
    1. ASVAB
    2. AFQT
    3. Study Guide
    4. Military
    5. Careers

Printed in the United States of America   œ-1

ASVAB Armed Services Vocational Aptitude Battery Study Guide
ISBN: 978-1-60787-107-1

Cover photo by David Furst/AFP.

Table of Contents

CHAPTER 4
MATHEMATICS KNOWLEDGE

CHAPTER 5
GENERAL SCIENCE

CHAPTER 6
MECHANICAL COMPREHENSION

CHAPTER 7
ELECTRONICS INFORMATION

CHAPTER 8
SHOP INFORMATION

CHAPTER 9
AUTO INFORMATION

CHAPTER 10
ASSEMBLING OBJECTS

SAMPLE TEST

ASVAB

ARMED SERVICES VOCATIONAL APTITUDE BATTERY

Available online:

 More Sample Tests: more ways to assess how much you know and how much further you need to study. Ultimately, makes you more prepared for all 10 subtests on the ASVAB.

Visit www.ASVABexamStudyGuide.com

WHAT IS THE ASVAB?

The Armed Services Vocational Aptitude Battery (ASVAB) is an aptitude test developed by the Department of Defense. The ASVAB determines whether you are qualified to join the military and which civilian and military occupations might be a good fit for you.

The ASVAB assesses your strengths and weaknesses in a wide range of areas—from math and vocabulary to automotive maintenance and electrical circuits. It is a timed multiple-choice test made up of the following ten subtests, each of which covers a different subject area:

- Word Knowledge
- Paragraph Comprehension
- Arithmetic Reasoning
- Mathematics Knowledge
- General Science
- Mechanical Comprehension
- Electronics Information
- Shop Information*
- Auto Information*
- Assembling Objects

   * In the paper-and-pencil version the ASVAB, Shop Information and Auto Information are combined into one subtest.

Information about the ASVAB is subject to change, so please speak to a recruiter for the most up-to-date information on any aspect of the test.

What Is an AFQT Score? Why Is It important?

Your Armed Forces Qualification Test (AFQT) score is critical if you desire to join the military. You must have a minimum qualifying score in order to enlist.

Your AFQT score is computed using four of the ten subtests:

- Word Knowledge
- Paragraph Comprehension
- Arithmetic Reasoning
- Mathematics Knowledge

AFQT scores are given as a percentile. For instance, if your score is 65 it means that you scored as well as or better than 65% of a nationally representative group of people who took the test.

Different service branches require different AFQT scores. Contact your local recruiter to learn the current minimum qualifying scores.

Why Is the ASVAB Score Important?

Composite scores from all of the subtests of the ASVAB help match new recruits to military occupations. Contact your local recruiter to learn which subtests are most important for specific military jobs.

Versions of the ASVAB

There are two versions of the ASVAB used for military enlistment: the CAT-ASVAB, which is taken on a computer, and the Paper and Pencil ASVAB (P&P-ASVAB).

Both versions cover the same subjects. However, the Paper and Pencil ASVAB combines Shop Information and Auto Information into one subtest.

CAT-ASVAB

Today, most people who want to enlist in the military take the CAT-ASVAB. CAT is short for computer adaptive testing.

You must take the CAT-ASVAB at a Military Entrance Processing Station (MEPS). Although you take the CAT-ASVAB on a computer, no computer experience is necessary. Everyone who takes the test receives training on all basic keyboard or mouse skills needed to take the test.

When you take the CAT-ASVAB, your answers are automatically recorded, your subtests are scored, and your AFQT score is computed. You will receive your scores as soon as you complete the test.

The CAT-ASVAB is made up of ten subtests, described in this table:

CAT-ASVAB			
Subtest	Questions	Minutes	Topics
Word Knowledge	16	8	Vocabulary knowledge, synonyms, and antonyms
Paragraph Comprehension	11	22	Reading comprehension, obtaining information from written passages
Arithmetic Reasoning	16	39	Solving word problems
Mathematics Knowledge	16	20	Mathematical concepts, algebra, and geometry
General Science	16	8	Biology, physics, chemistry, and earth and space science
Mechanical Comprehension	16	20	Principles of mechanics and mechanical devices
Electronics Information	16	8	Electrical current, circuits, and devices
Shop Information	11	6	Wood and metal shop tools and practices
Auto Information	11	7	Automotive knowledge, maintenance, and repair
Assembling Objects	16	16	Assembling parts into objects and connecting labeled parts
Total	145	154	

The CAT-ASVAB is an adaptive test, which means that the difficulty of the questions changes depending on how well you are doing. If you answer a question correctly, the next question will usually be more difficult. If you answer a question incorrectly, the next question will usually be easier. This way, you do not spend your time answering questions that are far too easy or too difficult for you. CAT-ASVAB scores are based not only on whether your answers are correct, but also on how difficult the questions are.

Unlike on the Paper and Pencil ASVAB, you cannot go back and change an answer on the CAT-ASVAB. However, the CAT-ASVAB allows you to go on to the next subtest if you finish a subtest early, and you can leave the room when you complete the entire test.

Paper and Pencil ASVAB

The Paper and Pencil ASVAB, which you may take in lieu of the CAT-ASVAB, is a test that you take on paper at a Mobile Examination Test site. The P&P-ASVAB is made up of nine subtests, described in this table:

P&P-ASVAB			
Subtest	Questions	Minutes	Topics
Word Knowledge	35	11	Vocabulary knowledge, synonyms, and antonyms
Paragraph Comprehension	15	13	Reading comprehension, obtaining information from written passages
Arithmetic Reasoning	30	36	Solving word problems
Mathematics Knowledge	25	24	Mathematical concepts, algebra, and geometry
General Science	25	11	Biology, physics, chemistry, and earth and space science
Mechanical Comprehension	25	19	Principles of mechanics and mechanical devices
Electronics Information	20	9	Electrical current, circuits, and devices
Auto and Shop Information	25	11	Automotive knowledge, maintenance, and repair; wood and metal shop tools and practices
Assembling Objects	25	15	Assembling parts into objects and connecting labeled parts
Total	225	149	

When you take the P&P-ASVAB, you write your answers on an answer sheet. You have a certain amount of time to finish each subtest. Within that time, you can go back and change an answer. However, you cannot go back to a previous subtest. You also cannot begin the next subtest until the test administer instructs you to.

After you have taken the test, your P&P-ASVAB answer sheet is sent to a MEPS. Your recruiter will let you know when your scores are available. It usually takes a few days for your test to be scored.

ASVAB Career Exploration Program for students

High school and college students can take the ASVAB as part of the ASVAB Career Exploration Program. The ASVAB helps students learn more about which careers might be a good match for their knowledge, skills, and abilities.

Students who take advantage of this program take the Paper and Pencil ASVAB. The Assembling Objects subtest is not included in this version given to students.

While this version of the ASVAB is used primarily for career exploration, you are also able to use your score to enlist in the military for up to two years.

CHAPTER 1
WORD KNOWLEDGE

The Word Knowledge subtest of the ASVAB is about one thing only—knowing the meaning of words. You will be given a word and then asked to select the word that has the same meaning as that word. Alternately, you will be given a word and then asked to select the word that has the opposite meaning of that word.

The Word Knowledge subtest of the ASVAB is about one thing only—knowing the meaning of words.

ASVAB tip!
The Armed Forces Qualification Test (AFQT) score is computed using four subtests, including the Word Knowledge subtest. Your AFQT score is critical because you must have a minimum qualifying score in order to enlist.

Understanding Synonyms

SYNONYMS are words that have the same or nearly the same meaning. For example, the pairs of words below are synonyms:

SYNONYMS: words that have the same or nearly the same meaning

car—automobile	huge—gigantic	unclear—vague
cry—weep	destruction—devastation	envoy—agent
poke—jab	excitement—thrill	expansive—broad
construct—assemble	under—beneath	competition—match

Often, synonyms can be used interchangeably. You could say that the instructions were *unclear* or *vague*. A movie made her *cry* or *weep*. The children loved the *excitement* or *thrill* of the fireworks.

Below are more examples of synonym pairs:

credible—plausible	temporary—interim	catapult—launch
doleful—sorrowful	wet—moist	traverse—cross
ghastly—dreadful	accomplice—partner in crime	couch—sofa
cynical—pessimistic	gloomy—bleak	aversion—distaste
beautiful—attractive	depart—exit	perfection—excellence

A running list of synonyms
Start your own list of synonyms now. As you learn the meanings of new words, add them to the list.

In test questions about synonyms, you will be asked to choose the word with the meaning that is closest to that of the tested word. Four possible answer choices will follow. Read all the answer choices carefully. Let's try one together.

Example
Affluent most nearly means:
  A. painful
  B. wealthy
  C. pensive
  D. native

Which answer choice could be used interchangeably with affluent? The answer is B, wealthy. *Affluent* and *wealthy* mean nearly the same thing.

Synonyms galore
A thesaurus is a reference book containing lists of synonyms. If you look up the word *energetic*, you might find the following words: dynamic, lively, peppy, robust, tireless, and vigorous. You can also find synonyms in many dictionaries at the end of the word's entry.

Now you can try some.

Practice Test Questions

1. **Defeat** most nearly means:
   A. Consider
   B. Devote
   C. Overcome
   D. Glare

2. **Hazard** most nearly means:
   A. Duty
   B. Risk
   C. Occupation
   D. Chamber

3. **Meddle** most nearly means:
   A. Interfere
   B. Reflect
   C. Merge
   D. Communicate

Answer Key

1. **C. Overcome**

   The word *overcome* has nearly the same meaning as the word *defeat*. They both mean *to win a victory over.*

2. **B. Risk**

   The word *risk* has nearly the same meaning to the word *hazard*. They both mean *something that can cause harm.*

3. **A. Interfere**

   The word *interfere* has nearly the same meaning as the word *meddle*. They both mean *to take part in someone's business without being asked.*

In other test questions, a word will be used in a sentence, and you will be asked to choose the synonym. If you don't know the answer, try substituting each answer choice for the word in the original sentence to see which answer choice has the same meaning.

For your convenience, the practice test questions also appear at the end of the book so you can sit down and go through them all at once.

The best study tool!

Each time you come across a new word, write it on an index card and write the meaning on the back. These will be your study flashcards. Create flashcards for words you see in this study guide (in this chapter and in all of the other chapters!), words you hear on the news, words you read in magazines—anywhere you see new words. Have friends or family members quiz you—or quiz yourself!

If you don't know the answer, try substituting each answer choice for the word in the original sentence to see which answer choice has the same meaning.

Example

Choose the word that has nearly the same meaning as the underlined word.

Sue will <u>endeavor</u> to teach her children patience.
   A. strive
   B. run
   C. fail
   D. allow

Which answer choice has nearly the same meaning as *endeavor*? Try substituting each answer choice in the original sentence. If the sentence doesn't make sense, you can eliminate that answer choice. ("Sue will *run* to teach her children patience?") The answer is A, *strive*. *Endeavor* and *strive* mean nearly the same thing. They both mean *to devote serious effort.*

ASVAB tip!
The CAT-ASVAB is the version of the ASVAB that is taken on a computer. It is an adaptive test, which means that the difficulty of the questions changes depending on how well you are doing.

Now you try some. Read the sentence and answer choices carefully.

Practice Test Questions

Choose the word that has nearly the same meaning as the underlined word.

1. Rainy days make me feel <u>languid</u>.

   A. Ill

   B. Lazy

   C. Lonely

   D. Isolated

2. Young children are known for their <u>incessant</u> questions.

   A. Loud

   B. Nosy

   C. Endless

   D. Thoughtful

3. In the end, the accused was <u>vindicated</u>.

   A. Charged

   B. Condemned

   C. Apologetic

   D. Acquitted

Answer Key

1. **B. Lazy**

   The word *languid* means *sluggish* or *without energy*. The word that has nearly the same meaning as *languid* is *lazy*.

2. **C. Endless**

   The word *incessant* means *never ending* or *going on for a long time*. The word that has nearly the same meaning as *incessant* is *endless*.

3. **D. Acquitted**

   The word *vindicated* means *to be cleared from accusation or wrongdoing*. The word that has nearly the same meaning as *vindicated* is *acquitted*.

Look it up!
This study guide is a great source of new vocabulary. If you don't know the meaning of any word in any of the examples or practice test questions, look it up in the dictionary, and remember to create a flashcard for each new word that you learn.

Understanding Antonyms

ANTONYMS are words that have opposite meanings. For example, the pairs of words below are antonyms, or opposites:

ANTONYMS: words that have opposite meanings

delay—rush	pursue—abandon	straight—crooked
public—private	assurance—doubt	escalate—lessen
lackluster—shiny	identical—dissimilar	unrelated—kindred
genuine—counterfeit	climb—decline	clamorous—hushed
humane—cruel	prominent—unknown	irreverent—respectful
laborious—easy	mistreat—coddle	natural—synthetic

In test questions about antonyms, you will be asked to choose the word that is the most opposite in meaning to the tested word. Let's try one together.

Example

The word most opposite in meaning to <u>stormy</u> is:

A. unruly

B. weathered

C. brief

D. calm

Which answer choice is the opposite of *stormy*? Think of a *stormy* relationship. Which answer choice is the most opposite in meaning? The answer is D, *calm*. *Stormy* means *marked by turmoil*. The word that is the opposite of *stormy* is *calm*.

Shuffling the deck

Review the vocabulary flashcards you created yesterday before learning new words today. Every few days, try shuffling the flashcards, and quiz yourself on the first 20 or 25 words.

Practice Test Questions

1. The word most opposite in meaning to <u>stifle</u> is:

   A. Guide

   B. Adjust

   C. Smother

   D. Encourage

2. The word most opposite in meaning to <u>condone</u> is:

   A. Pardon

   B. Rotate

   C. Disapprove

   D. Prevail

3. The word most opposite in meaning to <u>reprimand</u> is:

   A. Chatter

   B. Praise

   C. Scold

   D. Postpone

4. The word most opposite in meaning to <u>spontaneous</u> is:

   A. Deliberate

   B. Impulsive

   C. Magnificent

   D. Confined

5. The word most opposite in meaning to <u>proponent</u> is:

   A. Adversary

   B. Witness

   C. Dependent

   D. Supporter

Answer Key

1. **D. Encourage**

   To *stifle* means *to quell* or *to end by force; to smother*. The opposite of *stifle* is *encourage*.

2. **C. Disapprove**

   To *condone* means *to pardon or overlook*. The opposite of *condone* is *disapprove*.

3. **B. Praise**

   To *reprimand* means *to scold or find fault with*. The opposite of *reprimand* is *praise*.

4. **A. Deliberate**

   Spontaneous means *not planned or thought out in advance*. The opposite of *spontaneous* is *deliberate*.

5. **A. Adversary**

   A *proponent* is *a person who supports a cause or a belief*. The opposite of *proponent* is *adversary*.

Think "opposite"

Be careful when answering questions that ask for a word that is the opposite. It is easy to choose a word that is a synonym by accident. Keep the word *opposite* in your mind as you examine each answer choice. When you think you have the correct answer, ask yourself, "Is this word the opposite of the tested word?"

Using Root Words

The key to expanding your vocabulary is learning WORD ANALYSIS: examining word parts for clues to a word's meaning. A ROOT WORD is a word part to which a prefix, suffix, or another word part must be added. A root cannot stand alone.

> **WORD ANALYSIS:** examining word parts for clues to a word's meaning

> **ROOT WORD:** a word part to which a prefix, suffix, or another word part must be added

Roots are the key

If you do only one thing to prepare for the Word Knowledge subtest, learn roots. Knowing roots allows you to figure out the meaning of many words you don't know.

Example

The word *dermatology* includes two root words: *derma* and *logy*.

Each root has a meaning, but neither of the roots can stand alone. Together, they make up a word.

Derma means *skin*.

logy means *study of*.

Dermatology is *the science or study of skin and skin diseases*.

Example

The word *incredulous* is made up of the prefix *in-*, the root word *cred*, and the suffix *-ous*.

The prefix *in-* means *not*.

The root *cred* means *believe*.

The suffix *-ous* means *full of*.

Incredulous means *not believable; unbelieving*.

ASVAB tip!

On the CAT-ASVAB, the Word Knowledge subtest is 8 minutes long and has 16 questions.

Many of the roots used in our words today originated in Latin and Greek. Begin by learning the Greek and Latin roots below.

GREEK ROOTS		
Root	**Meaning**	**Example**
anthrop	human	anthropology, misanthropy
auto	self, alone	automobile, automatic, autonomous
bibl	book	bibliography, bibliophile
chron	time	chronology, chronicle
gen	birth, race	generation, genetics
graph	write	paragraph, autograph
ortho	straight, correct	orthodontist, orthography, orthopedist
phobia	fear	claustrophobia, acrophobia
therm	heat	thermometer, thermal, thermos

Know your roots

In addition to creating flashcards for new words, create them for new roots. Write the root on the front of the index card. On the back, write the meaning, along with two or three words that contain the root.

LATIN ROOTS		
Root	**Meaning**	**Example**
capt	take, hold, seize	capture, captivating
cede, ceed, cess	go, give way, yield	recession, proceed, exceed, recede
duc, duct	lead	conductor, induce, deduction
dys	abnormal, bad	dyspepsia, dyslexia, dystopia
ject	throw, hurl	eject, inject
port	carry	porter, portable

Continued on next page

spec, spic	look, see	spectacle, conspicuous
voc, vok	call	vocation, invoke
vor, vour	eat	carnivorous, devour

Searching for your roots...

This study guide lists common root words, but there are many, many more. To learn more root words, use an Internet search engine. Search for *root words* and you'll get hundreds of thousands of hits!

To practice using root words, try these test questions.

Practice Test Questions

1. **Recede** means:

   A. Carry

   B. Retreat

   C. Seize

   D. Throw

2. **Voracious** means:

   A. Willing

   B. Confused

   C. Hungry

   D. Exhausted

3. **Introspection** means:

   A. Self-examination

   B. Standard

   C. Cumbersome

   D. Go-between

4. **Dysfunctional** means:

   A. Old-fashioned

   B. Extreme

   C. Broken

   D. Appropriate

5. **Genocide** means:

   A. The killing of an entire species of animals

   B. The killing of a cultural, national, or racial group

   C. The killing of an entire group of mammals

   D. The killing of a species of plant

Answer Key

1. **B. Retreat**

   Recede contains the root *cede*, meaning *go, give way,* or *yield.* Answer choice B, *retreat,* is another way of saying *to give way* or *to yield.* The root provides a clue to the correct answer. The definition of *recede* is *to move away from; retreat; withdraw.*

2. **C. Hungry**

   Voracious contains the root word *vor,* meaning *eat.* Answer choice C, *hungry,* is related to eating. The root word provides a clue to the correct answer. The definition of *voracious* is *craving or consuming large amounts of food* or *exceedingly eager.*

3. **A. Self-examination**

   Introspection contains the root word *spec,* meaning *to look or see.* The definition of *introspection* is *the act of looking within oneself.*

4. **C. Broken**

   Dysfunctional contains the root *dys,* meaning *abnormal or bad.* The definition of *dysfunctional* is *not working normally or properly.*

5. **B. The killing of a cultural, national, or racial group**

   The word *genocide* is made up of the root *gen-* which means *birth* or *race.* Answer choice B includes *racial group.* The root is a clue to the correct answer.

Latin and Greek roots are often found in words related to the sciences, such as medicine, and in words related to law, the government, and the military.

Here are a few medical terms and their root words:

Root	Meaning	Medical Term
algia-	pain	myalgia
arthr-	joint, limb	arthritis
dent-	of or pertaining to teeth	dentist
onco-	tumor, bulk, volume	oncology

Here are a few related to law, the government, and the military:

Root	Meaning	Military Term
-cracy	government	autocracy
dem-	people	democracy
milit-	soldier	militia, military
jud-	law	judge, judiciary

Using roots
Look at all of the tables of roots. Which other words can you think of that come from these roots?

Using Prefixes

A PREFIX is a word part added to the beginning of another word or word part. Knowing the meaning of a prefix can help you figure out the meaning of an unfamiliar word.

PREFIX: a word part added to the beginning of another word or word part

Example

The prefix *sub-* means *under* or *below*.

When *sub-* is added to the base word *zero*, the definition changes. *Subzero* means *below zero.*

Here is a list of common prefixes and their meanings. You'll notice that some prefixes have more than one meaning.

A base word *is a word that can stand alone, like* human, color, *or* learn.

PREFIXES		
Prefix	Meaning	Example
ante-	before, prior to, in front of	antecedent, anteroom
bene-	good	benefit
circum-	around	circumvent
de-	away from, off, down, reverse action of	derail, decline, defrost

Continued on next page

hemi-	half	hemisphere
inter-	between, among	international
mal-	bad	maltreat
post-	after in time, space	postpone
super-	over and above, very large	supertanker
un-	not, reverse of	unhappy, unfasten

To practice using words with prefixes, try these test questions. Remember to look for the prefix and think about its meaning. Does the prefix somehow help reveal the meaning of the word? Look for connections to the meaning of the prefix in the four answer choices.

Practice Test Questions

1. **Circumfluent** means:

   A. Examining

   B. Marching

   C. Encompassing

   D. Preventing

2. **Antebellum** means:

   A. Before the war

   B. Afternoon

   C. Within reason

   D. Around midnight

3. **Benevolent** means:

   A. Greedy

   B. Hungry

   C. Confused

   D. Compassionate

Answer Key

1. **C. Encompassing**

   Circumfluent contains the prefix *circum-*, meaning *around*. Answer choice C, *encompassing*, means to *form circle around*. This answer choice is related to the prefix meaning *around*. The prefix provides a clue to the correct answer. *Circumfluent* means *flowing around; encompassing*.

2. **A. Before the war**

   Antebellum contains the prefix *ante-*, meaning *before*. Answer choice A, *before the war*, includes the meaning of the prefix. The prefix provides a clue to the correct answer. *Antebellum* means *of or during the period before a war, especially the United States Civil War.*

3. **D. Compassionate**

   Benevolent contains the prefix *bene-*, meaning *good*. The prefix provides a clue to the correct answer. *Benevolent* must be related to something good, such as the correct answer, *compassionate.*

Use it!
Use each new word that you learn immediately. For instance, send an email message to a friend and use the new word in a sentence. Or tell a family member about the new word, what it means, and when you might use it.

Using Suffixes

A SUFFIX is a word part added to the end of another word or word part. Suffixes are strong clues to a word's meaning. They also determine the part of speech. For example, a suffix can make a word a noun, an adjective, a verb, or an adverb.

SUFFIX: word part added to the end of another word or word part

Example
The suffix -*ant* means *relating to*. It is a NOUN SUFFIX, a suffix that creates a word that is a noun.

When added to the word *occupy* (a verb), it becomes *occupant* (a noun).

NOUN SUFFIX: a suffix that creates a word that is a noun

Example
The suffix -*ish* means *pertaining to* or *like*. It is an ADJECTIVE SUFFIX, a suffix that creates a word that is an adjective.

When added to the word *fool* (a noun), it becomes *foolish* (an adjective).

ADJECTIVE SUFFIX: a suffix that creates a word that is an adjective

Here is a list of common suffixes and their meanings.

SUFFIXES		
Suffix	Meaning	Example
-able, -ible	able to	understandable
-acious	full of	vivacious
-en	to become	widen
-fy	to make	simplify
-ible	able to	convertible
-ical	pertaining to	economical
-ism	doctrine	capitalism
-ize	to become	crystallize

Continued on next page

-less	without	homeless
-most	at the extreme	topmost
-ous	full of	furious
-ward	toward	westward

Know your prefixes and suffixes

Remember to create flashcards for prefixes and suffixes, too. Write the prefix or suffix on the front of the index card. On the back, write the meaning and at least one example. See how many examples you can think of.

To practice using words with suffixes, try the following test questions. Just like words with prefixes, remember to look for the suffix and think about its meaning. Does the suffix somehow help reveal the meaning of the word? Look for connections to the suffix meaning in the four answer choices.

Practice Test Questions

Choose the word that has nearly the same meaning as the underlined word.

1. Maggie was hoping to <u>modernize</u> her kitchen.

   A. To make modern

   B. With modern features

   C. Able to be modern

   D. Toward a modern style

2. Looking at the paper, Joe found it quite <u>legible</u>.

   A. To become clear

   B. With understanding

   C. Able to be read

   D. Pertaining to reading

3. Jordan's boss describes him as <u>ambitious</u>.

   A. Without ambition

   B. Like an ambition

   C. Pertaining to ambition

   D. Full of ambition

4. John studied <u>Thatcherism</u> in his government class.

   A. Tthe former leader, Margaret Thatcher

   B. The doctrine of Margaret Thatcher

   C. The biography of Margaret Thatcher

   D. The family of Margaret Thatcher

Answer Key

1. **A. To make modern**

   The suffix *-ize* means *to become*. When added to the base word *modern*, the definition is *to make or become modern*.

2. **C. Able to be read**

   The suffix *-ible* means able to. When added to the root word *leg-* (meaning *read*), the definition is *able to be read*.

3. **D. Full of ambition**

   The suffix *-ous* means *full of*. When added to the base word *ambition*, the definition is *full of ambition*.

4. **B. The doctrine of Margaret Thatcher**

   Because the suffix *-ism* means *doctrine of*, we know that the word's meaning is *the doctrine of Margaret Thatcher*.

Don't miss out on the chance to learn a new word

Is a word in the table of suffixes new to you? Did you not know the meaning of an answer choice in one of the practice test questions? Look up the meaning of each word that's new to you and then create a flashcard for it. It might be on the test!

Understanding Word Forms

Sometimes a familiar word can appear as a different part of speech. For example, many people might have heard that *fraud* involves a criminal misrepresentation, so when it appears as the adjective *fraudulent* (e.g., "He was suspected of *fraudulent* activities"), it is possible to make an educated guess about the meaning.

Sometimes a familiar word can appear as a different part of speech.

Example

You might not know the word *turbulent*, but you've probably heard of *turbulence* on airplanes. Thinking about the word *turbulence*, what might be the meaning of the word *turbulent*? Perhaps *bumpy, rough,* or *shaky*? In fact, those are all synonyms for *turbulent*. The definition of *turbulent* is *characterized by confusion or disorder*.

Mnemoni-what?

A mnemonic is any technique that helps you remember. There are lots of silly mnemonics you can use to help you learn new vocabulary. To remember the meaning of *grapple* (to grip or hold), you could think, "I grapple an apple." To remember the meaning of *parallel*, you could imagine the ll in the word parallel as parallel lines. To remember that *advent* means beginning, you could remember that *advent* begins with the first letter of the alphabet.

Using Context Clues

Words usually appear as part of a sentence, paragraph, or story. The words and ideas surrounding a word are called context, or CONTEXT CLUES. Using context clues can often help you determine the meaning of unfamiliar words.

When reading an unfamiliar word, think about the meaning of the words surrounding it. Think about the meaning of the whole sentence or entire paragraph. Then try to match the meaning of the unfamiliar word with the meaning of the known text.

> **CONTEXT CLUES:** the words and ideas surrounding a word

> *Using context clues can often help you determine the meaning of unfamiliar words.*

Example

Read the following sentence. Think about the meaning of the whole sentence. How does its meaning help you understand the meaning of the underlined word?

The young hikers nervously looked up as they carefully negotiated the <u>precipitous</u> mountain trail.

The definition of *precipitous* is *very steep*. The context clues help identify the meaning. The context includes hikers who are nervous and are being careful on a mountain trail. You could guess that the mountain trail is steep.

Example

Farmer John got a two-horse plow and went to work. Straight <u>furrows</u> stretched out behind him.

The word <u>furrows</u> means:

A. long cuts made by a plow

B. vast, open fields

C. rows of corn

D. pairs of hitched horses

What are *furrows*? Read the two sentences again. The word *straight* and the phrase *stretched out behind him* are the clues. Answer choice A, *long cuts made by a plow*, is the correct answer.

Take a guess

Before you look up the meaning of a word, try guessing the meaning using context clues. Figuring out the meaning of a word by context is a great skill—plus, the meaning will be much more firmly planted in your brain than if you simply looked up the definition of the word.

> ### Example
>
> The survivors struggled ahead, <u>shambling</u> through the terrible cold, doing their best not to fall.
>
> The word <u>shambling</u> means:
>
> A. frozen in place
>
> B. running
>
> C. shivering uncontrollably
>
> D. walking awkwardly
>
> What does the word *shambling* mean? Read the sentence again. The phrases *struggled ahead* and *doing their best not to fall* are the clues. They suggest slow movement. Answer choice D, *walking awkwardly*, is the correct answer.

> ### Millions of hits
>
> Ready to expand your vocabulary more? There are countless online sources for learning new words. Do an Internet search for phrases such as *word of the day* or *new vocabulary words* and you'll get millions of hits.

Signal words

There are several types signal words that can help alert you to context clues.

Comparison signal words include *also, both, like, resembling,* and *too.*

> ### Example
>
> *My voice began to <u>quaver</u> like a leaf in the wind.*
>
> The phrase *like a leaf in the wind* helps reveal the meaning of *quaver,* which is *to shake.*

Example signal words include *for example, for instance,* and *such as.*

> ### Example
>
> *The cost of the jewelry was <u>exorbitant</u>. For example, one bracelet sold for $25,000.*
>
> The example of the cost of the bracelet helps reveal the meaning of *exorbitant,* which is *excessive.*

Contrast signal words include *but, however, yet, instead,* and *unlike.*

> ### Example
>
> *My brother has a <u>concise</u> writing style, unlike my sister, who tends to go on and on.*
>
> The contrast between the two writing styles helps reveal the meaning of *concise,* which is *short and to the point.*

Definition or restatement signal words include *in other words, that is, is, which,* and *or.*

> **Example**
>
> *A good worker will not <u>malign</u>, or badmouth, any of his colleagues.*
>
> Stating a synonym for *malign* reveals the definition—*to badmouth or defame.*

> **Knowledge is power**
>
> Read about the ASVAB in the introduction to this study guide. Knowing the purpose, content, and format of the test will help you prepare and give you confidence.

To practice using context clues, try the following practice test questions.

Practice Test Questions

Choose the word that has nearly the same meaning as the underlined word.

1. A percentage of the budget was <u>appropriated</u> for advertisement costs.

   A. Decreased in volume

   B. Set aside for a specific use

   C. Obtained illegally

   D. Open for public viewing

2. We have to <u>amend</u>, or change, the rules to accommodate the new department.

   A. Alter

   B. Read

   C. Override

   D. Understand

3. The new living quarters are <u>commodious</u>, unlike my current cramped apartment.

   A. Small

   B. Messy

   C. Elegant

   D. Roomy

Answer Key

1. **B. Set aside for a specific use**

   The context of the sentence includes a percentage of the money for advertisement. It makes sense that this money is *set aside for a specific use.*

2. **A. Alter**

   The word *change* following the underlined word *amend* is the clue that reveals the correct answer, *alter. Alter* and *change* are synonyms.

3. **D. Roomy**

   The contrasting phrase, *unlike my current cramped apartment*, reveals that the word *commodious* means *roomy. Roomy* is the opposite of *cramped.*

> **Write a story**
> To help you remember the meaning of words, make a list of five or ten words you are learning and write a story that uses all of the words creatively and correctly.

Adjacent sentence clues

The context for a word goes beyond the sentence in which it appears. At times, the writer uses adjacent sentences to present an explanation or definition.

> **Example**
>
> Read the following passage:
>
> *The two hundred dollars for the car repair would have to come out of the <u>contingency</u> fund. Fortunately, Angela's father had taught her to keep some money set aside for just such emergencies.*
>
> In these sentences, where is the clue for the word *contingency*?
>
> The second sentence offers a clue to the definition of *contingency*—the word *emergencies*. Therefore, a fund for *contingencies* would be *money tucked away for unforeseen events or emergencies*.

Understanding words with multiple meanings

Another reason that context clues are so important is that so many words have multiple meanings. Without the context, it is impossible to know which meaning of a word with multiple meanings is intended.

Read the list of words below. Each has more than one meaning. Can you identify multiple meanings for these words?

- arrest
- dock
- nursery
- peddling

- slough
- snarl
- toast
- hamper

- commune
- buffer
- corporal
- chap

> **Example**
>
> Read the following sentence and choose the correct meaning for the underlined word:
>
> *The spread of the disease can be <u>arrested</u>.*
>
> A. stop or check progress
>
> B. seize by legal authority
>
> The correct definition is A, *stop or check progress*. Definition B does not make sense in this context. A legal authority would not seize a disease.

Example

Read the following sentence and choose the correct meaning for the underlined word:

The instructor's slide show <u>illuminated</u> the importance of recycling.

A. to brighten with light

B. to make clear

The correct definition is B, *to make clear*. Definition A does not make sense in this sentence. If you're not sure, try substituting each definition in the original sentence.

Using Experience Clues

Just like other context clues, EXPERIENCE CLUES can help you understand an unfamiliar word. Experience clues are the knowledge you have gained through personal experiences. You can sometimes draw on this knowledge to help understand unfamiliar words.

Example

When you are visiting your employer's family, you should show your best <u>decorum</u>.

Through experience, we know that we should behave properly and with the best manners when we are around our employers or superiors. Therefore, we can infer, or conclude, that the meaning of *decorum* is *good manners, politeness, good taste*.

Can you use that in a sentence, please?

Every time you learn a new word, be sure you can use it in a sentence. Using a word in a sentence ensures that you understand the meaning. It also helps you remember the meaning.

Practice using experience clues by answering the following test questions.

Practice Test Questions

Choose the word that has nearly the same meaning as the underlined word.

1. Hospitals are careful not to <u>adulterate</u> the blood supply.

   A. Organize

   B. Reveal

   C. Contaminate

   D. Spread

2. In every major metropolitan area, taxis are <u>ubiquitous</u>.

   A. Everywhere

   B. Mysterious

   C. Urban

   D. Scarce

3. Emma had many cats growing up, so she learned at a young age that cats are <u>tenacious</u> hunters.

   A. Hesitant

   B. Eccentric

   C. Agitated

   D. Persistent

4. When our team scored the home run, my <u>visceral</u> reaction was to jump out of my seat and cheer.

   A. Athletic

   B. Unnatural

   C. Heavy

   D. Instinctive

Answer Key

1. **C. Contaminate**

   It is through our experiences that we understand how important it is to protect the blood supply from contamination. Therefore, *adulterate* must mean *contaminate*.

2. **A. Everywhere**

   Through our experience, we know that there are many taxis in cities. Therefore, *ubiquitous* must mean *everywhere*. You might be tempted to choose answer choice C, but even though metropolitan areas are urban, it doesn't make sense to say that taxis are urban.

3. **D. Persistent**

   Anyone who has seen a cat chase a bird or mouse (or even a toy) knows that cats are determined, unrelenting hunters. Therefore, *tenacious* must mean *persistent*.

4. **D. Instinctive**

   Anyone who has been to a sporting event or watched one on television has seen the automatic reaction fans have to a touchdown or home run. Therefore, *visceral* must mean *instinctive*.

How would I use this?
In the military, legal specialists and court reporters assist lawyers and judges by researching military regulations, preparing legal documents, transcribing court proceedings, and performing many other duties. In this military career, the ability to decipher the meaning of legal terminology is a key to success.

CHAPTER 2
PARAGRAPH COMPREHENSION

In the Paragraph Comprehension subtest of the ASVAB, you will read short passages and then answer questions about the passages. This subtest tests your ability to understand written information.

Understanding the Main Idea

When reading a passage, it is important to think about the MAIN IDEA, the overall idea of the passage. The main idea the most important point about the topic.

To find a passage's main idea, first determine the topic. The TOPIC of a passage is a word or phrase that tells what the passage is about.

To find the topic of a passage, ask yourself, "What or whom is the passage about?"

Example

Read the following passage.

Climbing to the top of Mount Everest is an adventure. It is one that many—whether physically fit or not—seem eager to try. The trail leading to the top stretches for miles, the cold temperatures are usually frigid and brutal, and the altitude is a tremendous strain on the human body.

Ask yourself: What or whom is the passage about?

The answer is *Mount Everest*. Mount Everest is the topic of the passage.

What's in a title?

A passage may include clues about the topic. Pay special attention to titles, headings, and illustrations. These can save you time and point you in the right direction.

Once you have determined the topic, you are able to determine the main idea. The difference between a topic and a main idea is simple: A topic is only a general category, such as Mount Everest; a main idea is the topic *and* the single most important point about the topic.

In the Paragraph Comprehension subtest of the ASVAB, you will read short passages and then answer questions about the passages. This subtest tests your ability to understand written information.

MAIN IDEA: the overall idea of the passage

To find a passage's main idea, first determine the topic.

TOPIC: a word or phrase that tells what the passage is about

To find the topic of a passage, ask yourself, "What or whom is the passage about?"

Once you have determined the topic, you are able to determine the main idea. The difference between a topic and a main idea is simple: A topic is only a general category, such as Mount Everest; a main idea is the topic and the single most important point about the topic.

Example

Reread the passage about Mount Everest.

Climbing to the top of Mount Everest is an adventure. It is one that many—whether physically fit or not—seem eager to try. The trail leading to the top stretches for miles, the cold temperatures are usually frigid and brutal, and altitude is a tremendous strain on the human body.

What is the single most important point the author is making about Mount Everest?

The main idea of the passage can be stated as follows: Climbing Mount Everest is an extreme challenge for all who attempt it.

Let me repeat myself...

Another trick to finding the topic of a passage is to look for words that are repeated. Sometimes the topic is a word that appears many times in the passage.

Implicit and explicit main ideas

You may have noticed that the main idea of the passage about Mount Everest was not directly stated in the passage. The main idea was a statement that the reader had to determine based on the information in the passage.

A main idea that is not directly stated is an **IMPLICIT MAIN IDEA**. In more advanced reading selections, authors will typically not state the main idea directly but will use an implicit main idea.

As a reader, you must think about the entire passage and decide whether there is a stated main idea. If there is a sentence that states the main idea, the single most important point the author is making about the topic, it is called an **EXPLICIT MAIN IDEA**. The main idea is explicitly, or directly, stated.

Authors use both implicit and explicit main ideas in their writing. Understanding the difference between implicit and explicit main ideas will help you identify the main idea in a passage. You will recognize that sometimes the author will include a sentence stating the main idea, and sometimes the author will not state the main idea directly. When the author does not state the main idea directly, it will be up to you as the reader to put it into words.

IMPLICIT MAIN IDEA: a main idea that is not directly stated

In more advanced reading selections, authors will typically not state the main idea directly but will use an implicit main idea.

EXPLICIT MAIN IDEA: a main idea that is explicitly, or directly, stated

ASVAB tip!

The Armed Forces Qualification Test (AFQT) score is computed using four subtests, including the Paragraph Comprehension subtest. Your AFQT score is critical because you must have a minimum qualifying score in order to enlist.

Example

Read the following passage.

The plants of the rainforest are extremely important to the Earth's ecology. Rainforest plants provide homes to millions of plants, animals, and food resources. These plants also generate rich oxygen for much of the Earth, and if their destruction persists, the damage to the rainforests will pose a dangerous threat to the planet's ecological balance. If the trees and plants fail to grow, the planet will be deprived of many of the natural food resources of the rainforest, including cocoa, coffee, sugar cane, and many varieties of nuts, fruits, and spices.

Which of the following is the main idea of the passage?

A. Rain forest plants.

B. Dangers to the Earth's ecology.

C. The plants of the rainforest are extremely important to Earth's ecology.

D. Rainforest plants provide home to millions of plants, animals, and food resources.

Remember: The main idea is the topic and the single most important point about the topic. Answer choice A is the topic, not the main idea. Answer choice B is not specific enough. Answer choice D is just one detail from the passage. The correct answer is C, *The plants of the rainforest are extremely important to Earth's ecology.* This is also the first sentence in the paragraph, so the main idea is an explicit main idea.

What's the point?

When you're finding the main idea, be careful that you don't choose just the topic. Ask yourself, "What is the most important point about the topic?" The answer will most likely be the main idea.

The main idea of a passage would often make a good title for the passage. In some of the test questions, you will be asked, "What would be a good title for this passage?" When you see this question, think about the passage's main idea.

> *The main idea of a passage would often make a good title for the passage.*

Example

Read the following passage.

Disciplinary practices have been found to affect diverse areas of child development, such as the acquisition of moral values, obedience to authority, and performance at school. There are four types of disciplinary styles: assertion of power, withdrawal of love, reasoning, and permissiveness. Assertion of power involves the use of force to discourage unwanted behavior. Withdrawal of love involves making the love of a parent conditional on a child's good behavior. Reasoning involves persuading the child to behave one way rather than another. Permissiveness involves allowing the child to do as he or she pleases and to face the consequences of his or her actions.

Think about the main idea of the passage as you answer the following question.

What would be a good title for this passage?

A. Discipline

B. The Many Problems Associated with Discipline

C. Permissiveness: A Type of Discipline

D. The Four Types of Disciplinary Styles

The correct answer is D, *The Four Types of Disciplinary Styles*. This title states the topic, which is disciplinary practices, and includes the most important idea in the passage: There are four types of disciplinary styles.

Enjoy cars or cooking?

If you have trouble with reading comprehension, practice reading anything that interests you. Enjoy cars or cooking, tennis or travel? Buy a magazine, borrow a library book, or search the Internet for some interesting articles.

Practice Test Questions

Read the passage below and answer the question that follows.

Time magazine, which typically selects a person of the year, chose Earth as the "planet" of the year in 1988 to underscore the severe problems facing our planet, and therefore us. We hear dismal reports every day about water shortages, ozone depletion, and the obscene volume of trash generated by our society. By choosing Earth as the planet of the year, *Time* was hoping to alert people around the world to these issues and spur solutions to some of these problems.

1. **What would a good title be for this passage?**

   A. It's Time to Face Earth's Ecological Problems

   B. *Time* magazine's Person of the Year

   C. Water Shortages, Ozone Depletion, and Trash

   D. Earth's Issues and Solutions

Read the passage below and answer the question that follows.

Every job places different kinds of demands on employees. For example, jobs such as accounting and bookkeeping require mathematical ability, and graphic design requires creative and artistic ability. Medicine requires mainly scientific ability, and engineering requires scientific and mathematical ability. Those studying to be teachers need to be skilled in both psychology and pedagogy, and those wishing to become musicians must have musical and artistic ability.

2. **What would a good title for this passage be?**

   A. Training for a Job

   B. Different Demands for Different Jobs

   C. What Skills Do You Need to Become an Accountant?

   D. Skills Needed for Success

Answer Key

1. **A. It's Time to Face Earth's Ecological Problems**

   This title includes the topic— *ecological problems*—and the most important idea—we *need to address the problems*. Answer choice B isn't correct because this passage is about *Time* magazine's "planet" of the year. Answer choice C alludes to some of the details in the passage that support the main idea, but they are not the main idea. Answer choice D is too broad to be the main idea.

2. **B. Different Demands for Different Jobs**

   This title states the topic and the main idea. People need different skills for different jobs, so different jobs have different demands. Answer choices A and D are too broad. Answer choice C is too specific.

Mind your P's and Q's

Before you read, **p**review and **q**uestion. **P**review the passage—look at the length, titles, headings, italicized words, illustrations, and captions. After previewing, you might think to yourself, "It looks like this passage is about the rewards and challenges of horseback riding." Then **q**uestion—write down a few questions that you have about the topic. These steps will jumpstart your curiosity and help you become actively involved in the material.

Identifying Supporting Details

SUPPORTING DETAILS: any specific information that supports the main idea

Each passage includes a main idea and SUPPORTING DETAILS. The supporting details include any specific information that supports the main idea. Supporting details can include a host of information and often make the passage interesting.

Here are some examples of the types of supporting details you might find in a passage:

SUPPORTING DETAILS	
Type	**Example**
Facts	The Space Shuttle Discovery launched on February 24, 2011.
Sequences of events	The first stop for the shuttle is the International Space Station.
Descriptions	Discovery's launch was powerful and thrilling.
Examples	For example, one study conducted on the shuttle was to examine cell growth.
Anecdotes	While visiting the space museum, I saw an exhibit on Discovery.
Reasons	One reason we should continue the space program is that we have a need for adventure.

Read the questions first

One technique for finding the supporting details when taking a test is to read the questions before reading the passage. This will help the important information jump out at you. Be careful, though—it's best to read the questions, but not the answer choices. Reading the answer choices before reading the passage can send you down the wrong path.

Identifying the supporting details in a passage means reading carefully. Look for the details that make the passage interesting.

Identifying the supporting details in a passage means reading carefully.

Example

Read the following passage once again. This time, think about the details that support the main idea.

Climbing to the top of Mount Everest is an adventure. It is one that many—whether physically fit or not—seem eager to try. The trail leading to the top stretches for miles, the cold temperatures are usually frigid and brutal, and the altitude is a tremendous strain on the human body.

Creating a table listing the topic, main idea, and supporting details of a passage is an excellent way to improve reading comprehension. Look at the table below, which refers to the sample passage. The topic and main idea are identified and the details follow.

Creating a table listing the topic, main idea, and supporting details of a passage is an excellent way to improve reading comprehension.

Topic	Mount Everest
Main Idea	Climbing Mount Everest is an extreme challenge for all who attempt it.
Detail	The trail leading to the top stretches for miles.
Detail	The cold temperatures are usually frigid and brutal.
Detail	The altitude is a tremendous strain on the human body.

The details, as shown in the table, are *examples* of the extreme challenges of climbing Mount Everest.

The early bird…is relaxed!

On the day of your test, leave plenty of time to get to the testing site. Allow extra time for traffic or other delays, and plan to arrive at least 15 minutes early. If possible, visit the testing site before the day of the test so you know exactly where to go and how to get there. Arriving relaxed will help you excel on your test.

Example

Now, read a second passage about Mount Everest.

Training to climb Mount Everest is a long and grueling process. However, when the training is complete, climbers are met by the wonders of the mountain. Wide rock formations dazzle the climbers' eyes with shades of gray and white, while the peak forms a triangle that seems to touch the sky. The brilliance of the white snow and ice glimmers. Colorful prayer flags placed by the Tibetan people create a sea of color in the base camp. Climbers are reminded of the splendor and magnificence of our great Earth.

Now try filling out a table for the passage you just read. Identify the topic, the main idea, and the details and place them in the table below. This passage has five details. Some of the details appear in the same sentence, but separate them when you place them in the table.

Topic	
Main Idea	
Detail	
Detail	
Detail	

Detail	
Detail	

Look at the table below. The table you completed should be similar.

Topic	Mount Everest
Main Idea	Climbers of Mount Everest are met by many natural and manmade wonders.
Detail	Wide rock formations dazzle the climbers' eyes.
Detail	Rocks are shades of gray and white.
Detail	The peak forms a triangle that seems to touch the sky.
Detail	The brilliance of the white snow and ice glimmers.
Detail	Colorful prayer flags placed by the Tibetan people create a sea of color in the base camp.

Now practice using the information in the table to answer the questions below.

What would be a good title for this passage?

A. The Tibetan Prayer Flags on Mount Everest

B. The Natural and Manmade Wonders of Mount Everest

C. Preparing to Climb Mount Everest

D. The Wonders of Nature

Think about the main idea. The passage describes some of the beautiful sights that climbers will see. Therefore, a good title for this passage would be answer choice B, The Natural and Manmade Wonders of Mount Everest. Answer choice A is a detail, not the main idea, so it would not make a good title. Answer choice C does not relate to what the passage is mostly about. Answer choice D is too broad. Even though Mount Everest is a wonder of nature, the title in answer choice D does not identify that the passage is about Mount Everest.

According to this passage:

A. Prayer flags are placed in the base camp.

B. Mount Everest is the world's highest mountain.

C. Mount Everest is located in the Himalayan Mountain Range.

D. Mount Everest is a beautiful mountain.

Which piece of information is included in this passage? The passage states that prayer flags are placed in the base camp, so answer choice A is the correct answer. Answer choices B and C are true facts, but they are not included in the passage. Answer choice D is incorrect because it is too broad a statement.

It may be true but...

When answering a test question about a detail in a passage, be sure that the detail is actually found in the passage. Even if an answer choice is, in fact, true, if it is not in the passage or clearly implied based on the information in the passage, it is not the correct answer.

Here's another example.

Example

Read the passage below:

Climbers must endure several barriers on the way to the summit, including other hikers, steep jagged rocks, and lots of snow. But climbers often find that the most grueling part of the trip is their climb back down. They are thoroughly exhausted, and the lack of oxygen often causes problems with judgment. Sometimes climbers feel overconfident because they think the difficult part of the trip is over. They might become careless and not take the necessary precautions. Also, weather can become dangerous if a climber waits too long to descend.

Identify the topic, the main idea, and the supporting details, and place them in the table below. This passage has four details. Some of them appear in the same sentence, but separate them when you place them on the table.

Topic	
Main Idea	
Detail	
Detail	
Detail	
Detail	

Look at the table below. The table you completed should be similar.

Topic	Mount Everest
Main Idea	The descent from Mount Everest is sometimes the most difficult part of the climb.
Detail	They are thoroughly exhausted.
Detail	They lack oxygen.
Detail	They become overconfident, which leads to bad decisions.
Detail	The weather can become dangerous.

Now practice using the information in the table to answer the questions below.

What would be a good title for this passage?

A. The Dangers of Climbing Mount Everest

B. Mount Everest Descent

C. Dangers of Climbing Down Mount Everest

D. How to Climb Down Mount Everest

Again, think about the main idea. What is this passage about? A good title for this passage would be answer choice C, Dangers of Climbing Down Mount Everest.

Monitor your time
You have a set amount of time to answer all the questions. Don't get bogged down laboring over one question you're not sure about when there are ten others you could answer more readily. One question won't make or break the test.

According to this passage:

A. The best time to descend the mountain is early in the afternoon.

B. Climbers can use bad judgment when descending the mountain.

C. Oxygen tanks are not needed when climbing to the summit.

D. Not many climbers get tired when climbing down the mountain.

Which of these is a detail included in the passage? The correct answer is B, Climbers can use bad judgment when descending the mountain.

Not word-for-word
The correct answer is sometimes worded differently than the information in a passage. You are not necessarily looking for an answer pulled directly from the passage, word-for-word. Read each answer choice and think about the underlying *meaning*.

Now try answering some questions on your own.

Practice Test Questions

Read the passage below and then answer the practice test questions that follow.

Sometimes too much of a good thing can become a very bad thing indeed. In an earnest attempt to consume a healthy diet, dietary supplement enthusiasts have been known to overdose. Vitamin C, for example, long thought to help people ward off cold viruses, is currently being studied for its possible role in warding off cancer and other diseases that cause tissue degeneration. Unfortunately, an overdose of vitamin C—more than 10 mg on a daily basis—can cause nausea and diarrhea. Calcium supplements, commonly taken by women, are helpful in warding off osteoporosis. More than just a few grams a day, however, can lead to stomach upset and even kidney and bladder stones. Niacin, proven useful in reducing cholesterol levels, can be dangerous in large doses to those who suffer from heart problems, asthma, or ulcers.

1. **Which of the following best states the main idea?**

   A. Supplements taken in excess can be a bad thing

   B. Dietary supplement enthusiasts have been known to overdose

   C. Vitamins can cause nausea, diarrhea, and kidney or bladder stones

   D. People who take supplements are preoccupied with their health

2. **According to this passage:**

   A. Vitamin C cannot be taken in excess

   B. Too much calcium can cause tissue degeneration

   C. Niacin is dangerous for those with diabetes and lupus

   D. Vitamin C is being studied for its ability to prevent cancer

3. **What would be the best title for this passage?**

   A. A Warning about Calcium

   B. Vitamins Can Be Harmful

   C. The Benefits of Vitamins

   D. Vitamin C and Cancer

Answer Key

1. **A. Supplements taken in excess can be a bad thing**

   Answer choice A is a paraphrase of the first sentence and provides a general framework for the rest of the passage—excess supplement intake can be bad. This is the main idea. The rest of the passage discusses the consequences of taking too many supplements.

2. **D. Vitamin C is being studied for its ability to prevent cancer**

   The fact that vitamin C is being studied for its ability to prevent cancer is stated directly in the passage.

3. **B. Vitamins Can Be Harmful**

   Answer choice is B, Vitamins Can Be Harmful, is correct because it is the main idea of the passage. The other answer choices all address details in the passage, not the main idea, so they would not make good titles.

The buddy system

To practice reading comprehension, find a friend and choose a magazine article that you will both read. After reading the article, discuss it with your friend. What did you enjoy about the article? What questions did you have? What were some of the interesting facts?

Making Inferences and Drawing Conclusions

A writer will not always come right out and state all of the information about a story or a topic. As a careful reader, you must often come to your own conclusions about a passage. You can use evidence in the text and your own logical abilities to make INFERENCES, or educated guesses, about ideas that are not directly stated. By combining your inferences with the stated evidence, you can draw conclusions about a story or nonfiction passage.

An inference requires that you go beyond the strictly obvious to create additional meaning by taking the text one logical step further. Inferences and conclusions are based on the content of the passage—that is, on what the passage says or how the writer says it—and are derived by reasoning.

Inference is an essential and automatic component of most reading. Here are some examples:

- Making educated guesses about the meaning of unknown words

- Determining an author's main idea

- Determining if there is bias (prejudice) in an author's writing

> **INFERENCES:** educated guesses about ideas that are not directly stated

> By combining your inferences with the stated evidence, you can draw conclusions about a story or nonfiction passage.

Making an inference requires that you use your own ability to reason along with the evidence in the text in order to figure out what the writer has implied, or expressed indirectly.

ASVAB tip!
On the CAT-ASVAB, the Paragraph Comprehension subtest is 22 minutes long and has 11 questions.

Example

Consider the following example. Assume you are an employer, and you are reading over the letters of reference submitted by a prospective employee for the position of clerk in your real estate office. The position requires the applicant to be neat, careful, trustworthy, and punctual. You come across this letter of reference submitted by an applicant.

To Whom It May Concern:

Todd Finley has asked me to write a letter of reference for him. I am well qualified to do so because he worked for me for three months last year. His duties included answering the phone, greeting the public, and producing some simple memos and notices on the computer. Although Todd initially had few computer skills and little knowledge of telephone etiquette, he did acquire some during his stay with us. Todd's manner of speaking, both on the telephone and with the clients who came to my establishment, could be described as casual. He was particularly effective when communicating with peers. Please contact me by telephone if you wish to have further information about my experience with Todd.

Here the writer implies, rather than openly states, his real opinion of Todd. The tone of this letter is not enthusiastic. A truly positive letter would say something such as, "I have the distinct honor of recommending Todd Finley." Here, however, the letter simply verifies that Todd worked in the office. Also, the praise is obviously lukewarm. For example, when talking about Todd's computer skills, the writer says, "he did acquire some during his stay with us." As another example, the writer says that Todd "was particularly effective when communicating with peers." An educated guess translates that statement into a nice way of saying that Todd was not serious about his communication with clients.

After reading this letter, you can come to the conclusion that Todd is not an outstanding worker.

A conclusion is rarely stated, and an inference is never stated. You must rely on your common sense and clues.

In order to make inferences and draw conclusions, you must use prior knowledge and apply it to the current situation. A conclusion is rarely stated, and an inference is never stated. You must rely on your common sense and clues.

Don't assume
When drawing a conclusion, be sure there is evidence in the text that leads to the conclusion. Don't assume information unless there is some concrete clue in the passage that allows for the conclusion.

Practice Test Questions

Read the passage below and answer the question that follows.

Tim Sullivan had just turned fifteen. As a birthday present, his parents had given him a guitar and a certificate for ten guitar lessons. He had always shown a love of music and a desire to learn an instrument. Tim began his lessons, and before long, he was making up his own songs. At the music studio, Tim met Josh, who played the piano, and Roger, whose instrument was the saxophone. They all shared the same dream, to start a band, and each was praised by his teacher as having real talent.

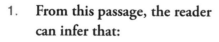

1. **From this passage, the reader can infer that:**

   A. Tim, Roger, and Josh are going to start their own band

   B. Tim is going to give up his guitar lessons

   C. Tim, Josh, and Roger will no longer be friends

   D. Josh and Roger are going to start their own band

Read the passage below and answer the question that follows.

The Smith family waited patiently around carousel number 7 for their luggage to arrive. They were exhausted after their five-hour trip and were anxious to get to their hotel. After about an hour, they realized that they no longer recognized any of the other passengers' faces. Mrs. Smith asked the person who appeared to be in charge if they were at the right carousel. The man replied, "Yes, this is it, but we finished unloading that baggage almost half an hour ago."

2. **From the man's response, the reader can infer that:**

   A. The Smiths were ready to go to their hotel

   B. The Smiths' luggage was lost

   C. The man had their luggage

   D. They were at the wrong carousel

Read the passage below and then answer the practice test questions that follow.

Student demonstrators lined the streets. They held picket signs and shouted at the cars that drove onto the campus. They were protesting the hiring of a new dean—one who had a record of discrimination against women. Charges had been brought against him, but they had been dropped.

3. **Where does this passage take place?**

   A. A bank

   B. A police station

   C. A shopping center

   D. A college

4. **Based on the passage, the reader can conclude that the:**

   A. Students believe it is okay for them to break the law

   B. Students believe that the new dean is guilty of discrimination

   C. Dean is a reasonable man who does not discriminate

   D. Dean is not likely to take the job

Practice Test Questions (cont.)

Read the passage below and answer the question that follows.

Climbers must endure several barriers on the way to the summit of Mount Everest, including other hikers, steep jagged rocks, and lots of snow. But climbers often find the most grueling part of the trip is their climb back down. They are thoroughly exhausted, and the lack of oxygen often causes problems with judgment. Sometimes climbers feel overconfident because they think that the most difficult part of the trip is over. They might become careless and not take the necessary precautions. Also, weather can become dangerous if a climber waits too long to descend.

5. The author of this passage would agree that:

   A. Accidents on Mount Everest are rare but serious

   B. Because of the altitude, the weather does not affect climbers

   C. Climbers must receive special training on how to descend

   D. Climbers should never climb Mount Everest without oxygen

Read the passage below and answer the question that follows.

Someone once said that the two most difficult jobs in the world—voting and being a parent—are given to rank amateurs. The consequences of this inequity are voter apathy and inept parenting leading to, on the one hand, an apparent failure of the democratic process and, on the other hand, misbehaving and misguided children.

6. **Based on this passage, the author would be most likely to agree that:**

   A. Parents should take parenting classes

   B. Schools should discipline children

   C. Most people should not have children

   D. Most children misbehave

Answer Key

1. **A. Tim, Roger, and Josh are going to start their own band**

   Tim wanted to be a musician and start his own band. After meeting others who shared the same dreams, you can infer that they worked together in an attempt to make their dreams become a reality.

2. **Answer: B. The Smiths' luggage was lost**

   Although not directly stated, it appears that their luggage was lost. All of the baggage had been unloaded at the carousel, but the Smiths' luggage still hadn't arrived. Answer choice A isn't correct, because the Smiths were still waiting for their luggage. Answer choice C isn't correct, because there is no suggestion that the man had their luggage. Answer choice D isn't correct, because the man told them that they were at the right carousel.

3. **D. A college**

   The passage does not directly state that it takes place at a college, but it uses words such as *student*, *campus*, and *dean*. These allow you to infer where the passage takes place and draw the conclusion that the location is a college campus.

4. **B. Students believe that the new dean is guilty of discrimination**

   Even though the passage does not state this, you can infer that the students think the dean is guilty because they are demonstrating against his hire. If they believed he was innocent of the charges, they would not likely be demonstrating.

5. **C. Climbers must receive special training on how to descend**

   Because the author stresses the dangers when climbing down the mountain, you can conclude that it is important to have special training on how to descend Mount Everest.

6. **A. Parents should take parenting classes**

   The author believes parenting is difficult job, therefore, it is logical to think that the author believes parents should have training.

Do a double take
Read test questions and answer choices twice. It's easy to misunderstand a question or misread an answer choice the first time.

Summarizing

SUMMARIZING is telling a shorter version of an event, piece of literature, or visual story.

An effective summary of a story includes the characters, conflict, setting (place and time), and main events.

An effective summary of a nonfiction (factual) passage includes the main idea stated in one sentence. Think about what you have learned about main ideas when you are asked to identify an effective summary.

> **SUMMARIZING:** telling a shorter version of an event, piece of literature, or visual story

> An effective summary of a story includes the characters, conflict, setting (place and time), and main events.

> An effective summary of a nonfiction (factual) passage includes the main idea stated in one sentence.

Example

Read the following passage. Think about the main idea and the details. Then complete the table below. Completing the table will help you write a good summary.

Chili peppers may turn out to be the wonder drug of the decade. The fiery fruit comes in many sizes, shapes, and colors, all of which grow on plants that are genetic descendants of the tepin plant, originally native to the Americas. Connoisseurs of the regional cuisines of the Southwest and Louisiana are already well aware that food flavored with chilies can cause a good sweat, but medical researchers are learning more every day about the medical power of capsaicin, the ingredient in the peppers that produces the heat.

Capsaicin, used as a pain medication, has been a part of medicine for centuries. It is, in fact, the active ingredient in several currently available over-the-counter liniments for sore muscles. Recent research has been examining the value of the compound for the treatment of other painful conditions. Capsaicin shows some promise in the treatment of phantom limb syndrome, as well as shingles and some types of headaches. Additional research focuses upon the use of capsaicin to relieve pain in post-surgical patients. Scientists speculate that application of the compound to the skin causes the body to release endorphins—natural pain relievers manufactured by the body itself. An alternative theory holds that capsaicin somehow interferes with the transmission of signals along the nerve fibers, thus reducing the sensation of pain.

In addition to its well-documented history as a painkiller, capsaicin has recently received attention as a phytochemical, one of the naturally occurring compounds from foods that show cancer-fighting qualities. Like the phytochemical sulfoaphane, which is found in broccoli, capsaicin might turn out to be an agent capable of short-circuiting the actions of carcinogens at the cell level before they can cause cancer.

Break it down

Having trouble understanding a sentence? Break it into pieces. A comma is usually a good place to make a break. Take this sentence: "The fiery fruit comes in many sizes, shapes, and colors, all of which grow on plants that are genetic descendants of the tepin plant, originally native to the Americas." Break it down in your mind: "The fiery fruit comes in many sizes, shapes, and colors. All of them grow on plants that are genetic descendants of the tepin plant. The tepin plant is originally native to the Americas."

Write the topic. Then write the main idea of the entire passage in *one* sentence. Finally, include six details. The main idea will be the summary of the passage.

Topic	
Main Idea and Summary	
Detail	
Detail	
Detail	
Detail	
Detail	
Detail	

Here's a completed table:

Topic	Chili Peppers
Main Idea and Summary	Chili peppers have proved useful in treating a variety of ailments, and they contain the chemical capsaicin, which is a phytochemical, or natural compound that may help fight cancer.
Detail	Chili peppers could be the wonder drug of the decade.
Detail	Chili peppers contain capsaicin.
Detail	Capsaicin can be used as a pain medication.
Detail	Capsaicin is a phytochemical.
Detail	Phytochemicals show cancer-fighting qualities.
Detail	Capsaicin might be able to short-circuit the effects of carcinogens.

Roar!
Be sure to eat a healthy meal before the test. You don't want to be distracted by a growling stomach!

FIGURATIVE LANGUAGE: language that is not literal but is symbolic in some way

Understanding Figurative Language

FIGURATIVE LANGUAGE is language that is not literal. In other words, it is language that is not used in its strict, dictionary meaning. Instead, it is language that is symbolic in some way. For example, read the following pair of sentences:

Because Emily had <u>cold feet</u>, *she put on an extra pair of wool socks.*

Dahlia had planned to sing a song tonight, but she didn't because she got <u>cold feet</u>.

In the first sentence, the phrase *cold feet* is literal. Emily's feet were cold, so she put on an extra pair of socks.

In the second sentence, Dahlia planned to sing, but she got nervous. The *cold feet* in this sentence is figurative language. *Cold feet* is an idiom, a type of figurative language, that means *a sudden loss of courage.*

Time to face the music

Idioms often have interesting origins. Why does *face the music* mean *accept the consequences of your actions*? A popular theory is that the expression comes from British military history. When someone was court marshaled, a drum squad would play; therefore, the court-marshaled soldier would have to *face the music*. Try looking up the origin of other idioms, such as *cross the line* and *nose to the grindstone*, on the Internet.

There are many types of figurative language. You don't need to know the names of all of them, but it's important to understand that language isn't always literal. By learning about figurative language, you'll better understand the intended meaning of the passages you read.

Here are some of the most common types of figurative language:

EXAMPLES OF FIGURATIVE LANGUAGE	
Simile	Comparison between two things using the word *like* or *as*. For example:
	He is as sharp *as* a tack.
	Lily danced around the room *like* a butterfly.
	I'm as hungry *as* a horse.

Continued on next page

Metaphor	Comparison between two things that does *not* use the word *like* or *as*. A word or phrase that has one meaning is used to represent something else. For example: Life is a rollercoaster. The math quiz was a piece of cake. After standing in the cold, her fingers were icicles.
Personification	Human characteristics attributed to an inanimate object, animal, or abstract quality. For example: The teacher enjoyed watching the dancing minds of her students. The sunshine reached into my kitchen and pulled me into my garden. Destiny whispered in his ear.
Euphemism	The substitution of an agreeable term for one that might offend or suggest something unpleasant. For example: *passed away* instead of *died* *let go* instead of *fired* *between jobs* instead of *unemployed*
Hyperbole	Deliberate exaggeration in order to add emphasis. For example: I could sleep for a week. He made enough chili to feed an army. What's in this box? It weighs a ton.
Oxymoron	A contradiction in terms, used deliberately for effect. It is usually made up of an adjective and a noun that contradict each other. For example: controlled chaos paid volunteer larger half

Continued on next page

Idiom	An expression that has a different meaning than the literal meaning of the words. For example:
	pass the buck means *blame someone else*
	under the weather means *sick*
	drag your feet means *procrastinate*

Figuratively speaking...

As a reader, notice the use of figurative language. Don't expect the meaning of every sentence to be literal. Think carefully when you encounter an idiom or other type of figurative language in a passage.

Putting Comprehension Skills Together

Now that you have learned comprehension skills, try putting it all together and answering questions about several passages.

Get involved

To improve reading comprehension, become actively involved with the material. What does that mean? After you read something, explain it to a friend, read part of it aloud, write a summary, write down follow-up questions you have about the topic, draw a picture describing what you read—anything that helps you become an *active participant* and not just a passive reader.

Practice Test Questions

Read the passage below and then answer the practice test questions that follow.

While one day recycling may be mandatory in all states, right now it is voluntary in many communities. Those of us who participate in recycling know just how important it is. By recycling glass, aluminum cans, and plastic bottles, we have reduced the volume of disposable trash by one-third, thereby extending the useful life of local landfills by over a decade. Imagine the difference if those dramatic results were achieved nationwide. The amount of reusable items we thoughtlessly throw away is staggering. For example, Americans dispose of enough steel every day to supply Detroit car manufacturers for three months. Additionally, we dispose of enough aluminum annually to rebuild the nation's air fleet. These statistics, available from the Environmental Protection Agency, should encourage us to watch what we throw away.

1. According to this passage:

   A. Through recycling, disposable trash as been reduced by one-half

   B. We throw away enough steel each day to supply Detroit car manufacturers for three months

   C. Most communities require citizens to recycle glass, aluminum cans, and plastic bottles

   D. The United States government has a plan to impose mandatory recycling in every state

2. The author of this passage would agree that recycling:

   A. Is beneficial

   B. Should be mandatory

   C. Is only slightly effective

   D. Causes several serious problems

3. According to this passage, recycling is:

   A. Effortless

   B. Time-consuming

   C. Mandatory

   D. Voluntary

Read the passage below and answer the question that follows.

Rainforests recycle air and clean water. The trees capture and remove a large amount of the carbon dioxide from the air. This decreases the overall temperature of the planet.

4. According to this passage, it's reasonable to assume that:

   A. Temperatures will decrease if rainforests are destroyed

   B. Carbon dioxide is harmful to plants and animals

   C. The rainforests affect people throughout the world

   D. The temperature of the rainforests is decreasing

Practice Test Questions (cont.)

Read the passage below and answer the question that follows.

Countless species of snakes, some more dangerous than others, still lurk on the urban fringes of Florida's towns and cities. They will often invade domestic spaces, frightening people and their pets.

5. **According to this passage, it is reasonable to assume that:**

   A. Snakes are a problem in Florida

   B. The people of Florida work to protect their snakes

   C. The snakes in Florida are harmless.

   D. Snakes are more prevalent in Florida than in other states

Read the passage below and answer the question that follows.

The local charity for the homeless is planning to open a new soup kitchen located on Main Street. Its objective is to provide three well-rounded meals to as many as 75 homeless people each day. The kitchen will open at 7:00 in the morning for breakfast and will continue to serve food throughout the day until dinner is over at 6:30 p.m. Local supermarkets have already agreed to supply food to the charity; however, they are still in need of volunteers to help run the food lines. In addition, further donations of money and food are needed to supply the patrons adequately.

6. **According to the passage:**

   A. The soup kitchen will serve up to 75 people each week

   B. All volunteers have been lined up

   C. People may contribute cash donations

   D. Local supermarkets will be providing all the food

Practice Test Questions (cont.)

Read the passage below and then answer the practice test questions that follow.

No one really knows how Valentine's Day started. There are several legends, however, which are often told. The first attributes Valentine's Day to a Christian priest who lived in Rome during the third century, under the rule of Emperor Claudius. Rome was at war, and apparently, Claudius felt that married men did not fight as well as bachelors. Consequently, Claudius banned marriage for the duration of the war. However, Valentinus, the priest, risked his life to marry couples secretly in violation of Claudius' law.

The second legend is even more romantic. In this story, Valentinus is a prisoner, having been condemned to death for refusing to worship pagan deities. While in jail, he fell in love with his jailer's daughter, who happened to be blind. He prayed daily for her sight to return, and, miraculously, it did. On February 14, the day that he was condemned to die, he was allowed to write the young woman a note. In this farewell letter, he promised eternal love, and signed at the bottom of the page the now famous words, "Your Valentine."

7. **According to this passage:**

   A. Emperor Claudius lived during the third century

   B. The legend is believed by all Romans

   C. Emperor Claudius believed in marriage

   D. Only two legends exist about Valentine's Day

8. **According to the second legend:**

   A. Valentinus was blind

   B. The daughter prayed for her father's sight

   C. Valentinus was condemned to die

   D. Valentinus was freed

9. **According to the passage, where does the first legend take place?**

   A. France

   B. Germany

   C. Russia

   D. Italy

Answer Key

1. **B. We throw away enough steel each day to supply Detroit car manufacturers for three months**

Read each answer choice carefully. Answer choice B is the only fact that is stated in the passage.

2. **A. Is beneficial**

The passage states the many benefits of recycling, such as extending the useful life of local landfills. Therefore, it is reasonable to infer that the author would agree that recycling is beneficial.

3. **D. Voluntary**

The passage states that recycling is voluntary, so answer choice D is the correct answer.

4. **C. The rainforests affect people throughout the world**

The final sentence of the passage is evidence that allows us to infer that the rainforests affect people throughout the world. It might be tempting to choose answer choice A, but be sure to read the passage carefully: According to the passage, it is fair to assume that temperatures would *increase*, not *decrease*.

5. **A. Snakes are a problem in Florida**

The passage states that the snakes scare people and have invaded towns and cities. The reader can therefore infer that the snakes are a problem.

6. **C. People may contribute cash donations**

According to the last sentence, the charity is seeking donations of money and food. Therefore, you know that people may contribute cash donations.

7. **A. Emperor Claudius lived during the third century**

The first paragraph states that a priest lived in Rome during the third century, under the rule of Emperor Claudius. Therefore, you know that Emperor Claudius lived during the third century. You might be tempted to choose answer choice D, but be careful: Two legends are discussed in the passage, but the first paragraph states that there are several legends, not just the two in this passage.

8. **C. Valentinus was condemned to die**

The passage states that he had been condemned to death. None of the other answer choices are facts that are in the passage.

9. **D. Italy**

The legend takes place in Rome, which is in Italy.

How would I use this?

Military recruiting specialists provide information about the military to civilians. They explain everything from training opportunities to ASVAB test results to military careers. In order to provide the most current information, recruiting specialists must read and accurately interpret written material, including enlistment requirements, updates about pay and benefits, and military career specifications.

CHAPTER 3
ARITHMETIC REASONING

The Arithmetic Reasoning subtest of the ASVAB is all word problems. A **WORD PROBLEM** is a real-world, applied math problem presented as a story.

Even hearing the words "word problem" can elicit groans from test takers. Word problems can be some of the most challenging math problems on a test. But the more types of word problems you practice solving, the better prepared and more confident you'll be for the test. In this chapter, you'll learn how to solve word problems involving fractions, percents, probability, averages, and more.

> *The Arithmetic Reasoning subtest of the ASVAB is all word problems.*

> **WORD PROBLEM:** a real-world, applied math problem presented as a story

> **ASVAB tip!**
> On the CAT-ASVAB, the Arithmetic Reasoning subtest is 39 minutes long and has 16 questions.

Basic Operations

Let's start with some problems you can solve using the basic operations: addition, subtraction, multiplication, and division. Choosing the correct operation is sometimes the key to solving the problem.

Using addition

Addition is the easiest operation to identify in word problems. Use addition when you want to find the sum of two or more numbers. The words "more," "additional," and "total" are often hints that you should add. Here's an example of a problem that you solve by adding the numbers.

Example: Marco went to the movies. He spent $8.50 for a ticket, $2.75 for popcorn, and $1.95 for a bottle of water. How much did he spend total?

He bought a ticket, popcorn, and water.	$8.50 + 2.75 + 1.95$
Add.	13.20

Therefore, he spent a total of $13.20.

Using subtraction

Use subtraction to find the difference between two numbers. Phrases like these are often hints that you should use subtraction.

SUBTRACTION PHRASES
what is the difference...
how much change did he get back...
how much does she have left...
how much did she save...
how much more...

Here are two examples of problems that you solve by subtracting one number from another.

Oh gross!
Gross pay is the amount someone is paid before deductions, such as taxes and insurance, are taken out. **Net pay** is "take-home pay." If a test question asks for net pay, you are being asked for the total pay minus the deductions.

Example: Gina bought 48 cans of cat food. Her cat eats one can of food a day. How many cans does she have left after 30 days?

| She started with 48 cans, and the cat ate 30. | $48 - 30$ |
| Subtract. | 18 |

Therefore, she has 18 cans left.

Example: Santiago bought a pair of running shoes. The regular price is $89.00, but they were on sale for $75.95. How much did he save?

| Subtract the sale price from the regular price. | $89.00 - 75.95$ |
| Do the math. | 13.05 |

Therefore, he saved $13.05.

Now you try one.

For your convenience, the practice test questions also appear the end of the book so you can sit down and go through them all at once.

Practice Test Question

1. Michael can do 23 pushups, Shin can do 31 pushups, and Dirk can do 17 more pushups than Michael. How many more pushups can Dirk do than Shin?

   A. 6
   B. 8
   C. 9
   D. 14

Answer Key

1. **C. 9**

   You have been asked *how many more* pushups Dirk can do than Shin. You need to subtract the number than Shin can do from the number that Dirk can do. Dirk can do 17 more than Michael (23 + 17), which equals 40. Subtract the number Shin can do, 31, from the number Dirk can do, 40. The answer is 9.

Using multiplication

Use multiplication to find the value of more than one of something—for example, the cost of 4 motorcycles, the number of students in 7 classes, the amount earned in 6 hours, the number of tires on 35 cars, or the number of hot dogs in 9 packages. Here's an example of a problem that you solve using multiplication.

The result when two or more numbers are multiplied together is called the product.

Example: Willem bought 14 packages of hamburger buns for a cookout. Each package contains 8 buns. How many hamburgers can he make with these buns?

He has 14 packages, each containing 8 buns. 14×8

Multiply.   112

Therefore, he can make 112 hamburgers.

Now you try one.

Practice Test Question

1. The Rosen family spends $150.00 to have cable television installed. They then spend $39.99 per month for cable television service. What is the total amount that they spend on cable television during the first year?

   A. $189.99

   B. $479.88

   C. $629.88

   D. $2,279.88

Answer Key

1. **C. $629.88**

   They spend $39.99 per month for cable television service, so for an entire year, they would spend $39.99 × 12, or $479.88. They also spend $150.00 to have cable television installed, so add $479.88 and $150.00. The answer is $629.88.

Estimate!

Sometimes you can estimate to find the correct answer—or at least to rule out incorrect answers. For the problem about cable television, you can estimate that the Rosen family pays about $40 per month, which is $480 a year. And $480 is about $500. Add that to the initial $150 charge, and you know that the answer will be about $650!

Using division

Use division to (as the word suggests!) divide something into parts. Look for questions with the words "each" and "per" in them. Here are some examples of division questions.

> The result when one number is divided by another is called the quotient.

How many players are on each team?	How much did he pay per month?
What is the cost of each baseball?	What is the cost of juice per ounce?
How much does he earn per hour?	How many crayons can each child have?

Practice Test Questions

1. Ellie buys bottles of water by the gross. One gross costs $72.00. What is the cost of each bottle of water?

   A. $0.50

   B. $0.72

   C. $3.00

   D. $6.00

2. Alicia bought 9 golden delicious apples for $4.23, and Glenn bought 7 red delicious apples for $3.64. Who got the better deal, and what was the difference in price per apple?

   A. Alicia; $0.05

   B. Alicia; $0.59

   C. Glenn; $0.05

   D. Glenn; $0.59

Answer Key

1. **A. $0.50**

    A gross is a dozen dozens, or 144. 144 bottles cost $72.00. To find the cost of each bottle, divide $72.00 by 144. The answer is $0.50.

2. **A. Alicia; $0.05**

    To find out who got the better deal, you need to find the price per apple. $4.23 ÷ 9 is $0.47, and $3.64 ÷ 7 is $0.52, so Alicia got the better deal. The difference between $0.47 and $0.52 is $0.52 − $0.47, or $0.05.

Variables

A **VARIABLE** is a letter, such as x, that represents an unknown value. Use a variable to solve a problem when one quantity is compared to another—for example, there are twice as many cars in a parking lot as trucks, a wool sweater costs $15.00 more than a cotton sweater, or Ming was driving 10 miles per hour faster than Eddie.

> **VARIABLE:** a letter, such as x, that represents an unknown value

Here are two examples of problems that you can solve by using a variable.

> Jane is three years older than Jose. The sum of their ages is 21. How old is Jose?

> A table costs four times as much as a chair. The cost of two chairs and a table is $90. How much does one table cost?

For each of these problems, let x equal one of the unknown quantities.

> Jane is three years older than Jose. The sum of their ages is 21. How old is Jane?
>
> Let x = Jose's age. Therefore, Jane's age is $x + 3$.

> A table costs four times as much as a chair. The cost of two chairs and a table is $90. How much does one table cost?
>
> Let x = the cost of a chair. Therefore, the cost of a table is $4x$.

Notice that you don't need to write ✕ between a number and a variable. For example, $5 \times x$ is simply written $5x$.

> Notice that you don't need to write x between a number and a variable. For example, $5 \times x$ is simply written 5x.

Let's try the first one.

Example: Jane is three years older than Jose. The sum of their ages is 21. How old is Jane?

Define the variable.	$x = $ Jose's age
Write the expression for Jane's age.	$x + 3 = $ Jane's age
The sum of their ages is 21.	$x + (x + 3) = 21$
$x + x$ is the same as $2 \times x$ or $2x$.	$2x + 3 = 21$
Subtract 3 from both sides of the equation.	$2x = 18$
Divide both sides of the equation by 2.	$x = 9$

The result is 9, but be careful! The variable, x, is Jose's age, but you were asked for Jane's age. The answer to the question is not 9. Jane is three years older than Jose, so the answer to the question is 12.

> **ASVAB tip!**
> The Armed Forces Qualification Test (AFQT) score is computed using four subtests, including the Arithmetic Reasoning subtest. Your AFQT score is critical because you must have a minimum qualifying score in order to enlist.

Example: A table costs four times as much as a chair. The cost of two chairs and a table is $90. How much does one table cost?

Define the variable.	$x = $ the cost of a chair
Write the expression for the cost of a table.	$4x = $ the cost of a table
2 chairs plus 1 table costs $90.	$2x + 4x = 90$
Add $2x$ and $4x$.	$6x = 90$
Divide both sides of the equation by 6.	$x = 15$

The result is 15, but, again, be careful: The variable, x, is the cost of a chair, but you were asked to find the cost of a table. A table costs four times as much as a chair, so the answer to the question is $60.

> **The big cover-up**
> After reading the examples in this chapter, try covering the steps with a blank piece of paper. Write each step, and then move the paper down to see if you're correct.

Practice Test Question

1. Three friends were playing a pickup game of basketball. Julia scored twice as many baskets as Aiden. Samir scored 3 more baskets than Aiden. Together, they scored 27 baskets. How many baskets did Julia score?

    A. 6
    B. 8
    C. 9
    D. 12

Answer Key

1. **D. 12**

    Let x = the number of baskets Aiden scored. Then $2x$ = the number of baskets Julia scored, and $x + 3$ = the number of baskets Samir scored. The sum of these is 27. When you solve for x, the result is 6, but be careful: The variable, x, is the number of baskets Aiden scored. You were asked for the number of baskets Julia scored. She scored twice as many as Aiden, so the correct answer is 12.

Fractions

A **FRACTION** is a number that represents part of a whole. For example, if 3 out of 4 students attended a football game, then $\frac{3}{4}$ of the students attended the game. If a family eats 3 out of 8 slices of pizza, then $\frac{5}{8}$ of the pizza is left uneaten. The top portion of the fraction is the **NUMERATOR**; the bottom portion is the **DENOMINATOR**.

> **FRACTION:** a number that represents part of a whole

> **NUMERATOR:** the top portion of a fraction

> **DENOMINATOR:** the bottom portion of a fraction

7 out of a dozen eggs are left in this egg carton. That fraction is written $\frac{7}{12}$.

A fraction is also a way of writing that one number is divided by another. For example, $\frac{50}{2}$ is the same as 50 divided by 2, which is 25.

Finding the fractional part of a whole

When you see the word "of," multiply.

You can use fractions to find a part of a whole. For instance, if $\frac{2}{5}$ (two out of five) of the vehicles on a dealer's lot are trucks, you might want to find the number of trucks. When you see the word "of," multiply.

Example: Find $\frac{1}{3}$ of 600.

When you see the word "of," multiply.	$\frac{1}{3} \times 600$
Rewrite 600 as $\frac{600}{1}$.	$\frac{1}{3} \times \frac{600}{1}$
Multiply the numerators and the denominators.	$\frac{600}{3}$
Divide 600 by 3.	2

Therefore, $\frac{1}{3}$ of 600 is 2.

Let's try the example discussed above.

Example: $\frac{2}{5}$ of the vehicles on a dealer's lot are trucks. If there are 375 vehicles on the lot, how many of the vehicles are trucks?

When you see the word "of," multiply.	$\frac{2}{5} \times 375$
Rewrite 375 as $\frac{375}{1}$.	$\frac{2}{5} \times \frac{375}{1}$
Multiply the numerators and the denominators.	$\frac{750}{5}$
Divide 750 by 5.	150

Therefore, $\frac{2}{5}$ of 375 vehicles is 150.

Adding and subtracting fractions

To add or subtract fractions that have the *same* denominator, simply add or subtract the numerators, and keep the same denominator.

To add or subtract fractions that have *different* denominators, first *convert* one or more of the fractions so that all of the fractions have the same denominator.

To convert a fraction, multiply both the numerator and denominator by the same number.

To convert a fraction, multiply both the numerator and denominator by the same number. Multiplying the numerator and denominator by the same number, for example, multiplying by $\frac{3}{3}$ or $\frac{5}{5}$, is equivalent to multiplying by 1.

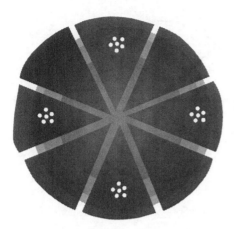

This cake cut into 8 slices shows that $\frac{8}{8}$ of a cake is equivalent to 1 whole cake.

Let's say you want to subtract $\frac{1}{8}$ from $\frac{3}{4}$. The denominators are different, so you need to find a **COMMON DENOMINATOR**. If you multiply $\frac{3}{4}$ by $\frac{2}{2}$, the denominators of both fractions will be 8.

COMMON DENOMINATOR: a denominator that is the same for two or more fractions

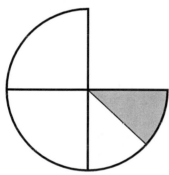

The figure above is $\frac{3}{4}$ of a circle. The slice shaded in gray is $\frac{1}{8}$ of a circle. What fraction of a circle will remain when $\frac{1}{8}$ is subtracted from $\frac{3}{4}$?

Example: Subtract $\frac{1}{8}$ from $\frac{3}{4}$.

Write out the problem.

$$\frac{3}{4} - \frac{1}{8}$$

Multiply the first fraction by $\frac{2}{2}$.

$$\left(\frac{3}{4} \times \frac{2}{2}\right) - \frac{1}{8}$$

Simplify.

$$\frac{6}{8} - \frac{1}{8}$$

Subtract the numerators.

$$\frac{5}{8}$$

Therefore, $\frac{1}{8}$ subtracted from $\frac{3}{4}$ is $\frac{5}{8}$.

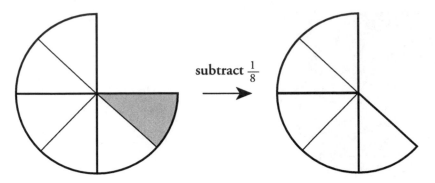

These figures show $\frac{1}{8}$ of a circle subtracted from $\frac{3}{4}$ (or $\frac{6}{8}$) of a circle.
Notice that the result is 5 "slices," each $\frac{1}{8}$ of a circle, or $\frac{5}{8}$.

Practice Test Question

1. Juan and Niki plow a field. Juan plows $\frac{1}{12}$ of the field, and Niki plows $\frac{1}{3}$ of the field. How much of the field is left unplowed?

   A. $\frac{1}{6}$

   B. $\frac{5}{12}$

   C. $\frac{7}{12}$

   D. $\frac{5}{6}$

Answer Key

1. **C.** $\frac{7}{12}$

First, add the fractional parts that are plowed. To add the fractions, they need to have a common denominator. If you multiply $\frac{1}{3}$ by $\frac{4}{4}$, the common denominator will be 12. Now add the fractions. Be careful: The result, $\frac{5}{12}$, is the amount of the field that has been *plowed*. You are asked how much is left *unplowed*. If $\frac{5}{12}$ of the field has been plowed, $\frac{12}{12} - \frac{5}{12}$, or $\frac{7}{12}$, is unplowed.

Dividing by a fraction

Dividing by a fraction is a funny concept. When would you divide by a fraction? Let's say you have 20 pounds of top soil and you want to divide it into 4-pound bags. How many bags can you fill? Five. How did you find the answer? It's simple to find the answer by using division. The same idea applies to fractions.

If you have 6 pounds of potato salad and you want to divide it up into $\frac{3}{4}$-pound containers, how many containers can you fill? Just do the division: $6 \div \frac{3}{4}$. But how do you divide by a fraction?

To divide by a fraction, just "flip" the fraction and then multiply.

$6 \div \frac{3}{4}$ is equivalent to $6 \times \frac{4}{3}$

Therefore, you can fill 8 containers of potato salad.

> *To divide by a fraction, just "flip" the fraction and then multiply.*

Practice Test Question

1. A farmer has 10 acres of land. He wants to allot $\frac{2}{5}$ of an acre for each kind of vegetable. How many different kinds of vegetables can he plant?

   A. 25
   B. 20
   C. 6
   D. 4

Answer Key

1. **A. 25**

   He's going to *divide* 10 acres into plots that are $\frac{2}{5}$ of an acre, so you need to divide 10 by $\frac{2}{5}$.

   To divide by $\frac{2}{5}$, "flip" the fraction, and then multiply. $10 \times \frac{5}{2} = 25$.

Reducing fractions

REDUCING A FRACTION is making it simpler. For example, the fractions $\frac{3}{21}$, $\frac{15}{50}$, $\frac{5}{5}$, and $\frac{2}{12}$ can all be reduced. To reduce a fraction, divide the numerator and the denominator by the same number. A number that divides two numbers evenly is called a COMMON FACTOR. In the example below, you need to find a common factor of the numerator, 15, and the denominator, 50. (The common factor is 5.)

> **REDUCING A FRACTION:** making a fraction simpler

> *To reduce a fraction, divide the numerator and the denominator by the same number.*

> **COMMON FACTOR:** a number that divides two numbers evenly

Example: Reduce $\frac{15}{50}$.

Begin with the unreduced fraction. $\qquad\qquad\qquad\qquad\qquad$ $\frac{15}{50}$

Divide the numerator and denominator by 5. $\qquad\qquad\qquad$ $\frac{3}{10}$

The reduced fraction is $\frac{3}{10}$. Therefore, $\frac{15}{50}$ is equivalent to $\frac{3}{10}$.

Important reminder

When reducing a fraction, remember to divide **both** the numerator and the denominator by the same number.

Example: Reduce $\frac{180}{630}$.

Begin with the unreduced fraction. $\qquad\qquad\qquad\qquad\qquad$ $\frac{180}{630}$

Divide the numerator and denominator by 10. $\qquad\qquad\qquad$ $\frac{18}{63}$

Divide the numerator and denominator by 9. $\qquad\qquad\qquad$ $\frac{2}{7}$

The reduced fraction is $\frac{2}{7}$. Therefore, $\frac{180}{630}$ is equivalent to $\frac{2}{7}$. Notice that, in this example, we reduced the fraction in two steps. When the numerator and denominator of a fraction are large numbers, it can be helpful to divide them by common factors until the fraction can't be reduced anymore.

Percents

PERCENT means "per hundred." 37% of voters means 37 out of 100 voters. 6% of the population means 6 out of 100 people. A 20% discount means 20 cents off of every dollar.

Since 37% is 37 out of 100, it is equivalent to $\frac{37}{100}$. It is also equivalent to 0.37. 6% is equivalent to $\frac{6}{100}$ and 0.06. 20% is equivalent to $\frac{20}{100}$ and 0.20.

Converting from fractions to decimals or percents

Numbers are numbers. The same number can be written as a fraction, decimal, or percent. 25% of the fish in a fish tank is the same as $\frac{1}{4}$ of the fish in a fish tank. 20% of all teachers is the same as $\frac{1}{5}$ of all teachers.

To convert a fraction to a decimal, divide the numerator by the denominator. For example, to convert $\frac{2}{5}$ to a decimal, divide 2 by 5. The answer is 0.4.

To write a decimal as a percent, move the decimal point two places to the right and add a percent sign. Therefore, 0.4 (which is equivalent to 0.40) can be written as 40%.

PERCENT: quantity per hundred

Numbers are numbers. The same number can be written as a fraction, decimal, or percent.

To convert a fraction to a decimal, divide the numerator by the denominator.

To write a decimal as a percent, move the decimal point two places to the right and add a percent sign.

> **When you're learning anything new...**
> Make sure you understand the concept before you dive into the details. For example, if you're learning about percents, read the definition and understand what percents are used for before diving into answering the math problems.

Example: Write $\frac{1}{8}$ as a percent.

Begin with a fraction.	$\frac{1}{8}$
Divide 1 by 8.	0.125
Move the decimal point two places to the right.	12.5
Add a percent sign.	12.5%

Therefore, $\frac{1}{8}$ can also be written as 12.5%. (For example, you might say that $\frac{1}{8}$, or 12.5%, of the products at a sporting goods store are on sale.)

A decimal that contains one or more digits that repeat indefinitely is called a **REPEATING DECIMAL**. To write a repeating decimal, put a line over the digit or digits that repeat. For example, the number 5.272727... is written $5.\overline{27}$.

> **REPEATING DECIMAL:**
> a decimal that contains one or more digits that repeat indefinitely

Example: Convert $\frac{2}{3}$ to a decimal.

Begin with a fraction.	$\frac{2}{3}$
Divide 2 by 3.	0.666...
Put a line over the digit that repeats.	$0.\overline{6}$

Therefore, $\frac{2}{3}$ is equivalent to $0.\overline{6}$.

Common fraction, decimal, and percent equivalents

The table below shows common fractions and their equivalent decimals and percents. Knowing just a few of the common ones will save you time—you'll recognize that one number is equivalent to another without having to perform a calculation.

COMMON FRACTIONS AND THEIR DECIMAL AND PERCENT EQUIVALENTS		
Fraction	**Decimal**	**Percent**
$\frac{1}{10}$	0.1	10%
$\frac{1}{9}$	$0.\overline{1}$	$11.\overline{1}\%$
$\frac{1}{8}$	0.125	12.5%
$\frac{1}{5}$	0.2	20%

Continued on next page

$\frac{1}{4}$	0.25	25%
$\frac{1}{3}$	$0.\bar{3}$	$33.\bar{3}\%$
$\frac{2}{5}$	0.4	40%
$\frac{1}{2}$	0.5	50%
$\frac{2}{3}$	$0.\bar{6}$	$66.\bar{6}\%$
$\frac{3}{4}$	0.75	75%

Finding the percent of a whole

You will often use percents to find part of a whole. As with fractions, when you see the word "of," multiply. Let's try an example using COMMISSION, the amount of money a salesperson earns on a sale.

As with fractions, when you see the word "of," multiply.

COMMISSION: the amount of money a salesperson earns on a sale

Example: Rani sells stereo equipment. He makes a 12% commission on his sales. What is his commission on a $260 sale?

You need to find 12% of $260.   12% of 260
Remember: When you see "of," multiply.   0.12 × 260
Do the math.   31.2
Therefore, Rani's commission is $31.20.

Practice Test Questions

1. Bruno received a score of 80 on his midterm science test. On his final exam, his score increased by 15%. What was the score on his final exam?

   A. 95
   B. 92
   C. 81.5
   D. 12

2. A baseball player got 5% fewer hits in 2010 than he did in 2009. If he got 140 hits in 2009, how many hits did he get in 2010?

   A. 70
   B. 126
   C. 133
   D. 147

The savings or the sale price?
Read the exam question carefully. Have you been asked for the tip only—or for the entire price of a meal? For the savings on a sweater—or for the sale price?

Answer Key

1. **B. 92**

   To find 15% of 80, multiply 0.15 by 80. The result, 12, is the increase from his midterm to his final exam. To find the score on the final exam, add 12 to 80.

2. **C. 133**

   To find 5% of 140, multiply 0.05 by 140. The result, 7, is the decrease. Be careful: The player got fewer hits in 2010, not more. To find the number of hits in 2010, subtract 7 from 140.

Mental math!
There are quick ways to find percentages in your head. To find 10%, just (mentally) move the decimal point of a number one place to the left. 140 becomes 14, and 600 becomes 60. From that, you can find many percentages. For example, 5% is half that number; 20% is twice that number; and 30% is three times that number.

Finding the percent one number is of another

You might want to find out what percent one number is of another. For example, if 68 out of 80 rooms at a motel are booked, what percent of the rooms are books? Or, if Art spends 12 minutes of each hour on the phone, what percent of his time does he spend on the phone? To find the percent that one number is of another, divide the first number by the second number.

To find the percent that one number is of another, divide the first number by the second number.

Practice Test Question

1. There are 39 men and 21 women in a softball league. What percent of the players are women?

   A. 35%
   B. 46%
   C. 54%
   D. 65%

Answer Key

1. **A. 35%**

   To find what percent one number is of another, divide the first number by the second. You want to find out what percent of the players are women; in other words, what percent 21 is of the total number of players. Be careful not to divide 21 by 39. You need to divide 21 by the total number of players, which is 60.

Finding percent increase or decrease

To find percent increase or decrease, find the amount that the value has changed, and then divide by the original value.

To find percent increase or decrease, find the amount that the value has changed, and then divide by the *original* value. For example, to find the percent increase of the price of a home, find the amount that the price has changed, and then divide that by the original price of the home.

Test-taking tip!
To *depreciate* means to decrease in value. If a test question says that something has depreciated a certain percent, the value has fallen.

Practice Test Questions

1. The cost of an Indian lunch buffet increased from $6.50 to $7.15. What was the percent increase?

   A. 65%

   B. 10%

   C. 6.5%

   D. 0.1%

2. When Vinny moved to Centerville, his car insurance premium increased from $795.00 to $969.90. What was the percent increase?

   A. 0.18%

   B. 0.22%

   C. 18%

   D. 22%

Answer Key

1. **B. 10%**

First, find the amount that the price changed, and then divide that amount by the original price. The price increased by $0.65. Divide $0.65 by $6.50. The result is 0.1, or 10%.

2. **D. 22%**

First, find the amount that the premium changed, and then divide that amount by the original cost. The premium increased $174.90. Divide $174.90 by $795.00. The result is 0.22, or 22%.

If you get stuck...

If you're having trouble answering a question, read the entire question, write down exactly what you need to *find*, and then write down everything you *know*.

Solving interest rate problems

An **INTEREST RATE** is the percent that someone needs to pay in order to borrow money, or the percent that someone earns on invested money. Interest rate is a percent of a whole—similar to a tip, a commission, or a percent discount. If you *borrow* $100 at annual interest rate of 5%, you have to *pay back* an additional 5% of $100.00 at the end of one year. If you *invest* money that earns an annual interest rate of 5%, you will *receive* an additional 5% at the end of one year.

INTEREST RATE: the percent that someone needs to pay in order to borrow money, or the percent that someone earns on invested money

Interest rate is a percent of a whole—similar to a tip, a commission, or a percent discount.

Just the highlights...

When people are studying, they tend to highlight too much. A full page of highlighted text isn't helpful! Instead, use a highlighter sparingly. Or, better yet, use arrows to point to important pieces of information. Add short notes in the margins to reword important details in your own words.

Practice Test Question

1. Sasha deposits $250.00 into a savings account that earns an annual interest rate of 5.5%. He doesn't withdraw from the account or deposit any additional money in the account. What is the balance after one year?

    A. $13.75
    B. $137.50
    C. $263.75
    D. $387.50

Answer Key

1. **C. $263.75**

    First, find the interest earned; then add the interest to the amount invested. The interest is 5.5% of $250.00, or

    0.055 × 250, which equals 13.75. To find the balance, add the interest, $13.75, to the amount invested, $250.00. The answer is $263.75.

Be careful!
When converting a percent to a decimal, move the decimal point *two* places to the left. For example, 5.5% becomes 0.055, *not* 0.55. The number 0.55 is equal to 55%.

Ratios

A ratio shows the relationship between two numbers.

A ratio shows the relationship between two numbers. If there is one coach for every eight baseball players, the ratio of coaches to players is "1 to 8," which can be written 1:8 or $\frac{1}{8}$. If there are two chaperones for every five students on a field trip, the ratio of chaperones to students is 2:5 or $\frac{2}{5}$.

Just like fractions, ratios can be reduced by dividing both numbers by a common factor. For example, the ratio 8:12 or $\frac{8}{12}$ can be reduced by dividing both numbers by 4. The reduced ratio is 2:3 or $\frac{2}{3}$.

Practice Test Questions

1. Jorge has 78 action DVDs and 26 comedy DVDs. What is the ratio of action DVDs to comedy DVDs?

   A. $\frac{1}{3}$

   B. $\frac{3}{1}$

   C. $\frac{2}{3}$

   D. $\frac{3}{2}$

2. Janine has an annual salary of $22,000 per year. Leonard's annual salary is 25% higher than Janine's. What is the ratio of Janine's salary to Leonard's salary?

   A. $\frac{1}{4}$

   B. $\frac{4}{1}$

   C. $\frac{4}{5}$

   D. $\frac{5}{4}$

Answer Key

1. **B.** $\frac{3}{1}$

   The ratio of action DVDs to comedy DVDs is $\frac{78}{26}$. A common factor of both 78 and 26 is 26. Divide each number by 26, and the reduced ratio is $\frac{3}{1}$.

2. **C.** $\frac{4}{5}$

   Leonard's annual salary is 25% higher than Janine's. To find Leonard's salary, first find 25% of $22,000. Remember, when you hear the word "of," multiply. 0.25 times $22,000 is $5,500, so Leonard's salary is $5,500 more than Janine's. To find his salary, add her salary, $22,000, to $5,500. His salary is $27,500. The ratio of Janine's salary to Leonard's salary is $\frac{22,000}{27,500}$. This ratio reduces. To reduce the ratio, divide the numerator and denominator by common factors until it can't be reduced anymore. The ratio of her salary to his is $\frac{4}{5}$.

Are your ratios flipped?
When answering a ratios question, double check to see which ratio you've been asked for—girls to boys, or boys to girls? Cars to trucks, or trucks to cars?

Proportions

PROPORTION: one ratio set equal to another

A PROPORTION is one ratio set equal to another. Use a ratio when you hear something that sounds like, "This is to that, as this is to that." Here are some examples of problems that can be solved quickly using proportions.

> If 6 people can shovel 4 driveways in one hour, how many driveways can 9 people shovel in the same amount of time?
>
> This question is asking, "6 people is to 4 driveways, as 9 people is to how many driveways?"

> If you can buy 10 homemade muffins for $15, how many can you buy for $24?
>
> This question is asking, "10 muffins is to $15, as how many muffins is to $24?"

> If a landscaper charges $200 to plant 3 trees, how much will he charge to plant 10 trees?
>
> This question is asking, "$200 is to 3 trees, as how much is to 10 trees?"

Solving a problem by using a proportion

To solve a problem by using a proportion, write a proportion that shows the relationship between the numbers. For the unknown value, use a variable, such as x. Then solve for x. Here are proportions for the examples above.

> If 6 people can shovel 4 driveways in one hour, how many driveways can 9 people shovel in the same amount of time?
>
> $\frac{6}{4} = \frac{9}{x}$

> If you can buy 10 homemade muffins for $15, how many can you buy for $24?
>
> $\frac{10}{15} = \frac{x}{24}$

> If a landscaper charges $200 to plant 3 trees, how much will he charge to plant 10 trees?
>
> $\frac{200}{3} = \frac{x}{10}$

Example: If 8 security guards can watch 32 security monitors, how many security monitors can 2 security guards watch?

Notice that this question is asking, "8 guards is to 32 monitors, as 2 guards is to how many monitors?"

Set up the proportion. $\frac{8}{32} = \frac{2}{x}$

Multiply both sides of the equation by x. $\frac{8x}{32} = 2$

Multiply both sides of the equation by 32. $8x = 64$

To solve for x, divide both sides by 8. $x = 8$

Therefore, 2 security guards can watch 8 monitors.

You might have found a quicker way to solve this problem. If you did, great! But be sure that you are able to solve it the "long way." Understanding how to use proportions will help you solve many word problems.

Is there a shortcut?

Are you missing an easy way to solve a problem? Let's say you're asked, "If 4 boxes contain 24 cans of paint, how many cans of paint are in 8 boxes?" You could set up a proportion, but take a moment to read the question carefully. Twice as many boxes contain twice as many cans of paint!

Practice Test Question

1. If Lynn can set up 26 computers in 6 hours, how many computers can she set up in 15 hours?

   A. 65
   B. 62
   C. 60
   D. 52

Answer Key

1. **A. 65**

   The question is asking, "26 computers is to 6 hours, as how many computers is to 15 hours?"

   Set up the proportion $\frac{26}{6} = \frac{x}{15}$. To solve for x, multiply both sides of the equation by 15. Then do the math. The answer is 65.

SCALE: a ratio that shows the relationship between a drawing or model and the actual object

Solving problems involving scale drawings and scale models

Scale drawings and scale models are scaled down (or sometimes scaled up) versions of real objects. A SCALE is a ratio that shows the relationship between a drawing or model and the actual object. For example, the scale 1:30 shows that the real object is 30 times larger than it is in the drawing or model.

To solve problems involving scale, set up a proportion. For example, if the scale is 1:30, set up this proportion:

$$\frac{\text{length on drawing or model}}{\text{actual length}} = \frac{1}{30}$$

Example: Roger is building a scale model of a boat. The scale is 1:20. The actual boat is 40 feet long. How long should the model of the boat be?

Remember how to write the proportion.

$$\frac{\text{length on model}}{\text{actual length}}$$

Set up the proportion.

$$\frac{x}{40} = \frac{1}{20}$$

Multiply both sides of the equation by 40.

$$x = \frac{40}{20}$$

Reduce.

$$x = 2$$

Therefore, the model of the boat should be 2 feet long.

Practice Test Question

1. The wingspan on a scale model of an airplane is 1.5 feet. The scale of the model is 1:50. What is the actual wingspan of the plane?

   A. 33 feet

   B. 50 feet

   C. 75 feet

   D. 150 feet

Answer Key

1. **C. 75 feet**

   Set up the proportion $\frac{1.5}{x}$. To solve for x, multiply both sides of the equation by x, and then multiply both sides of the equation by 50. The answer is 75.

SIMILAR: having the same shape but not necessarily the same size

Using proportions to solve similarity problems

If two shapes are SIMILAR, they have the same shape but not necessarily the same size. Here are some examples of similar shapes.

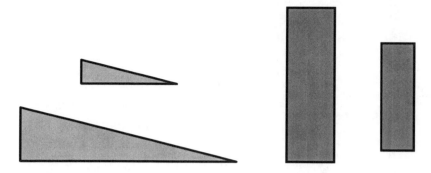

Here are a pair of similar triangles and a pair of similar rectangles. Notice that the figures in each pair have the same shape but not the same size.

How can proportions help you solve problems involving similar shapes? The lengths of the corresponding sides are proportional. In other words, the ratios of the corresponding sides are equal.

For example, in a pair of similar triangles, if the shortest sides of the two triangles are 1 inch and 4 inches, then you know that the other sides are in the same proportion—the sides of the larger triangle are all 4 times longer than the sides of the shorter triangle.

Practice Test Question

1. **A contractor remodeling a kitchen is installing two triangular tiles on the floor. Two triangular pieces of tile are similar. If the shortest sides of the tiles are 4 inches and 6 inches, and the longest side of the larger tile is 15 inches, how long is the longest side of the smaller tile?**

   A. 7.5 inches

   B. 10 inches

   C. 12 inches

   D. 13 inches

Answer Key

1. **B. 10 inches**

   In similar shapes, the ratios of the corresponding sides are equal. Write the ratios and set them equal to each other. The ratio of the shortest sides is $\frac{4}{6}$, and the ratio of the longest sides is $\frac{x}{15}$. Set them equal to each other and write the proportion $\frac{4}{6} = \frac{x}{15}$. To solve for x, multiply both sides of the equation by 15. Then do the math. The answer is 10.

Probability

PROBABILITY: the measure of how likely it is that an event will occur

PROBABILITY is the measure of how likely it is that an event will occur. What is the probability that it will rain? That a game spinner will land on red? That you will choose grape when you reach into a bag of candy?

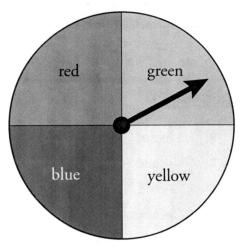

When this spinner is spun, what is the probability that it will land on yellow? Yellow is one of four sections, so the probability is 1 out of 4.

To find the probability that an event will occur, divide the number of acceptable outcomes by the total number of possible outcomes.

Probability can be expressed in words, as a fraction, as a ratio, or as a percent.

1 out of 4 $= \frac{1}{4} =$ 1:4 $=$ 25%

To find the probability that an event will occur, divide the number of acceptable outcomes by the total number of possible outcomes.

Example: Find the probability of rolling an even number when you roll a six-sided die.

Three numbers on a die are even (2, 4, and 6), so the number of acceptable outcomes is 3. There are six numbers on a die, so the total number of possible outcomes is 6.

Divide the number of acceptable outcomes by the total number of possible outcomes.

Acceptable outcomes divided by total outcomes. $\frac{3}{6}$

Reduce. $\frac{1}{2}$

Therefore, the probability of rolling an even number is $\frac{1}{2}$, or 50%.

Practice Test Question

1. DeShawn reaches into a bag of candy. There are 10 butterscotch candies and 14 chocolate candies in the bag. What is the probability that he will choose a butterscotch candy?

   A. $\frac{5}{7}$

   B. $\frac{14}{24}$

   C. $\frac{5}{12}$

   D. $\frac{1}{10}$

Answer Key

1. **C.** $\frac{5}{12}$

   To find the probability, divide the number of acceptable outcomes, in this case, the number of butterscotch candies, by the total number of possible outcomes. There are 10 butterscotch candies and a total of 24 candies, so the probability is $\frac{10}{24}$, which reduces to $\frac{5}{12}$.

Finding probability of compound events

You can also find the probability of a COMPOUND EVENT, an event that includes two or more events. What is the probability of a coin landing on tails twice in a row? That a game spinner will land on red the first time you spin it, and blue the next time you spin it? To find the probability of two or more events, multiply the probabilities of each separate event.

COMPOUND EVENT: an event that includes two or more events

To find the probability of two or more events, multiply the probabilities of each separate event.

Practice Test Question

1. Sanjay is playing a board game that has a spinner that is divided into four equal sections of different colors. He spins the spinner twice. What is the probability that the spinner will land on red both times?

   A. $\frac{1}{2}$

   B. $\frac{1}{4}$

   C. $\frac{1}{8}$

   D. $\frac{1}{16}$

Answer Key

1. **D.** $\frac{1}{16}$

   The probability that the spinner will land on red each time he spins is 1 out of 4, or $\frac{1}{4}$. To find the probability of a compound event, multiply the probabilities.

   In this case, to find the probability that it will land on red twice, multiply $\frac{1}{4}$ by $\frac{1}{4}$. Therefore, the chance that it will land on red both times is $\frac{1}{16}$.

Have a healthy snack while you study
It gives you energy and helps you concentrate. Try carrot sticks, an apple, or peanut butter and crackers. Water, juice, and milk are good beverage choices. Avoid sugar and caffeine.

Unit Rates

UNIT RATE: the amount of one quantity per one unit of another quantity

A UNIT RATE describes the amount of one quantity per one unit of another quantity. There are many examples of unit rates.

miles per hour	rate of pay per hour
students per class	pickles per sandwich
cost per item	miles per gallon
balloons inflated per minute	candies per box

Here is the general rule.

unit rate × quantity = total

For example:

miles per hour × number of hours = total miles
cost per item × number of items = total cost
rate of pay per hour × number of hours = total pay
candies per box × number of boxes = total number of candies

Example: Jada hails a taxi, which takes her 5.5 miles to the train station. The taxi charges $3.00 plus $2.70 per mile. What is the total fare for Jada's trip?

Find rate per mile × number of miles	2.70 × 5.5
Multiply.	14.85
The taxi charges an additional $3.00.	14.85 + 3.00
Add.	17.85

Therefore, Jada's total fare is $17.85.

A key to solving word problems

Read the entire question before you begin working. It might sound simple, but it's key. Read the entire question, make sure you have all of the information, and then begin working. If you follow this simple but important rule, you'll become a better problem solver.

Practice Test Questions

1. A window washer is paid 35¢ per window washed. If he can wash 24 windows per hour, how much money can he earn in one hour and 15 minutes?

    A. $10.50

    B. $9.66

    C. $9.24

    D. $8.40

2. Maria works four days a week selling hot dogs from a street cart. She pays $325.00 per week to rent the cart, and she pays $145.00 per week for hot dogs, buns, and other supplies. She sells the hot dogs for $2.50 each. How many hot dogs does she need to sell each week in order to make a profit?

    A. 189

    B. 188

    C. 48

    D. 47

Answer Key

1. **A. $10.50**

First, find the amount earned in one hour. He can wash 24 windows in one hour. 35¢ (or $0.35) per window × 24 windows is $8.40. To find the amount earned in one hour and 15 minutes (or one and one-quarter hour), multiply $8.40 by 1.25. The answer is $10.50.

2. **A. 189**

In order to make a profit, she needs to earn more than she spends. Her expenses are rent ($325.00) plus supplies ($145.00). Her total expenses are $470.00. To make a profit, she needs to make more than $470.00 per week. She sells hot dogs for $2.50 each. $2.50 times what number is more than $470.00? Divide $470.00 by $2.50, and the result is 188. However, be careful: If she sells 188 hot dogs, she'll make exactly $470.00, so she'll break even. In order to make a profit, she needs to sell one more hot dog, so the answer is 189.

Equivalent Units of Measurement

Converting units of measurement allows you to express a measurement using different units. If you're given a measurement in feet, you can express it in inches. If you're given a measurement in gallons, you can express it in quarts.

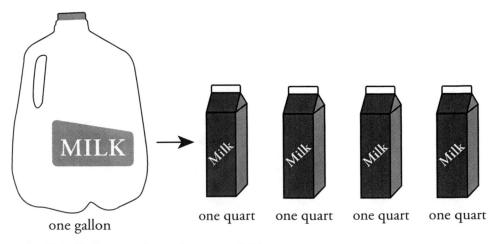

one gallon   one quart   one quart   one quart   one quart

One gallon of milk is equivalent to four quarts of milk.

Often you need to convert from one unit to another so that all of the measurements in a word problem are in the same units. If you are given measurements in meters and centimeters, convert the measurements so that they are all in meters or all in centimeters. If you are given measurements in yards and feet, convert the measurements so that they are all in yards or all in feet.

This table below lists some common equivalent measurements. Study these and know them by heart!

EQUIVALENT MEASUREMENTS	
1 foot	12 inches
1 yard	3 feet
1 meter	100 centimeters
1 kilometer	1,000 meters
1 pint	2 cups
1 quart	2 pints
1 gallon	4 quarts
1 pound	16 ounces
1 ton	2,000 pounds

Often you need to convert from one unit to another so that all of the measurements in a word problem are in the same units.

Two cents' worth

To help you remember that there are 100 <u>centi</u>meters in 1 meter, remember that there are 100 years in a <u>cent</u>ury and 100 <u>cent</u>s in a dollar.

Converting units of measurements

To convert between units, multiply by a CONVERSION FACTOR. A conversion factor is a fraction that is equal to 1 that allows you to convert from one unit to another. Use equivalent measurements in the table above to write conversion factors like the ones below.

CONVERSION FACTOR: a fraction that is equal to 1 that allows you to convert from one unit to another

EXAMPLES OF CONVERSION FACTORS			
$\frac{1 \text{ pound}}{16 \text{ ounces}}$	$\frac{2,000 \text{ pounds}}{1 \text{ ton}}$	$\frac{12 \text{ inches}}{1 \text{ foot}}$	$\frac{1 \text{ gallon}}{4 \text{ quarts}}$

Four quarters in a dollar

Remember that a *quart* is one *quarter* of a gallon. Just like there are four quarters in a dollar, there are four quarts in a gallon.

Example: A middle school is having a pancake breakfast to raise money for charity. Francisco and Denise volunteered to bring milk. Francisco brought 5 quarts and Denise brought 3 gallons. How many quarts of milk did the two students bring altogether?

Write the amount of milk brought.	5 quarts + 3 gallons
Multiply by the conversion factor.	5 quarts + (3 gallons × $\frac{\text{4 quarts}}{\text{1 gallon}}$)
Multiply. Notice that the gallons "cancel out."	5 quarts + 12 quarts
Add.	17 quarts

Therefore, there are 17 quarts of milk altogether.

Include the units in calculations

When solving unit conversion problems, write the units in every single step. Including the units helps you solve the problem because you can see how the units "cancel out." Writing the units will also help you avoid mistakes!

Example: A delivery truck is carrying 3.5 tons of dog food. What is the largest number of 8-pound bags of dog food that the truck could be carrying?

Write the number of tons of dog food.	3.5 tons
Multiply by the conversion factor.	3.5 tons × $\frac{\text{2,000 pounds}}{\text{1 ton}}$
Multiply. Notice that the tons "cancel out."	7,000 pounds

Now you know that the truck is carrying 7,000 pounds of dog food. How many 8-pound bags of dog food could be in the truck? To find the answer, divide.

Divide the total by the size of the bag of dog food.	7,000 pounds ÷ 8 pounds
Do the math.	875

Therefore, the truck could be carrying up to 875 8-pound bags of dog food.

Ready for more?

Common equivalent measurements are listed in the table above, but there are many, many more. To learn more equivalent measurements, use an Internet search engine. Search for a phrase such as *equivalent measurements*, *measurement conversion*, or *units of measure*.

Practice Test Question

1. Janelle buys 14 pieces of ribbon from a fabric store. Each piece is 18 inches long. If the ribbon costs $3.70 per foot, what is the total cost of the ribbon Janelle buys?

   A. $51.80
   B. $68.11
   C. $77.70
   D. $932.40

Answer Key

1. **B. $77.70**

   The total length of ribbon she bought is 14 × 18 inches, or 252 inches. The cost of the ribbon is given per foot, not per inch, so you need to convert from inches to feet. Multiply 252 inches by the conversion factor $\frac{1 \text{ foot}}{12 \text{ inches}}$. Therefore, 252 inches is equal to 21 feet. To find the total cost, multiply the number of feet of ribbon, 21, by the cost per foot, $3.70.

Is this reasonable?

After doing the math, look to see if your answer is reasonable. Is it reasonable that 14 pieces of ribbon would cost over $900? (Maybe if it's made of gold!) An unreasonable answer is a great guide. It allows you to eliminate an answer choice—and it is a sign that you need to redo your work to find where your calculation went wrong.

Practice Test Question

1. A medical device manufacturer has a 12-foot piece of plastic tubing. The manufacturer is going to cut it into pieces that are 3 inches long. How many pieces will there be?

   A. 3
   B. 4
   C. 40
   D. 48

Answer Key

1. **D. 48**

   You need to divide the total length of the tubing into 3-inch pieces, but you're given the total length in feet, so you need to convert units. To convert 12 feet to inches, multiply 12 feet by the conversion factor $\frac{12 \text{ inches}}{1 \text{ foot}}$. Therefore, 12 feet is equal to 144 inches. To divide the 144-inch piece into 3-inch pieces, divide 144 by 3. The answer is 48.

Averages

AVERAGE: a measure of the middle value of a set of numbers

The **AVERAGE** of a set of numbers is a measure of the middle value. The average represents all of the values in the set. You might want to know the average number of students in a graduating class, or the average price of a house in a neighborhood. The average tells you the typical number of students or the typical price of a home.

Fri	Sat	Sun	Mon
Partly Cloudy	Cloudy	Sunny	Mostly Sunny
74° High	61° High	58° High	65° High
58° Low	48° Low	49° Low	53° Low

Finding the average high temperature of these four days would tell you the typical high temperature during this period of time.

To find the average of a set of values, add up the numbers in the set, and then divide by the number of values in the set.

To find the average of a set of values, add up the numbers in the set, and then divide by the number of values in the set. That's it!

Example: Shantelle is shopping online for a FastSpeed Wireless Router. ABC Electronics sells it for $32.50, Cheapo Computers sells it for $29.90, XYZ Superstore sells it for $43.45, and Good Deal Computers has it on sale for $35.95. What is the average price that Shantelle found for the router?

Add up the numbers.	32.50 + 29.90 + 43.45 + 35.95
Do the math.	141.80
Divide by the number of values.	141.80 ÷ 4
Do the math.	35.45

Therefore, the average price that Shantelle found for the router is $35.45.

Make up word problems for a friend

Find a friend and make up word problems for each other—find the average of the high temperatures this week, or find the percent discount on a pair of pants. There are endless possibilities. Begin with examples from this book.

Practice Test Question

1. On Monday, the price of a gallon of gas was $3.25. The price increased 9¢ per gallon Tuesday. The price increased an additional 2¢ per gallon Wednesday. The price then dropped 4¢ per gallon Thursday. By Friday, the price per gallon was $3.33. What was the average price per gallon of gas during the five days?

   A. $3.28
   B. $3.29
   C. $3.32
   D. $4.15

Answer Key

1. **C. $3.32**

   First, find the price per gallon each day. The prices were $3.25, $3.34, $3.36, $3.32, and $3.33.

   Now add all the prices together. The total is $16.60. Divide by the number of values, 5. The answer is $3.32.

How would I use this?

In the military, dieticians are the nutritional experts for hospital patients. They manage food service operations, plan meals for patients who have special diets, create food service budgets, and more. Converting units of measurement is a required skill for dieticians. When planning meals or interpreting doctors' instructions, they must have the math skills to readily convert from teaspoons to cups or from ounces to pounds.

CHAPTER 4
MATHEMATICS KNOWLEDGE

The Mathematics Knowledge subtest of the ASVAB tests your understanding of mathematical concepts. In contrast to the Arithmetic Reasoning subtest, which is all word problems, the Mathematics Knowledge subtest is made up of more straightforward mathematical problems. Your job is to be familiar with the mathematical concepts so you can answer the questions. This chapter covers concepts from exponents to algebra to geometry.

Factorials

The **FACTORIAL** of a number is that number times the number one less than that number, times the number one less than that number, etc., until you reach 1. The factorial of a number is indicated by an exclamation point. Here's an example.

$$6! = 6 \times 5 \times 4 \times 3 \times 2 \times 1$$

When you multiply the numbers, you see that $6! = 720$.

> *The Mathematics Knowledge subtest of the ASVAB tests your understanding of mathematical concepts. In contrast to the Arithmetic Reasoning subtest, which is all word problems, the Mathematics Knowledge subtest is made up of more straightforward mathematical problems.*

> **FACTORIAL:** a number times the number one less than that number, times the number one less than that number, etc., until you reach 1

Practice Test Question

1. $5! = ?$

   A. 20

   B. 25

   C. 60

   D. 120

Answer Key

1. **D. 120**

   5! is 5 factorial. $5! = 5 \times 4 \times 3 \times 2 \times 1$, which equals 120.

> **Batter up!**
> The factorial of a number can be used to find the number of ways that a group of objects (or people!) can be arranged. How many different ways can 9 baseball players be ordered to hit in a line-up? To find the answer, simply find 9!. (And, by the way, the answer is a whopping 362,880!)

Exponents

EXPONENTS: a shorthand way to write repeated multiplication

EXPONENTS are a shorthand way to write repeated multiplication. A number raised to an exponent indicates that the number is multiplied by itself the number of times indicated by the exponent. Here are some examples:

6^4 is a shorthand way of writing $6 \times 6 \times 6 \times 6$.

12^5 is a shorthand way of writing $12 \times 12 \times 12 \times 12 \times 12$.

x^6 is a shorthand way of writing $x \times x \times x \times x \times x \times x$.

6^4 is read, "6 raised to the power of 4." If a number is **SQUARED**, it is raised to the power of 2. If a number is **CUBED**, it is raised to the power of 3. Here are some examples:

SQUARED: a number raised to the power of 2

13 squared is 13^2, which equals 13×13.

8 cubed is 8^3, which equals $8 \times 8 \times 8$.

CUBED: a number raised to the power of 3

Example: What is the value of 4 cubed?

4 cubed is 4^3.	4^3
4^3 is the same as $4 \times 4 \times 4$.	$4 \times 4 \times 4$
Perform the multiplication.	64
Therefore, 4 cubed, or 4^3, equals 64.	

> **ASVAB tip!**
> On the CAT-ASVAB, the Mathematics Knowledge subtest is 20 minutes long and has 16 questions.

Performing operations on numbers raised to exponents

There are easy rules for performing operations on numbers raised to exponents.

RULES FOR PERFORMING OPERATIONS WITH EXPONENTS	
Rule	**Example**
$n^a \times n^b = n^{a+b}$	$3^4 \times 3^5 = 3^9$
$\dfrac{n^a}{n^b} = n^{a-b}$	$\dfrac{7^{12}}{7^4} = 7^8$
$(n^a)^b = n^{a \times b}$	$(2^4)^3 = 2^{12}$

Notice that the rules for performing operations with exponents apply only when the bases (the numbers raised to exponents) are the same.

Notice that the rules for performing operations with exponents apply only when the bases (the numbers raised to exponents) are the same.

Practice Test Questions

1. $\dfrac{3^{16}}{3^4} = ?$

 A. 3^4

 B. 3^6

 C. 3^{12}

 D. 3^{20}

2. $(x^6)^3 = ?$

 A. x^2

 B. x^3

 C. x^9

 D. x^{18}

Answer Key

1. **C. 3^{12}**

 The rule is $\dfrac{n^a}{n^b} = n^{a-b}$, so you need to subtract the exponents. $\dfrac{3^{16}}{3^4} = 3^{16-4} = 3^{12}$.

2. **D. x^{18}**

 The rule is $(n^a)^b = n^{a \times b}$, so you need to multiply the exponents. $(x^6)^3 = x^{6 \times 3} = x^{18}$.

The notation for square root is $\sqrt{n}$.

Roots

The **SQUARE ROOT OF A NUMBER** is the number that, when multiplied by itself, produces that number. The square root of 25 is 5, because 5 times 5 is 25. The notation for square root is $\sqrt{n}$.

SQUARE ROOT OF A NUMBER: the number that, when multiplied by itself, produces that number

CUBE ROOT OF A NUMBER: the number that, when multiplied by itself, and then multiplied by itself again, produces that number

The notation for cube root is $\sqrt[3]{n}$.

The **CUBE ROOT OF A NUMBER** is the number that, when multiplied by itself, and then multiplied by itself again, produces that number. The cube root of 27 is 3, because 3 times 3 times 3 is 27. The notation for cube root is $\sqrt[3]{n}$.

Here are some common square roots and cube roots. Memorize these so you won't have to spend time to figuring them out during an exam!

COMMON SQUARE ROOTS AND CUBE ROOTS	
$\sqrt{16} = 4$	$\sqrt[3]{8} = 2$
$\sqrt{25} = 5$	$\sqrt[3]{27} = 3$
$\sqrt{36} = 6$	$\sqrt[3]{64} = 4$
$\sqrt{100} = 10$	$\sqrt[3]{125} = 5$
$\sqrt{144} = 12$	$\sqrt[3]{1,000} = 10$

Example: Find $\sqrt[3]{64}$.

We need to find the cube root of 64. What number when multiplied by itself, and then multiplied by itself again, equals 64? That number is 4. Therefore, $\sqrt[3]{64} = 4$.

Tip for cube roots

If you don't know the answer to a cube root problem, try small numbers and work your way up until you find the correct answer. For example, try $2 \times 2 \times 2$, and then $3 \times 3 \times 3$, etc. Using this method, you'll quickly find the cube root of 64.

Practice Test Question

1. $\sqrt[3]{216}$

    A. 4

    B. 6

    C. 7

    D. 8

Answer Key

1. **B. 6**

   $6 \times 6 \times 6 = 216$.
   Therefore, $\sqrt[3]{216} = 6$.

Test-taking tip!
Sometimes you can find the answer to a question by simply trying each answer choice. When finding the cube root of 216, you can try answer choice A, then answer choice B, etc., until you find the correct answer.

Practice Test Question

1. $\sqrt{(25 + 36 + y)^2} = ?$

   A. $11 + y$

   B. $11 + y^2$

   C. $61 + y$

   D. $61 + y^2$

Answer Key

1. **C. $61 + y$**

   The square root of a number is the number that, when multiplied by itself, produces the number. What number when multiplied by itself produces $(25 + 36 + y)^2$? The answer is $(25 + 36 + y)$, because $(25 + 36 + y)$ times $(25 + 36 + y)$ equals $(25 + 36 + y)^2$. Simplify $(25 + 36 + y)$, and the answer is $61 + y$.

Order of Operations

The trick to answering many math questions correctly is to simply know the order of operations, the order in which operations should be performed. Why? Because often if you *multiply* first, you'll get a different answer than if you *add* first!

ORDER OF OPERATIONS
1. Perform operations inside of parentheses.
2. Perform operations involving exponents and roots from left to right.
3. Perform multiplication and division from left to right.
4. Perform addition and subtraction from left to right.

You might not need to do every step in the order of operations. For example, here's a problem where there are no roots and no division.

Parenthetically speaking…

If there is no symbol next to a parenthesis, the implied operation is multiplication. For example, $4(3 + 7)$ is same as $4 \times (3 + 7)$, and $(6 - 2)(8 + 4)$ is the same as $(6 - 2) \times (8 + 4)$.

Example: $3(12 + 7) + 2^4 \times 4 - (6 - 1) = ?$

Begin with the equation.	$3(12 + 7) + 2^4 \times 4 - (6 - 1) = ?$
Perform operations inside parentheses.	$3 \times 19 + 2^4 \times 4 - 5$
Perform operations involving exponents and roots.	$3 \times 19 + 16 \times 4 - 5$
Perform multiplication and division.	$57 + 64 - 5$
Perform addition and subtraction.	116

Therefore, the answer is 116.

Practice Test Questions

1. $5 + 3 \times \sqrt{16} + (11 - 9) \times 6 = ?$

   A. 29

   B. 44

   C. 114

   D. 288

2. $20 - 5(7 + 2) - 8^2 \div 4 = ?$

   A. -41

   B. $17\frac{3}{4}$

   C. 119

   D. 131

Answer Key

1. **A. 29**

First, perform the operation inside parentheses. Next, find the square root of 16, which is 4. Then multiply from left to right. Finally, add and subtract from left to right.

2. **A. -41**

First, perform the operation inside parentheses. Next, find 8 squared, which is 64. Then multiply and divide from left to right. Finally, subtract from left to right.

ASVAB tip!

The Armed Forces Qualification Test (AFQT) score is computed using four subtests, including the Mathematics Knowledge subtest. Your AFQT score is critical because you must have a minimum qualifying score in order to enlist.

Algebra

A variable is a letter, such as x, that represents an unknown value. When working with variables, you can add or subtract LIKE TERMS, terms that contain the same variable raised to the same power. For example, x and $4x$ are like terms, and $2y$ and $6y$ are like terms.

> **LIKE TERMS:** terms that contain the same variable raised to the same power

Solving an equation

To solve an equation for x, isolate x on one side of the equation. By solving an equation for x, you find the value that makes an equation true. Here's an example.

> To solve an equation for x, isolate x on one side of the equation.

Example: Solve for x: $7x + 16 - 3x = (4 \times 3)x$

Begin with the equation.	$7x + 16 - 3x = (4 \times 3)x$
Perform the operation inside parentheses.	$7x + 16 - 3x = 12x$
Put the like terms together.	$7x - 3x + 16 = 12x$
Subtract the like terms.	$4x + 16 = 12x$
Subtract $4x$ from both sides of the equation.	$4x + 16 - 4x = 12x - 4x$
Subtract.	$16 = 8x$
Divide both sides of the equation by 8.	$\frac{16}{8} = \frac{8x}{8}$
Do the math.	$2 = x$

Therefore, $x = 2$. To check your answer, substitute 2 for x in the original equation, and you'll see that the equation is true.

Example: Solve for x: $7x + \sqrt{36} = 26 - 12 \times 2 + 3x$

Begin with the equation.	$7x + \sqrt{36} = 26 - 12 \times 2 + 3x$
Take the square root of 36.	$7x + 6 = 26 - 12 \times 2 + 3x$
Perform the multiplication.	$7x + 6 = 26 - 24 + 3x$
Perform the subtraction.	$7x + 6 = 2 + 3x$
Subtract 3x from both sides of the equation.	$7x + 6 - 3x = 2 + 3x - 3x$
Subtract.	$4x + 6 = 2$
Subtract 6 from both sides of the equation.	$4x + 6 - 6 = 2 - 6$
Do the math.	$4x = -4$
Divide both sides of the equation by 4.	$\frac{4x}{4} = \frac{-4}{4}$
Do the math.	$4x = -4$
	$x = -1$

Therefore, $x = -1$. To check your answer, substitute -1 for x in the original equation, and you'll see that the equation is true.

Remember the order of operations!
Remember the order of operations—even when solving for *x* in an equation.

Practice Test Questions

1. Solve for x: $2 - 4 \times 10 - 3x = 7x + 3 - 2x - 9$

   A. -16

   B. -4

   C. $-1\frac{3}{4}$

   D. $3\frac{1}{4}$

2. Solve for x: $y^4 + (10 - 2)(7 - 5) = y^2 \times y^3$

   A. 4

   B. 10

   C. 16

   D. 24

Answer Key

1. **B. -4**

First, perform the multiplication. Then add and subtract like terms. The result is $-38 - 3x = 5x - 6$. Add $3x$ to both sides of the equation and add 6 to both sides of the equation. The result is $-32 = 8x$. Divide both sides of the equation by 8, and the result is $-4 = x$.

2. **C. 16**

First, perform the operations inside parentheses. The result is $y^4 + 8 \times 2 = y^2 \times y^3$. Then multiply from left to right. Remember: According to the rules of exponents, when you multiply, you add exponents. The result is $y^4 + 16 = y^5$. Subtract y^4 from both sides of the equation, and the answer is 16.

Using the distributive property

When solving for x, how do you approach a problem like the one below?

$$4(3 + x) - 10$$

The DISTRIBUTIVE PROPERTY allows you to *distribute* a number across numbers enclosed in parentheses. In the equation above, you can *distribute* the 4 to the 3 and the x. You multiply 4 by 3, and you multiply 4 by x.

$$4(3 + x) = 10$$

This is the result.

$$12 + 4x = 10$$

> **DISTRIBUTIVE PROPERTY:** a property that allows you to distribute a number across numbers enclosed in parentheses

You can then solve for x. Here's an example.

Example: Solve for x: 8(x − 3) = 12

Begin with the equation.	$8(x - 3) = 16$
Distribute 8 to the x and the 3.	$8x - 24 = 16$
Add 24 to both sides of the equation.	$8x = 40$
Divide both sides of the equation by 8.	$x = 5$

Therefore, $x = 5$. You can check your answer by substituting 5 for x in the original equation.

Don't forget!
When distributing, remember to distribute all the way through! It's easy to forget to distribute to the second number.

Practice Test Questions

1. Solve for x: $12(x - 2) + 7 = 19$

   A. $\frac{1}{6}$

   B. $1\frac{1}{6}$

   C. 2

   D. 3

2. Solve for d: $100 - 5(d + 8) = 7(d - 3) - 9d$

   A. 23

   B. 27

   C. 37

   D. $53\frac{2}{3}$

Answer Key

1. **D. 3**

   After distributing 12 to the x and the 2, the equation becomes $12x - 24 + 7 = 19$. Add -24 and 7 and you have the equation $12x - 17 = 19$. Add 17 to both sides of the equation, and the equation becomes $12x = 36$. Finally, divide both sides of the equation by 12. The answer is 3.

2. **B. 27**

   After distributing on both sides of the equation, the equation becomes $100 - 5d - 40 = 7d - 21 - 9d$. Simplify both sides of the equation, and the equation becomes $60 - 5d = -21 - 2d$. Add 21 to both sides of the equation, and the equation becomes $81 - 5d = -2d$. Add $5d$ to both sides of the equation, and the equation becomes $81 = 3d$. Finally, divide both sides by 3. The answer is 27.

Got ten minutes?
In ten minutes you can: quiz yourself with vocabulary flashcards, read a short newspaper article, review an explanation in this study guide, or do a math practice test question. Even if you don't fully understand something on the first pass, your mind stores it for recall, which is why frequent reading or review increases chances of retention and comprehension.

Evaluating an expression

An **EXPRESSION** is a combination of numbers, variables, and operations. Unlike an equation, an expression doesn't contain an equals sign. Here are some examples of expressions:

$2x - 5 + 4x$ $(x^2)^3$

$3y$ $4x + 3y - 9$

$2 + m - (20 + 2)$ $20 + 4$

EVALUATING AN EXPRESSION is finding the value of the expression when you substitute specific values for the variables. Here's an example.

Example: Evaluate the expression $(x^3)^2$, if $x = 2$.

Begin with the expression. $(x^3)^2$

Substitute 2 for x. $(2^3)^2$

Remember the rules for exponents. 2^6

2^6 is $2 \times 2 \times 2 \times 2 \times 2 \times 2$. 64

Therefore, when you substitute 2 for x in the expression, the result is 64.

Example: Evaluate the expression $3a + b \times 5ab + (7 - a) - \sqrt{9}$, if $a = 2$ and $b = 6$.

Begin with the expression. $3a + b \times 5ab + (7 - a) - \sqrt{9}$

Substitute 2 for a, and substitute 6 for b. $3 \times 2 + 6 \times 5 \times 2 \times 6 + (7 - 2) - \sqrt{9}$

Perform the operation inside parentheses. $3 \times 2 + 6 \times 5 \times 2 \times 6 + 5 - \sqrt{9}$

Take the square root of 9. $3 \times 2 + 6 \times 5 \times 2 \times 6 + 5 - 3$

Multiply from left to right. $6 + 360 + 5 - 3$

Add and subtract from left to right. 368

> **EXPRESSION:** a combination of numbers, variables, and operations

> **EVALUATING AN EXPRESSION:** finding the value of the expression when you substitute specific values for the variables

Don't be intimidated
Don't be intimidated by long expressions or equations. Just work through them step by step.

Practice Test Questions

1. Evaluate the expression $\frac{m^6}{m^3} \times 4m$, if $m = 5$.

    A. 500

    B. 1,000

    C. 1,500

    D. 2,500

2. Evaluate the expression $9p - 8q \times (p - q) + q^2$, if $p = 8$ and $q = 6$.

    A. 12

    B. 50

    C. 84

    D. 112

Answer Key

1. **D. 2,500**

    When you substitute 5 for m, the expression becomes $\frac{5^6}{5^3} \times 4 \times 5$. According to the rules of exponents, when you divide, you subtract exponents, so the expression becomes $5^3 \times 4 \times 5$. 5 cubed is 125. Finally, do the multiplication. The answer is 2,500.

2. **A. 12**

    Substitute 8 for p and 6 for q, and the expression becomes $72 - 48 \times 2 + 36$. Then remember the order of operations: multiply, and then add and subtract. The answer is 12.

It's not worth it
Don't try to save time by doing many steps in your head. Avoid mistakes by writing down every step.

Don't forget the order of operations
Remember the order of operations when evaluating an expression!

> **INEQUALITY:** a statement that one number or expression is less than or greater than another

Solving an inequality

An **INEQUALITY** is a statement that one number or expression is less than or greater than another. These symbols are used in inequalities:

INEQUALITY SYMBOLS	
<	less than
≤	less than or equal to
>	greater than
≥	greater than or equal to

Solving an inequality is very much like solving an equation. The most important thing to remember about inequalities is that if you multiply or divide both sides of the inequality by a negative number, you need to "flip" the inequality sign.

Example: Solve: $3(c + 6) + 5c < 3^3 - 4^2$

Begin with the inequality.	$3(c + 6) - 5c < 3^3 - 4^2$
Simplify the right side of the inequality.	$3(c + 6) - 5c < 27 - 16$
Subtract 16 from 27.	$3(c + 6) - 5c < 11$
Distribute on the left side of the inequality.	$3c + 18 - 5c < 11$
Combine like terms. (Subtract $5c$ from $3c$.)	$18 - 2c < 11$
Subtract 18 from both sides of the inequality.	$-2c < -7$
Divide both sides by –2. Flip the inequality sign!	$c > 3\frac{1}{2}$

The solution is $c > 3\frac{1}{2}$. Therefore, the inequality is true for all numbers greater than $3\frac{1}{2}$.

Flip it!
If you multiply or divide both sides of an inequality by a negative number, remember to flip the inequality sign!

Practice Test Questions

1. **Solve:** $2 + 5(s - 4) > \sqrt{49}$

   A. $s < 1$

   B. $s > 1$

   C. $s < 5$

   D. $s > 5$

2. **Solve:** $-2t < 2 - (7 - 4)^2 + \sqrt{121}$

   A. $t < -2$

   B. $t > -2$

   C. $t < 2$

   D. $t > 2$

Answer Key

1. **D.** $s > 5$

   On the left side of the inequality, distribute. The inequality becomes $2 + 5s - 20 > \sqrt{49}$. On the right side of the inequality, take the square root of 49, which is 7. Subtract 20 from 2 and the inequality becomes $5s - 18 > 7$. Add 18 to both sides of the inequality, and then divide both sides by 5. The answer is $s > 5$.

2. **B.** $t > -2$

   First, perform the operation inside parentheses. The inequality becomes $-2t < 2 - 3^2 + \sqrt{121}$. Square the 3 and take the square root of 121, and the inequality becomes $-2t < 2 - 9 + 11$. Simplify the right side, and the inequality becomes $-2t < 4$. Finally, divide both sides by -2. Remember: When you divide both sides of an inequality by a negative number, you need to flip the inequality sign. The answer is $t > -2$.

Bright eyed and bushy tailed
Get at least eight hours of sleep the night before the test. You'll be well rested, relaxed, and focused.

> Geometry *is the branch of mathematics that covers lines and shapes.*

> **TWO-DIMENSIONAL SHAPES:** shapes that are flat

> **THREE-DIMENSIONAL SHAPES:** shapes that have length, width, and height

> **POLYGON:** a two-dimensional shape with straight sides

Shapes and Figures

TWO-DIMENSIONAL SHAPES are shapes that are flat. They have length and width. Circles and triangles are examples of two-dimensional shapes. THREE-DIMENSIONAL SHAPES are shapes that are not flat. They have length, width, and height. Cubes and pyramids are examples of three-dimensional shapes.

A POLYGON is a two-dimensional shape with straight sides. Squares and triangles are examples of polygons.

Identifying shapes

Here are some common two-dimensional and three-dimensional shapes.

Two-Dimensional Shapes

Rectangle

Square

Triangle

Parallelogram
(two pairs of parallel sides)

Trapezoid
(one pair of parallel sides)

Pentagon
(five sides)

Hexagon
(six sides)

Octagon
(eight sides)

Three-Dimensional Shapes

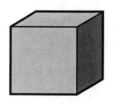

Cube

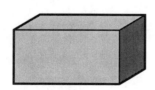

Rectangular prism
(or box)

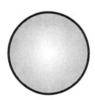

Sphere

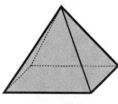

Pyramid

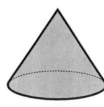

Cone

Cylinder

Did you notice?
A cube is just a special type of rectangular prism—it's a rectangular prism in which every side is the same length.

Practice Test Question

1. What is the name of the shape below?

   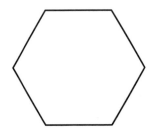

   A. Trapezoid

   B. Parallelogram

   C. Hexagon

   D. Pentagon

Answer Key

1. **C. Hexagon**

   A hexagon is a two-dimensional figure with six sides.

Identifying types of angles

In order to understand triangles, it helps to learn the three types of angles.

RIGHT ANGLE: a 90° angle

ACUTE ANGLE: an angle that is less than 90°

OBTUSE ANGLE: an angle that is more than 90°

- A RIGHT ANGLE is a 90° angle, the angle made by the corner of a piece of paper. A right angle is indicated by a small square.

- An angle that is less than 90° is an ACUTE ANGLE.

- An angle that is more than 90° is an OBTUSE ANGLE.

Here are examples of the three types of angles.

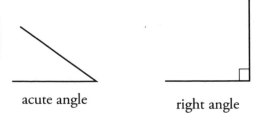

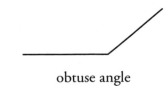

acute angle   right angle   obtuse angle

Practice Test Question

1. The angle below is what type of angle?

   A. Scalene

   B. Acute

   C. Obtuse

   D. Right

Answer Key

1. **B. Acute**

   An acute angle is less than 90°, the angle made by the corner of a piece of paper.

> **RIGHT TRIANGLE:** a triangle that contains a right angle

Identifying triangles

You can name triangles by the types of angles they have.

- A **RIGHT TRIANGLE** is a triangle that contains a right angle.

> **ACUTE TRIANGLE:** a triangle that contains three acute angles

- An **ACUTE TRIANGLE** is a triangle that contains three acute angles.

- An **OBTUSE TRIANGLE** is a triangle that contains one obtuse angle.

> **OBTUSE TRIANGLE:** a triangle that contains one obtuse angle

Here are examples of the three types of triangles according to their angles.

> **EQUILATERAL TRI-ANGLE:** a triangle that has three sides of the same length

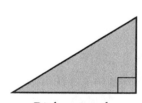
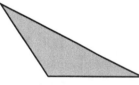

| Acute triangle | Right triangle | Obtuse triangle |

You can also name triangles by lengths of their sides.

> **ISOSCELES TRIANGLE:** a triangle that has two sides of the same length

- An **EQUILATERAL TRIANGLE** is a triangle that has three sides of the same length.

- An **ISOSCELES TRIANGLE** is a triangle that has two sides of the same length.

- An **SCALENE TRIANGLE** is a triangle that has three sides of different lengths.

> **SCALENE TRIANGLE:** a triangle that has three sides of different lengths

Here are examples of the three types of triangles according to the lengths of their sides.

Equilateral triangle

Isosceles triangle

Scalene triangle

Practice Test Question

1. The triangle below is what type of triangle?

A. Equilateral

B. Isosceles

C. Obtuse

D. Right

Answer Key

1. **B. Isosceles**

   An isosceles triangle has two sides of the same length.

Finding perimeter and area of a square, rectangle, or triangle

PERIMETER is the distance around the edge of a two-dimensional shape. The distance around the shape is simply the sum of the measurements of all of the sides. You would find the perimeter of a field to see how much fencing you would need to enclose it.

AREA is the amount of space inside a two-dimensional shape. You would find the area of a room to see how much carpeting you would need to cover the floor.

PERIMETER: the distance around the edge of a two-dimensional shape

AREA: the amount of space inside a two-dimensional shape

Here are the formulas for perimeter and area of common figures.

Square

s is the length of one side

Perimeter = 4*s*
Area = s^2

Rectangle

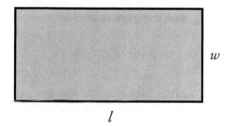

l and *w* are the length and width

Perimeter = 2*l* + 2w
Area = *lw*

Triangle

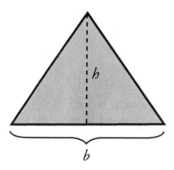

h is the height, and *b* is the length of the base

Area = $\frac{1}{2}bh$
The perimeter of a triangle is simply the sum of the three sides.

Since area is found by multiplying one dimension by another, such as length × width, the answer is given in units squared—for example, ft², m², or km².

Since area is found by multiplying one dimension by another, such as length × width, the answer is given in units squared—for example, ft², m², or km².

Tip for finding perimeters

Instead of memorizing the formulas for perimeter, you can just remember that the perimeter of the shape is the sum of all of the sides.

Example: Joan has a rectangular garden that is 62 feet long and 14 feet wide. What are the perimeter and area of the garden?

Write the formula for perimeter of a rectangle.	Perimeter $= 2l + 2w$
Substitute the length and width of the garden.	$(2 \times 62) + (2 \times 14)$
Multiply.	$124 + 28$
Add.	152
Write the formula for area of a rectangle.	Area $= lw$
Substitute the length and width of the garden.	62×14
Multiply.	868

Therefore, the perimeter of the garden is 152 ft, and the area is 868 ft².

Draw a picture

When solving a word problem, it often helps to draw a sketch of the problem. For a question about area of a rectangle, make a sketch and label the figure with the length and width.

Example: What is the area of the triangle below?

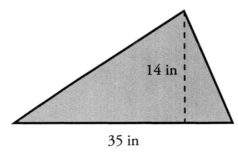

14 in

35 in

Write the formula for area of a triangle.	Area $= \frac{1}{2}bh$
Substitute the base and height of the triangle.	$\frac{1}{2} \times 35 \times 14$
Multiply.	245

Therefore, the area of the triangle is 245 in².

Practice!

The best way to improve your math scores on the ASVAB is to practice. Nothing replaces the act of doing a math problem, and then doing another. Work through all of the questions in this study guide several times.

Practice Test Questions

1. Bernie is going to tile his kitchen floor. One side of his square kitchen is 14 feet long. Tiles that are 1 square foot cost $1.15 each. How much will it cost to tile the floor?

   A. $28.00

   B. $32.20

   C. $196.00

   D. $225.40

2. The perimeter of a rectangle is 42 cm, and the length of one side is 9 cm. What is the area of the rectangle?

   A. 12 cm^2

   B. 42 cm^2

   C. 108 cm^2

   D. 441 cm^2

Answer Key

1. **D. $225.40**

   You need to find the area of the square kitchen. The formula for area of a square is Area $= s^2$. Therefore, the area of the square is 196 ft^2, so he needs 196 square foot tiles. Square foot tiles cost $1.15 each. To find the total cost, multiply 196 by $1.15. The total cost is $225.40.

2. **C. 108 cm^2**

   The perimeter of the rectangle is 42 cm. Perimeter $= 2l + 2w$, and the length of one side is 9 cm. Therefore, $42 = 2 \times 9 + 2w$. When you solve for w, you find that the length of the other side is 12. You are asked for the area of the rectangle. The formula for area of a rectangle is Area $= lw$. Substitute 9 for length and 12 for width. The answer is 108 cm^2.

Strrretch!
Take a five-minute break every half hour while you're studying. Go outside to get some fresh air, or walk around and stretch.

Finding circumference and area of a circle

The **CIRCUMFERENCE** of a circle is the distance around the edge of the circle. The area of a circle, like the area of a rectangle or triangle, is the amount of space inside the circle.

> **CIRCUMFERENCE:** the distance around the edge of a circle

In order to find the circumference and area of a circle, there are a couple of terms that you need to know.

RADIUS: the distance from the center of a circle to the edge of the circle

The **RADIUS** of a circle is the distance from the center of the circle to the edge of the circle.

The **DIAMETER** of a circle is the width of the circle.

DIAMETER: the width of a circle

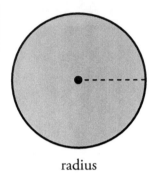 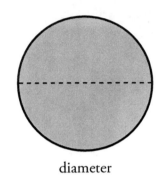

radius   diameter

Notice that the diameter of a circle is twice as long as the radius.

Notice that the diameter of a circle is twice as long as the radius.

Here are the formulas for the circumference and area of a circle.

Circle

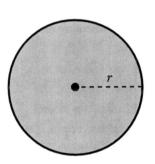

r is the radius

π is approximately equal to 3.14.

Circumference = $2\pi r$

Area = πr^2

The number π is in both formulas. π (also called pi) is a number used in calculations related to circles. π is approximately equal to 3.14.

When solving problems, you can either substitute 3.14 for π (pi), or you can leave the answer "in terms of pi." Leaving the answer "in terms of pi" means leaving the number π in the answer and not substituting 3.14 for π.

When solving problems, you can either substitute 3.14 for π (pi), or you can leave the answer "in terms of pi." Leaving the answer "in terms of pi" means leaving the number π in the answer and not substituting 3.14 for π.

Example: What is the circumference of the circle below?

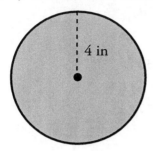

4 in

Write the formula for circumference of a circle.	Circumference = $2\pi r$
Substitute the radius of the circle.	$2 \times \pi \times 4$
Substitute 3.14 for π.	$2 \times 3.14 \times 4$
Multiply.	25.12

Therefore, the circumference of the circle is approximately 25.12 inches. The answer is approximate because π is only *approximately* equal to 3.14.

Example: What is the area of the circle below?

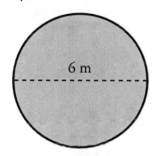

6 m

Write the formula for area of a circle.	Area = πr^2
Substitute the radius (half the diameter).	$\pi \times 3^2$
3 squared is 9.	$\pi \times 9$
Rewrite $\pi \times 9$ as 9π.	9π

Therefore, the area of the circle is 9π m². This answer is exact because we did not substitute 3.14 for π.

Tip!
Remember that the diameter of a circle is twice as long as the radius.

Practice Test Question

1. Jim installed an above-ground round swimming pool in his backyard. The pool is 12 feet wide. What is the approximate area of the ground that the pool covers?

   A. 37.68 ft²

   B. 75.36 ft²

   C. 113.04 ft²

   D. 452.16 ft²

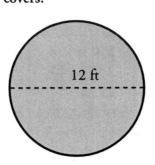

12 ft

Jim's pool shown from above.

Answer Key

1. **C. 113.04 ft²**

   Area = πr^2. Be careful: You are given the diameter, not the radius. The radius is half the diameter, or 6 ft. Therefore, the area is $\pi \times 6^2$, or $\pi \times 36$. Substitute 3.14 for π, and the answer is 113.04. Therefore the area is approximately 113.04 ft².

Tip!
Remember that π is approximately equal to 3.14.

Practice Test Question

1. There is a round fountain in Sawyer Park. The radius of the fountain is 3 meters. Billy walked around the edge of the fountain twice. How far did he walk?

    A. 3π m

    B. 6π m

    C. 9π m

    D. 12π m

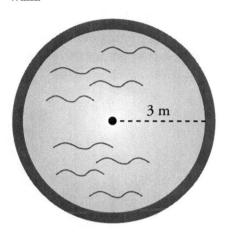

3 m

Fountain shown from above.

Answer Key

1. **D. 12π m**

    Billy walked around the edge of the fountain. The distance around the edge of a circle is the circumference, and the formula for circumference = $2\pi r$. You can see that the answer choices are given in terms of pi, so you should *not* substitute 3.14 for π. Substitute 3 for the radius, and the result is 6π. Be careful, though: The question states that he walked around the fountain *twice*. Therefore, the answer is 12π meters.

Be comfortable

Wear comfortable clothes on exam day. You'll be distracted if your belt is too tight, or if you're too cold or too hot.

Finding the volume of a cube, box, or cylinder

VOLUME: the amount of space inside a three-dimensional object

VOLUME is the amount of space inside a three-dimensional object. For example, if you have two moving boxes, and you want to find out which box would hold more clothing, you would find the *volume* of each box to see which one is larger.

Here are formulas for the volume of a cube, rectangular prism (or box), and cylinder.

> **Formula tip!**
> Create a master list of all of the formulas that you learn for the ASVAB. Rewriting them will help commit them to memory, and having them in one place will help you study.

Cube

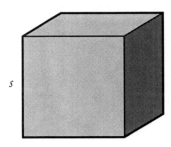

s is the length of one side

Volume $= s^3$

Rectangular Prism (or Box)

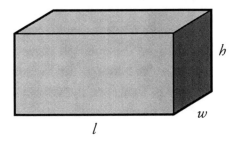

l, w, and *h* are the length, width, and height

Volume $= lwh$

Cylinder

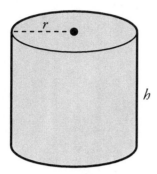

r is the radius, and *h* is the height

Volume $= \pi r^2 h$

> **Volume tip!**
> The formula for the volume of a cylinder is easy to remember if you just remember that the volume is simply the area of a circle (πr^2) times the height.

Since volume is found by multiplying one dimension by another by another, such as length $\times$ width $\times$ height, the answer is given in units *cubed*—for example, ft^3, cm^3, or in^3.

Since volume is found by multiplying one dimension by another by another, such as length $\times$ width $\times$ height, the answer is given in units cubed—for example, ft^3, cm^3, or in^3.

Example: What is the volume of the cube below?

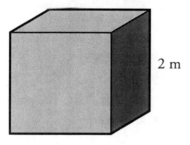

2 m

Write the formula for volume of a cube.	Volume $= s^3$
Substitute the length of one side.	2^3
2 cubed is $2 \times 2 \times 2$.	$2 \times 2 \times 2$
Do the math.	8

Therefore, the volume of the cube is 8 m^3.

Example: What is the volume of the box below?

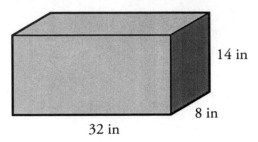

Write the formula for volume of a box.　　　Volume = *lwh*
Substitute the length, width, and height.　　32 × 8 × 14
Do the math.　　　　　　　　　　　　　　3,584
Therefore, the volume of the box is 3,584 in³.

Example: What is the approximate volume of the cylinder below?

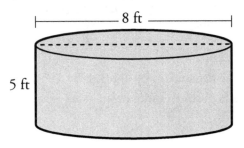

Write the formula for volume of a cylinder.　　Volume = $\pi r^2 h$
Substitute the radius (half the diameter).　　$\pi \times 4^2 \times h$
Substitute the height.　　　　　　　　　　$\pi \times 4^2 \times 5$
Substitute 3.14 for π.　　　　　　　　　3.14 × 4² × 5
Do the math.　　　　　　　　　　　　　　251.2
Therefore, the volume of the cylinder is approximately 251.2 ft³. The answer
is approximate because π is only *approximately* equal to 3.14.

Test-taking tip!
Be careful when solving problems related to circles and cylinders: You are often given
the diameter (width of a circle), but a formula will call for the radius (the distance from
the center of the circle to the edge of the circle). Just remember that the radius is half
the length of the diameter.

Practice Test Questions

1. Office Supplies Unlimited sells the small plastic storage cube shown below. What is the volume of the cube?

    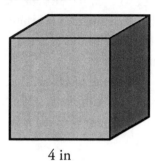

    4 in

    A. 8 in³
    B. 12 in³
    C. 16 in³
    D. 64 in³

2. Maria built the storage box below to hold tools. What is the volume of the box?

    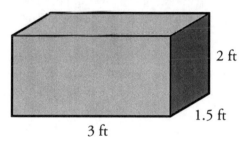

    2 ft

    1.5 ft

    3 ft

    A. 4.5 ft³
    B. 6 ft³
    C. 9 ft³
    D. 27 ft³

3. What is the approximate volume of a can that has a diameter of 6 inches and a height of 8 inches?

    A. 72 in³
    B. 226.08 in³
    C. 301.44 in³
    D. 904.32 in³

Answer Key

1. **D. 64 in³**

   The formula for volume of a cube is Volume = s^3, where s is the length of one side. Substitute 4 for s, and the volume is $4^3 \times 4^3$ is the same as $4 \times 4 \times 4$, which equals 64. Therefore, the volume of the cube is 64 in³.

2. **C. 9 ft³**

   The formula for volume of a rectangular prism (or box) is Volume = lwh. Substitute the length, width, and height, and the volume is $3 \times 1.5 \times 2$, which equals 9. Therefore, the volume of the box is 9 ft³.

3. **B. 226.08 in³**

   Volume of a cylinder = $\pi r^2 h$. Be careful: You are given the diameter (6 inches), but you need the radius. Remember that the radius is half the diameter. Substitute the radius and the height, and the volume is $\pi \times 3^2 \times 8$, or 72π. Substitute 3.14 for π, and the result is 226.08. Therefore, the approximate volume is 226.08 in³. The answer is approximate because π is only *approximately* equal to 3.14.

How would I use this?

In the military, construction specialists build and repair buildings, bridges, dams, and other structures. In this military career, geometry skills are essential. For example, a construction specialist might lay roofing materials, install floor tiles, or pour a concrete floor. Each of these jobs requires knowing how much material is needed, which requires finding the area of a two-dimensional shape.

CHAPTER 5
GENERAL SCIENCE

The General Science subtest of the ASVAB tests your knowledge of general science, including chemistry, physics, earth and space science, and biology.

The General Science subtest of the ASVAB tests your knowledge of general science, including chemistry, physics, earth and space science, and biology.

Chemistry

Everything in our world is made up of matter—rocks, mushrooms, animals, and people. In chemistry, you learn how matter changes and how different kinds of matter interact. When matter changes, energy is often absorbed or released. Energy appears in many forms, including heat, light, and chemical energy.

States of matter

Matter primarily occurs in three states: solid, liquid, and gas. A SOLID has a definite shape and volume. A LIQUID has a definite volume, but no definite shape. A GAS has no definite shape or volume because it will spread out to occupy the entire space of whatever container it is in.

Matter is made up of tiny particles called molecules. The molecules in a solid are held together tightly. The molecules in a liquid are more loosely bound. Molecules in a gas move around freely.

When a material is heated, the molecules begin moving faster. The PRESSURE of a gas is the force exerted by molecules that are moving on each unit of area of a surface. As the temperature of a fixed volume of gas increases, its pressure increases. At a constant pressure, an increase in temperature causes an increase in the volume of a gas. At a constant temperature, a decrease in the volume of a gas causes an increase in its pressure.

SOLID: matter that has a definite shape and volume

LIQUID: matter that has a definite volume, but no definite shape

GAS: matter that has no definite shape or volume

PRESSURE: the force exerted by molecules that are moving on each unit of area of a surface

What's volume again?
Remember that volume is the amount of space inside a three-dimensional object. For example, as you blow up a beach ball, its volume increases.

Example

Your car tires typically have a pressure of 32 pounds per square inch (psi). On a cold winter day, you check the pressure in your front right tire and find that the pressure is only 26 psi! What's wrong? Has your tire sprung a leak?

Fortunately, you remember that when the temperature of a fixed volume of gas increases, its pressure increases. The reverse is true as well. When the temperature falls, the pressure does, too. So you pump a little more air into your tires and you are on your way.

Practice Test Question

1. **An inflated balloon is left in a refrigerator for a few hours. What do you predict will happen?**

   A. The balloon will shrink

   B. The balloon will expand

   C. The balloon volume will remain the same

   D. The pressure in the balloon will increase

Answer Key

For your convenience, the practice test questions also appear the end of the book so you can sit down and go through them all at once.

1. **A. The balloon will shrink**

   A balloon is very flexible and will change shape easily. Therefore, the pressure inside the balloon won't decrease—if the pressure decreased inside the balloon, it would simply get smaller. You know that the temperature decreased, and the pressure remained the same. According to the gas laws, at a constant pressure, a decrease in temperature will cause a decrease in volume. In other words, the balloon will shrink.

PHASE CHANGES: changes in matter from one state to another

MELTING POINT: the temperature at which a particular solid starts melting

Phase changes

Applying heat energy to a frozen liquid, such as ice, changes it from solid to liquid. Continue heating it, and it will boil and vaporize, changing it into a gas.

These changes from one state to another are called **PHASE CHANGES**.

- The temperature at which a particular solid starts melting is known as its **MELTING POINT**.

- The temperature at which a liquid begins to solidify when cooled is known as its FREEZING POINT. In general, the melting point and freezing point of a substance are the same.

- The BOILING POINT of a liquid is the temperature at which it begins to change into gas.

FREEZING POINT: the temperature at which a liquid begins to solidify when cooled

Example

The boiling point of water at normal atmospheric pressure is about 100°C (Celsius) or 212°F (Fahrenheit). The melting point of water and the freezing point of ice is about 0°C or 32°F. This is why roads become icy and driving can be hazardous when the temperature outside is about 32°F.

BOILING POINT: the temperature at which a liquid begins to change into a gas

Man, that's cold!

Why is dry ice, or solid carbon dioxide, a good choice to keep food cold during transportation? For one thing, it is colder than water ice. Also, it leaves no messy puddles as it warms up. Under standard temperature and pressure conditions, dry ice skips the liquid stage and goes straight from a solid state to a gas.

Atomic structure

An ELEMENT is a pure chemical substance, such as sodium, copper, or oxygen. An ATOM is the smallest particle of an element. Atoms consist of a nucleus surrounded by a cloud of moving electrons. There are two types of particles in the nucleus of an atom: protons and neutrons.

ELEMENT: a pure chemical substance

ATOM: the smallest particle of an element

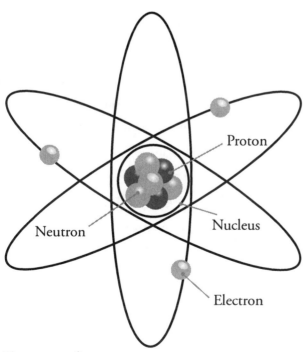

The structure of an atom.

Protons have a positive charge; neutrons are uncharged. Protons and neutrons have about the same mass. Electrons have a negative charge (equal in magnitude to the charge of a proton) and are about 2,000 times less massive than protons or neutrons.

The number of protons in the nucleus of an atom is called the ATOMIC NUMBER. All atoms of the same element have the same atomic number. In an atom, the number of protons (which have a positive charge) is equal to the number of electrons (which have a negative charge). This makes an atom neutral. The MASS NUMBER of an atom is the sum of its protons and neutrons.

> **ATOMIC NUMBER:** the number of protons in the nucleus of an atom

> **MASS NUMBER:** the sum of the protons and neutrons in an atom

Think positively
Remember that **p**rotons have a **p**ositive charge, and **n**eutrons are **n**eutral.

Example
Carbon-12, the most common isotope, or form, of carbon has an atomic number of 6 and a mass number of 12. How many protons, neutrons, and electrons does an atom of Carbon-12 have?

Since the atomic number is 6, each atom has 6 protons. Since the number of protons is equal to the number of electrons in an atom, each atom has 6 electrons. The mass number is the total number of protons and neutrons. Therefore, the number of neutrons is $12 - 6 = 6$.

Practice Test Questions

1. The nucleus of an atom is:

   A. Positively charged

   B. Negatively charged

   C. Neutral

   D. Sometimes positively charged, sometimes negatively charged

2. The atomic number of an oxygen atom is 8, and its mass number is 17. This means that the atom of oxygen has:

   A. 8 neutrons

   B. 9 neutrons

   C. 17 neutrons

   D. No neutrons

Answer Key

1. **A. Positively charged**

   The nucleus contains only protons, which have a positive charge, and neutrons, which are uncharged. Therefore, the nucleus is positively charged. The atom as a whole is neutral because the negative charge of the electrons equals the positive charge of the protons.

2. **B. 9 neutrons**

   Because the atomic number is 8, the number of protons is 8. The mass number is the total number of protons and neutrons. Therefore, the number of neutrons is $17 - 8 = 9$

The periodic table

The PERIODIC TABLE is an arrangement of the elements in rows and columns so that it is easy to locate elements with similar properties. The elements of the modern periodic table are arranged in numerical order by atomic number. The PERIODS are the rows numbered down the left side of the periodic table. They are called first period, second period, and so on. The columns of the periodic table are called GROUPS, OR FAMILIES. Elements in a family have similar properties.

> **PERIODIC TABLE:** an arrangement of the elements in rows and columns

> **PERIODS:** the rows numbered down the left side of the periodic table

> **GROUPS, OR FAMILIES:** the columns of the periodic table

	IA																	O
1	1 H	IIA											IIIA	IVA	VA	VIA	VIIA	2 He
2	3 Li	4 Be											5 B	6 C	7 N	8 O	9 F	10 NE
3	11 Na	12 Mg	IIIB	IVB	VB	VIB	VIIB	——VII——		IB	IIB		13 Al	14 Si	15 P	16 S	17 Cl	18 Ar
4	19 K	20 Ca	21 Sc	22 Ti	23 V	24 Cr	25 Mn	26 Fe	27 Co	28 Ni	29 Cu	30 Zn	31 Ga	32 Ge	33 As	34 Se	35 Br	36 Kr

The first few rows of the periodic table of elements.

Some groups are described below:

- **Group 1A:** Alkali metals; very reactive; never found free in nature; react readily with water (e.g., sodium)

- **Group 2A:** Alkaline earth elements; all are metals; occur only in compounds (e.g., magnesium)

- **Group 3A:** Metalloids; includes aluminum (the most abundant metal on Earth)

- **Group 8A:** Nobel gases; not abundant on Earth; not reactive with other elements (e.g., neon and argon)

Are you a morning person?
Many people concentrate best in the morning. You're rested and your mind is fresh. Make yourself a light breakfast, find a comfortable place to work, and begin studying.

> *A* compound *is a chemical substance made up of a combination of elements.*

Example

What is a possible reason that the elements Lithium (Li), Sodium (Na), Potassium (K), Rubidium (Rb), Cesium (Cs), and Francium (Fr) all have the same silvery white color? All of these are alkali metals that belong to the same group (1A) of the periodic table. Elements in the same group or family have similar properties.

Practice Test Question

1. The rows of the periodic table are called:

   A. Families

   B. Elements

   C. Groups

   D. Periods

Answer Key

1. **D. Periods**

   The periods are the rows numbered down the left side of the periodic table. The columns of the periodic table are called groups or families.

> **PHYSICAL CHANGE:** a change that does not produce a new substance, but changes the appearance of the substance

> **CHEMICAL CHANGE, OR CHEMICAL REACTION:** a change that turns a substance into one or more different substances with different chemical compositions

Physical and chemical changes

A PHYSICAL CHANGE is a change that does not produce a new substance, but changes the appearance of the substance. A CHEMICAL CHANGE, OR CHEMICAL REACTION, is a change that turns a substance into one or more different substances with different chemical compositions. Energy is released or absorbed during some chemical reactions. For example, when a piece of paper is burned, energy is released in the form of heat and light.

Example

Chopping and mixing salad ingredients is a physical change. A slice of tomato is still tomato. Chopped-up onion is still onion. But baking a cake is a chemical change. A cake is not egg, flour, and milk, but something entirely new.

Practice Test Question

1. **Which of these is a physical change?**

    A. Fireworks are set off

    B. A nail becomes rusty

    C. Ice melts into water

    D. An antacid makes you feel better

Answer Key

1. **C. Ice melts into water**

    The melting of ice is a physical change because the water molecules remain unchanged. It is the same substance, water, in two different states—solid and liquid. The other choices involve chemical reactions. There is a rapid release of heat and light energy when fireworks are set off. When a nail becomes rusty, the iron of the nail combines with oxygen to create a red coating. An antacid neutralizes stomach acid in a chemical reaction.

Physics

PHYSICS is the study of matter, forces, and energy and how they are connected. For example, you can use physics principles to study how a stone falls under the

> **PHYSICS:** the study of matter, forces, and energy and how they are connected

> *The law of conservation of energy states that energy can neither be created nor destroyed.*

> **ENERGY:** the ability to do work

> **KINETIC ENERGY (KE):** the energy of a moving object

> **POTENTIAL ENERGY (PE):** the energy stored in an object due to its position relative to other objects

> **MECHANICAL ENERGY:** the sum of an object's kinetic and potential energy

action of the force of gravity. You can calculate its position, speed, and energy content at different times during its fall. You can also study how a ripple moves through water or how a mirror reflects light.

Potential and kinetic energy

ENERGY is the ability to do work. The law of conservation of energy states that energy can neither be created nor destroyed. Therefore, the sum of all energies in a system remains constant.

KINETIC ENERGY (KE) is the energy of a moving object. The more quickly an object moves, the higher its kinetic energy. **POTENTIAL ENERGY (PE)** is the energy stored in an object due to its position relative to other objects. **MECHANICAL ENERGY** is the sum of the kinetic energy and potential energy.

Two familiar forms of potential energy are gravitational potential energy and the energy stored in a compressed or expanded spring. The higher an object is raised, the greater its gravitational potential energy. The more a spring is compressed or expanded, the greater its stored potential energy.

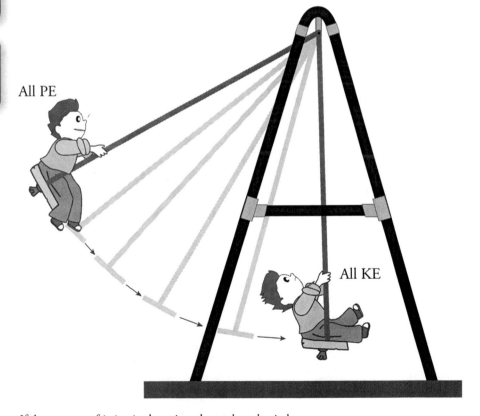

All PE

All KE

If there were no friction in the swing, the total mechanical energy would stay the same. The energy is all potential at the highest point where the swing is not moving, all kinetic at the lowest point where it is moving the fastest, and part potential part kinetic in between.

Think of the potential…
Potential energy is energy waiting to be *used*; kinetic energy is energy in *motion*.

If the law of conservation of energy is true, why does a swing gradually slow down? FRICTION is the force that resists the movement of one surface against another. In an ideal swing with no friction, the total mechanical energy would be conserved and the swing would keep going forever, with its energy switching between potential and kinetic. In the real world, though, some of the mechanical energy of the swing is lost to friction and is transformed into heat. The principle of conservation of energy still holds—the sum of the mechanical energy plus the lost heat energy is equal to the total energy the swing had in the beginning.

> **FRICTION:** the force that resists the movement of one surface against another

Practice Test Question

1. **A marble rolls down a smooth curved track. Why does it move more quickly as it goes down?**

   A. Some of its potential energy is changed into kinetic energy

   B. Some of its kinetic energy is changed into potential energy

   C. The total energy of the marble increases

   D. The mechanical energy of the marble increases

Answer Key

1. **A. Some of its potential energy is changed into kinetic energy**

   As the marble moves to lower heights, its potential energy is lowered. Since little energy is lost to friction on a smooth track, the total mechanical energy (PE + KE) stays about the same. Therefore, the kinetic energy of the marble increases. In other words, the marble moves more quickly.

Waves

Waves transfer energy through space without transferring matter. In many kinds of waves, material particles simply vibrate in place and help to transmit the wave.

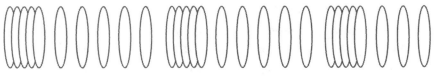

Longitudinal Wave

Transverse Wave

In transverse waves, the particles move perpendicular to the direction in which the wave is going; in longitudinal waves, particles move parallel to the direction in which the wave is moving.

Sound waves are longitudinal. They move through compression and expansion of the medium (for example, air) that carries the sound. Sound can be transmitted through any gas, liquid, or solid. However, it cannot be transmitted through a vacuum, because there are no particles present to vibrate and bump into their adjacent particles to transmit the wave. The speed of sound in air is about 343 meters per second.

Light waves are transverse. They are not made up of moving particles. Changing electric and magnetic fields perpendicular to the direction of propagation carry light waves. Light waves don't need a material medium for transmission and can move through a vacuum. Light waves travel at a speed of about 300,000,000 meters per second. Nothing travels faster than light.

Perpendicular means at a 90 degree angle. For example, the two lines of a plus sign are perpendicular to each other.

A vacuum is a space that is free of everything— even air!

Example

You throw a pebble into a lake and watch waves ripple out from it. Are these waves transverse or longitudinal?

If you look closely, you will see that the particles of water are moving up and down perpendicularly to the horizontal direction in which the ripples are spreading out. This is characteristic of a transverse wave.

Practice Test Question

1. You see a flash of lightning, but the rumble of thunder only gets to you after several seconds. Why is that?

A. Thunder happens several seconds after the lightning flash

B. The thunder and lightning are from two different locations

C. The sound of thunder moves much more slowly than light from the lightning flash

D. The light from the lightning flash moves much more slowly than the sound of thunder

Answer Key

1. **C. The sound of thunder moves much more slowly than light from the lightning flash**

The speed of light is about 300,000,000 meters per second, while the speed of sound is 343 meters per second, so sound is about a million times slower than light. Therefore, even though the thunder and lightning happen at the same place and at the same time, the light gets to you much more quickly than the sound.

Optics

When light hits a surface, it undergoes REFLECTION, a change in direction in which the angle of the incoming light ray (angle of incidence) is the same as the angle of the reflected light ray (angle of reflection). When light enters a different medium, such as water or glass, it bends. This bending, due to change of wave speed, is called REFRACTION.

REFLECTION: a change in direction in which the angle of the incoming light ray (angle of incidence) is the same as the angle of the reflected light ray (angle of reflection)

REFRACTION: the bending of light due to change of wave speed

Example

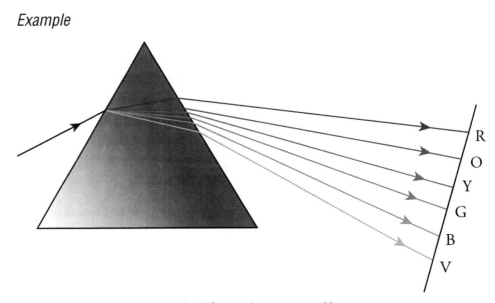

When you look at an object in the mirror, its reflection appears to be on the other side of the mirror. The reflection of the object is the same size as the object.

Example

When white light falls on a prism, the different colors in it are visible because they get refracted at different angles.

Practice Test Question

1. **Refraction does not occur in:**

   A. Eyeglasses

   B. Rearview mirrors

   C. Rainbows

   D. A lighted fountain

Answer Key

1. **B. Rearview mirrors**

   Refraction occurs whenever light moves from one medium to another. For choice A, light passes from air to glass and back. For choices C and D, light rays move between air and water. In the case of a rearview mirror, light is reflected and stays in the air. It does not enter another medium.

Heat transfer

Heat is transferred in three ways: conduction, convection, and radiation.

CONDUCTION is the transfer of heat from one end of an object to another, or between two things that are in contact with each other. Some materials, such as metals, are better conductors of heat than others.

CONVECTION is the transfer of heat energy within a fluid. The particles in a fluid (which could be a gas or a liquid) transfer the thermal energy from hot areas to cooler areas by convection currents.

RADIATION is the transfer of energy by waves, such as the electromagnetic waves emitted by stars. It does not need any material medium. The sun warms the earth by emitting radiant energy.

> **CONDUCTION:** the transfer of heat from one end of an object to another, or between two things that are in contact with each other

> **CONVECTION:** the transfer of heat energy within a fluid

> **RADIATION:** the transfer of energy by waves

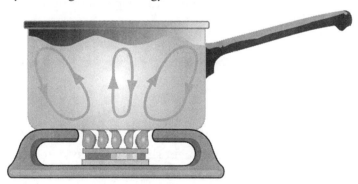

When water is heated in a pan, hot water from the bottom rises and cooler water from the top sinks creating convection currents that heat the whole pan of water.

Example

You are enjoying the heat of a campfire on a calm, clear night. How does the heat get to you: by conduction, convection, or radiation?

It is not by conduction; air is not a good conductor of heat. It is not by convection because the air is calm and the air would need to move in order to transfer heat by convection. The campfire is warming you by radiating heat.

Practice Test Question

1. You add insulation to your walls to avoid heat loss in winter through:

   A. Conduction

   B. Convection

   C. Radiation

   D. Both convection and radiation

Answer Key

1. **A. Conduction**

   Because the temperature outside your walls in winter is colder than the temperature on the inside, heat flows from the inside to the outside through conduction. Putting in insulation of material with low heat conductivity helps to reduce this loss.

Astronomy

ASTRONOMY: the study of the universe outside the earth

ASTRONOMY is the study of the universe outside the earth. It is a very old science, because people have always been fascinated by the night sky. Modern astronomers are able to study celestial objects in detail using powerful telescopes.

Basic definitions

- Big Bang Theory: A theory of the origin of the universe, according to which the universe originated from a massive explosion about 15 billion years ago.

- Black Hole: A volume of space from which no form of radiation can escape. A black hole is created when a supergiant star implodes.

- **Comet:** A mass of frozen gases, cosmic dust, and small rocky particles. A comet consists of a nucleus, a coma, and a tail, which always points away from the sun. The most famous comet, Halley's comet, returns to the skies near the earth every 75 to 76 years.

- **Constellation:** A group of prominent stars forming a pattern in the sky. Familiar constellations include Ursa Major (big bear) and Ursa Minor (little bear).

- **Eclipse:** A phenomenon that occurs when an astronomical body is shadowed by another and made invisible to some part of the earth. A lunar eclipse occurs when the moon is in the earth's shadow. A solar eclipse happens when the earth is in the moon's shadow.

- **Galaxy:** A vast collection of billions of stars. Galaxies are classified as irregular, elliptical, and spiral. Our sun is a minor star in the spiral Milky Way galaxy.

- **Meteoroids:** Particles of rock and metals of various sizes floating in space.

> *The most famous comet, Halley's comet, returns to the skies near the earth every 75 to 76 years.*

The solar system

There are eight established planets in our solar system that orbit around the sun: Mercury, Venus, Earth, Mars, Jupiter, Saturn, Uranus, and Neptune. Pluto was an established planet in our solar system, but as of the summer of 2006, its status was downgraded to a dwarf planet.

The planets are divided into two groups based on distance from the sun. The inner planets that are made of rock and other solid materials are Mercury, Venus, Earth, and Mars. The outer planets, which are gas giants made primarily of gaseous matter, are Jupiter, Saturn, Uranus, and Neptune. Earth is the only planet that supports life. In the region between the inner and outer planets is the asteroid belt that consists of thousands of asteroids or rocky fragments.

> *There are eight established planets in our solar system that orbit around the sun: Mercury, Venus, Earth, Mars, Jupiter, Saturn, Uranus, and Neptune.*

Mmm... nachos
Use this mnemonic to remember the first letters of the planet names in order: **M**y **V**ery **E**ducated **M**other **J**ust **S**erved **U**s **N**achos.

Example
Which is the hottest planet in our solar system?

You may be tempted to think it is Mercury because Mercury is closest to the sun. But it's not! The hottest planet is Venus. The dense cloud cover and the large amount of carbon dioxide in Venus' atmosphere keeps heat trapped.

Example

What is the difference between a meteor and a meteorite?

A meteoroid that enters the earth's atmosphere and burns is known as a meteor or shooting star. A meteoroid that reaches the ground is called a meteorite.

Practice Test Question

1. The planet that has an atmosphere composed mainly of oxygen and nitrogen is:

    A. Jupiter

    B. Venus

    C. Neptune

    D. Earth

Answer Key

1. **D. Earth**

    Earth's atmosphere is about 80% nitrogen and 20% oxygen. It is the only planet that supports life.

Phases of the moon

Just as the earth follows an orbit around the sun, the moon follows an eastward-moving orbit around the earth. Because the moon's rotational period matches the earth's and its period of revolution is 27.3 days, one side of the moon is always facing the earth. The side always facing us is called the near side, and the darkened side we never see is called the far side.

The PHASES OF THE MOON are the apparent changes in the shape of the moon caused by the absence or presence of reflected sunlight as the moon orbits around the earth. The orbital pattern of the moon in relation to the sun and earth determines how much of the moon is lit from our point of view on Earth.

> **PHASES OF THE MOON:** the apparent changes in the shape of the moon caused by the absence or presence of reflected sunlight as the moon orbits around the earth

The Moon as seen from Earth

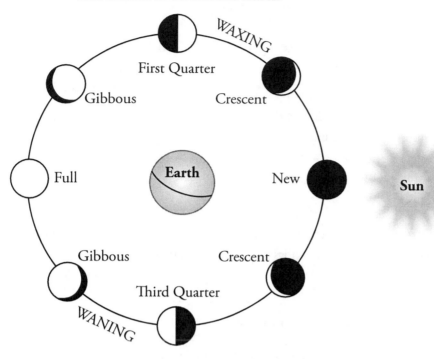

When the Moon is between the sun and the earth, the side facing us is darkened, and we refer to this as a new moon. The opposite pattern occurs in the second half of the lunar cycle, when the moon is fully illuminated and bright in the night sky. This is called a full moon.

Example

Does the waxing crescent phase occur before or after the new moon?

The waxing part of the cycle is when the moon is "growing" from a new moon to a full moon. Therefore, the waxing crescent phase is seen just after the new moon. The waning crescent is seen during the "shrinking" stage, just before the new moon.

Practice Test Question

1. **The gibbous moon:**

   A. Is between the sun and the earth

   B. Is less illuminated than the crescent moon, as seen from the earth

   C. Has more than half of its earth-facing side illuminated

   D. Has exactly half of its earth-facing side illuminated

Geology

GEOLOGY is the study of the structure of the earth, the history of its formation, and the processes that take place in its interior and on its surface.

Layers of the earth

The interior of the Earth is divided into distinct layers.

The CRUST of the earth is the outermost layer and is between 5 and 70 km thick. Thin areas generally exist under ocean basins (oceanic crust), and thicker crust underlies the continents (continental crust). Oceanic crust is composed largely of iron magnesium silicate rocks, while continental crust consists mainly of sodium potassium aluminum silicate rocks.

The earth's MANTLE begins about 35 km beneath the surface and stretches all the way to 3,000 km beneath the surface. Within the mantle, there are silicate rocks that are rich in iron and magnesium. The mantle is semisolid and plastic.

The OUTER CORE of the earth begins about 3,000 km beneath the surface and is a liquid.

Even deeper, approximately 5,000 km beneath the surface, is the solid INNER CORE which is extremely dense. Temperatures in the core exceed 4,000°C. The core is about 80% iron.

GEOLOGY: the study of the structure of the earth, the history of its formation, and the processes that take place in its interior and on its surface

CRUST: the outermost layer of the Earth that is between 5 and 70 km thick

MANTLE: the layer of the earth that begins about 35 km beneath the surface and stretches down to 3,000 km beneath the surface

OUTER CORE: the layer of the earth that begins about 3,000 km beneath the surface; it is a liquid

INNER CORE: the solid innermost layer of the earth, approximately 5,000 km beneath the surface

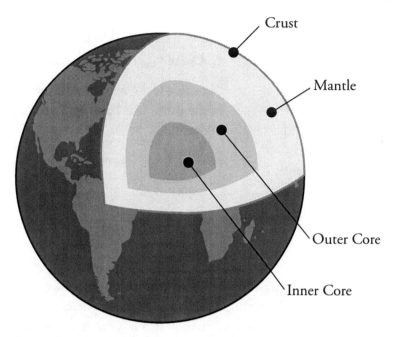

Starting from the middle of the earth and moving toward the surface are the inner core, the outer core, the mantle, and the crust.

Practice Test Questions

1. The inner core of the earth is solid because:

   A. Otherwise the earth would collapse

   B. It is cooler than the outer core

   C. It is under very high pressure

   D. It is between 5 and 70 km thick

2. The outermost layer of the earth is called the:

   A. Inner core

   B. Outer core

   C. Crust

   D. Mantle

Answer Key

1. **C. It is under very high pressure**

   Even though the inner core of the earth is very hot, it is solid because it is under very high pressure and is extremely dense.

2. **C. Crust**

   The crust is the outermost layer of the earth. It is between 5 and 70 km thick.

Plate tectonics

Plate tectonics *explains not only the movement of the continents, but also the changes in the earth's crust caused by internal forces.*

LITHOSPHERE: the crust and upper mantle of the earth, which is broken into tectonic plates

TECTONIC PLATES: the nine large and several smaller slabs of rock into which the lithosphere is broken

The earth's LITHOSPHERE, crust and part of upper mantle, is broken into nine large sections and several small ones. These huge slabs of rock (lithosphere) are called TECTONIC PLATES. The plates float on and move with a layer of hot, plastic-like rock in the upper mantle. These movements produce many major features of the earth's surface, including mountain ranges, volcanoes, and earthquake zones. Most of these features are located at plate boundaries, where the plates interact by spreading apart, pressing together, or sliding past each other. These movements are very slow, averaging only a few centimeters a year.

Example

Faults are fractures in the earth's crust caused by stretching or compression of plates or by plates sliding sideways past one another. Which famous fault makes California an area prone to earthquakes?

The San Andreas Fault that runs through California is at the boundary between the Pacific Plate and the North American Plate.

Practice Test Question

1. Plate movements are **not** responsible for producing:

   A. Earthquake zones

   B. Tornadoes

   C. Mountain ranges

   D. Volcanoes

Answer Key

1. **B. Tornadoes**

   Plate movements produce many features of the earth's surface, including mountain ranges, volcanoes, and earthquake zones. Tornadoes have no direct link with plate tectonics.

Meteorology

METEOROLOGY is the study of weather. It deals with topics such as the structure and properties of the atmosphere, air circulation patterns and winds, clouds and precipitation, high and low pressure systems, air masses and frontal systems, and climate.

> **METEOROLOGY:** the study of weather

Types of clouds

A CLOUD is a mass of condensed water vapor. The following are the major types of clouds:

- **Cirrus:** White and feathery; high in the sky
- **Cumulus:** Thick, white, fluffy
- **Stratus:** Layers of clouds
- **Nimbus:** Heavy, dark clouds; thunderstorm clouds

> **CLOUD:** a mass of condensed water vapor

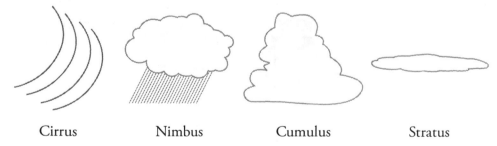

| Cirrus | Nimbus | Cumulus | Stratus |

There are four basic cloud types.

Example

Fog is essentially cloud formation at or near ground level. This occurs when moist air near ground level cools enough to condense into water droplets.

Practice Test Question

1. Thick, fluffy dark rain clouds are called:

A. Cumulonimbus

B. Stratonimbus

C. Stratocumulus

D. Cirrocumulus

Answer Key

1. **A. Cumulonimbus**

   Since "cumulo" refers to thick, fluffy clouds, and "nimbus" refers to dark rain clouds, cumulonimbus clouds combine both of these characteristics.

Shhh! It's study time

Remove distractions from the room where you're studying. Remove everything from the table where you're working except your book, notebook, and pen or pencil. Turn off your cell phone, turn off the television, and close the door. Tape a sign to the door that says, "Important study time! Please come back at 8:00."

Frontal systems

A FRONT is a narrow zone of transition between air masses of different densities and temperatures. The four types of fronts are:

FRONT: a narrow zone of transition between air masses of different densities and temperatures

1. Warm front: A front whose movement causes the lighter warm air to advance, while the denser cold air retreats. A warm front usually triggers a cloud development sequence of cirrus, cirrostratus, altostratus, nimbostratus, and stratus. It may result in an onset of light rain or snowfall immediately

ahead of the front, which gives way, as the cloud sequence forms, to steady precipitation (light to moderate) until the front passes.

2. Cold front: A front whose movement causes the denser cold air to displace the lighter warm air. The results of cold front situations depend on the stability of the air. If the air is stable, nimbostratus and altostratus clouds may form, and brief showers may immediately precede the front. If the air is unstable, there is greater uplift. Cumulonimbus clouds may tower over nimbostratus, and cirrus clouds may be blown downstream from the cumulonimbus by high-altitude winds. Thunderstorms may occur, accompanied by gusty surface winds and hail, as well as other, more violent weather. If the cold front moves quickly (roughly 28 mph or greater), a squall line of thunderstorms may form either immediately ahead of the front or up to 180 miles ahead of it.

3. Occluded front: A front formed when a cold front has caught up to a warm front and has intermingled, usually by sliding under the warmer air. Cold fronts generally move more quickly than warm fronts, and therefore occasionally overrun slower-moving warm fronts. The weather ahead of an occluded front is similar to that of a warm front during its advance, but switches to that of a cold front as the cold front passes through.

4. Stationary front: a front that shows no overall movement. The weather produced by this front can vary widely and depends on the amount of moisture present and the relative motions of the air pockets along the front. Most of the precipitation falls on the cold side of the front.

Example

From what direction does the wind blow after a warm front passes by you?

Before the warm front arrives, the wind is generally cool and from the east. As the front passes by you, the wind direction shifts toward the southeast and south with an accompanying rise in temperature.

Practice Test Question

1. **Thunderstorms are typically associated with:**

   A. Warm fronts

   B. Cold fronts

   C. Occluded fronts

   D. Stationary fronts

> ## Answer Key
>
> 1. **B. Cold fronts**
>
>   Cold fronts are associated with violent weather more often than other kinds of fronts.

Biology

Cell basics

CELL: the fundamental unit of life

The CELL is the fundamental unit of life. All known ORGANISMS, or living things, are composed of cells and the products of cells. Cells are also the smallest organizational units that are classified as living.

ORGANISMS: living things

Some organisms, like bacteria, are unicellular—that is, the entire organism is made up of one cell. Other organisms, like humans, are multicellular. While some multicellular organisms are made up of only a few cells, humans are made up of about 100 trillion cells.

Cells can be divided into two major types—prokaryotic and eukaryotic. Prokaryotic cells, such as bacteria, are relatively simple in structure. Eukaryotic cells, such as human cells, are much more complex and feature extensive internal structure and compartmentalization.

> **Keep learning new vocabulary!**
> Remember that your score on the Word Knowledge subtest is critical, so continue to learn new vocabulary throughout this study guide. For example, while you're reading about biology, create flashcards for the new vocabulary terms *organism* and *cilia*.

ORGANELLES: subcellular components that perform some function or functions in the cell

Principle components of all cells include the cellular membrane (the "skin" of the cell), the cytoskeleton (the "skeleton" of the cell), genetic material (e.g., DNA), and organelles. ORGANELLES are subcellular components that perform some function or functions in the cell, much like a human body's organs perform functions in the body. Plant cells also have a fairly rigid cell wall surrounding the cell.

FLAGELLA: tail-like structures that help cells move

Prokaryotic cells are filled with cellular fluid called cytoplasm, genetic material, and organelles called ribosomes. Mobile prokaryotic cells may have one or more FLAGELLA, tail-like structures that help them move. Prokaryotic cells don't have a nucleus.

Eukaryotic cells also are filled with cytoplasm, genetic material, and numerous organelles including ribosomes. Mobile eukaryotic cells may have flagella or CILIA, hair-like structures that help a cell move. Eukaryotic cells also have a nucleus. The nucleus is separated from the rest of the cell by the nuclear membrane, which is structurally much like the cellular membrane.

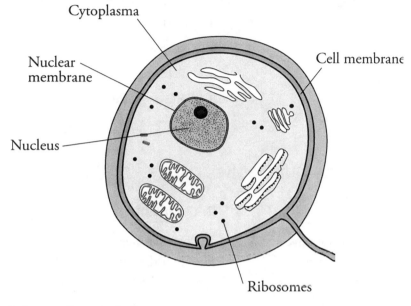

Basic parts of an animal cell.

The interior of all cells is filled with a thick liquid called cytosol. The cytosol is composed of water and dissolved proteins, carbohydrates, lipids, and genetic material. The cytosol also surrounds many organelles. Taken together, the cytosol and the organelles are referred to as cytoplasm.

ASVAB tip!
On the CAT-ASVAB, the General Science subtest is 8 minutes long and has 16 questions.

Practice Test Questions

1. What structure would not be found in a prokaryotic cell?

   A. Cellular membrane

   B. Nucleus

   C. Cytoplasm

   D. Ribosome

2. Which term describes the entire contents of the cell, including the organelles?

   A. Cytosol

   B. Cytoplasm

   C. Nucleus

   D. Cellular membrane

Answer Key

1. **B. Nucleus**

   Prokaryotic cells do not have a nucleus; they do have a cellular membrane, cytoplasm, and ribosomes. Any cell with a nucleus is, by definition, a eukaryotic cell.

2. **B. Cytoplasm**

   The cellular membrane surrounds and bounds the cell. The cytosol is the fluid inside the cell. The cytosol and the organelles are collectively known as the cytoplasm.

Parts of cells

The interior of all eukaryotic cells is divided into numerous compartments and full of various organelles. Each organelle performs a specific function for the cell.

RIBOSOMES, present in prokaryotic and eukaryotic cells, are the site of protein synthesis. A cell may contain five hundred thousand or so ribosomes.

In eukaryotic cells, many ribosomes are bonded to the ENDOPLASMIC RETICULUM, a folded membrane that transports materials throughout the cell.

Extensions of the endoplasmic reticulum are known as GOLGI BODIES; they sort, modify, and package molecules made elsewhere in the cell.

Lysosomes, found mainly in animal cells, contain digestive enzymes that break down food.

RIBOSOMES: the site of protein synthesis in cells

ENDOPLASMIC RETICULUM: a folded membrane that transports materials throughout the cell

GOLGI BODIES: extensions of the endoplasmic reticulum

MITOCHONDRIA are the site of cellular respiration, the conversion of nutrients in the cell into energy.

PLASTIDS (including the common chloroplast) are found in photosynthetic organisms (such as plants) and convert light energy into chemical energy.

> **MITOCHONDRIA:** the site of cellular respiration

> **PLASTIDS:** found in photosynthetic organisms (such as plants) and convert light energy into chemical energy

Practice Test Questions

1. **What type of structure would identify a cell as a plant cell?**

   A. Chloroplast

   B. Nucleus

   C. Cytoplasm

   D. Ribosome

2. **What is the function of the mitochondria in an animal cell?**

   A. To transport materials throughout the cell

   B. To produce usable energy

   C. To package molecules made elsewhere in the cell

   D. To protect the genetic material

Answer Key

1. **A. Chloroplast**

   Plant cells contain all of these structures—a nucleus, cytoplasm, ribosomes, and chloroplasts. But *all* eukaryotic cells contain a nucleus, cytoplasm, and ribosomes. Only a chloroplast would definitively identify a cell as a plant cell. Chloroplasts are found in photosynthetic organisms, such as plants.

2. **B. To produce usable energy**

   Mitochondria are the site of cellular respiration, which converts nutrients in the cell into energy.

Biological classification

Scientists estimate that there are more than ten million different species of living things on Earth. Of these, 1.5 million have been named and classified. Systems of classification show similarities and provide scientists with a worldwide system of organization.

TAXONOMY: the science of classification

Carolus Linnaeus is known as the father of taxonomy. **TAXONOMY** is the science of classification. The following levels are used to classify living things.

Kingdom

    Phylum

        Class

            Order

                Family

                    Genus

                        Species

Kingdom is the largest and least specific group. For example, all plants are in the same kingdom. The groups become smaller and more specific as you move down to the level of species. For example, the white oak is one species of oak tree. All white oak trees are much more alike than all plants!

Create posters

To help you remember new concepts, create posters and post them on your wall. Create a poster listing the classification levels, from kingdom to species—or a poster with a diagram of the layers of the earth from earlier in this chapter.

Binomial nomenclature

The modern classification system uses binomial nomenclature, a two-word name, for every species. The genus is the first part of the name and the species is the second part.

The modern classification system uses binomial nomenclature, a two-word name, for every species. The genus is the first part of the name and the species is the second part.

Notice in the example below that *Homo sapiens* is the scientific name for humans.

Example

Kingdom: Animalia

    Phylum: Chordata

        Class: Mammalia

            Order: Primate

                Family: Hominidae

                    Genus: Homo

                      Species: sapiens

Kingdoms

The current five-kingdom system separates living things into five groups:

1. **Monera**: Single-celled, prokaryotic organisms. Examples include bacteria.

2. **Protista**: Eukaryotic, usually single-celled organisms. Examples include amoebae and some algae.

3. **Fungi**: Eukaryotic, multicullular organisms. Examples include mushrooms, yeast, and mold.

4. **Plantae**: Eukaryotic, multicellular, and photosynthetic organisms. Examples include mosses, flowering plants, and trees.

5. **Animalia**: Eukaryotic, multicellular, and motile organisms. Examples include insects, fish, dogs, and people.

Practice Test Question

1. **The scientific name for humans is *Homo sapiens*. Choose the proper classification, beginning with kingdom and ending with order.**

   A. Animalia, Mammalia, Primate, Hominidae

   B. Animalia, Chordata, *Homo, sapiens*

   C. Animalia, Chordata, Mammalia, Primate

   D. Chordata, Primate, *Homo, sapiens*

Answer Key

1. **C. Animalia, Chordata, Mammalia, Primate**

   The order of classification for humans is as follows: Kingdom, Animalia; Phylum, Chordata; Class, Mammalia; Order, Primate; Family, Hominadae; Genus, *Homo*; Species, *sapiens*.

Ecology

ECOLOGY is the scientific study of the relationships between living organisms and their environments. The largest functional unit of ecology is usually understood to

> **ECOLOGY:** the scientific study of the relationships between living organisms and their environments

ECOSYSTEM: a community of organisms and their environment

BIOTIC: living

ABIOTIC: nonliving

A producer is the first organism in a food chain.

be an **ECOSYSTEM**, a community of organisms and their environment. Ecosystems contain **BIOTIC**, living, and **ABIOTIC**, nonliving, components. Most ecosystems are thought to be stable through prolonged periods of time. Ecosystem stability usually is sustained by biodiversity.

Many ecological studies focus on the flow of energy throughout an ecosystem. These types of "who eats whom" studies establish food networks that demonstrate key players in ecosystems and illustrate the interconnectedness of life and the importance of biodiversity.

Here are some key terms related to ecology.

- Food chain: A "who-eats-whom" diagram showing the flow of energy within an ecosystem. For example:

  grass → mouse → snake → owl

- Producer: An organism that makes its own food, usually through photo-synthesis; for example, grasses and flowering plants. A producer is the first organism in a food chain.

- Consumer: An organism that eats other organisms. For examples, mice eat grass, and people eat fish.

- Decomposer: A true "recycler"; an organism that breaks down dead plants and animals so they can be used again by plants. Decomposers include bugs and worms.

- Predator: An animal that hunts other animals.

- Prey: An animal that is hunted.

ASVAB tip!
If you take the P&P-ASVAB (the paper-and-pencil version), you can go back and change an answer within a subtest. However, you cannot go back to a previous subtest. If you take the CAT-ASVAB (the version on the computer), you cannot go back and change an answer within a subtest. However, this version allows you to go on to the next subtest if you finish a subtest early, and you can leave the room when you complete the entire test.

Practice Test Question

1. Which of the following is an
   example of a producer?

   A. A mouse

   B. A person

   C. A worm

   D. A tree

Answer Key

1. **D. A tree**

   A producer is an organism that
   makes its own food, usually
   through photosynthesis. All
   plants are producers; therefore, a
   tree is a producer.

Anatomy and Human Systems

ANATOMY is the study of the structure of organisms. Human anatomy is usually
considered to be a foundational and basic medical science. Comparative anatomy
focuses on the similarities and differences among the anatomies of different species.

> **ANATOMY:** the study of
> the structure of organisms

Put it in your own words

After reading a section in this book, try paraphrasing it, or putting it in your own words
in a short summary. Rephrasing what you have read helps you understand the material
and makes it sink in.

Here are some of the primary organ systems:

The function of the digestive system is to break down food into nutrients
and absorb it into the bloodstream, where it can be delivered to all cells of the
body for use in cellular respiration.

The function of the circulatory system (cardiovascular system) is to
carry oxygenated blood and nutrients to all cells of the body and return carbon
dioxide waste to the lungs for expulsion. The heart, blood vessels, and blood make
up the cardiovascular system.

> The heart, blood vessels,
> and blood make up the
> cardiovascular system.

The function of the respiratory system is to take in oxygen and remove carbon dioxide from the body. Different animal groups have different types of respiratory organs that perform gas exchange. Some animals use their entire outer skin for respiration (e.g., worms). Fish and other aquatic animals have gills for gas exchange. All vertebrates, including humans, have lungs as their primary respiratory organ.

The excretory system eliminates waste (primarily nitrogenous wastes) and unneeded fluids from the body. Vertebrates have kidneys as the primary excretion organ.

Most animals use a complex system of nervous control to respond to internal and environmental stimuli. In humans, the nervous system is composed of the central nervous system (e.g., brain and spinal column) and the peripheral nervous systems (the nerves that run throughout the body). The central nervous system makes "decisions," while the peripheral nervous system conveys messages to and from the brain.

The musculoskeletal system allows movement and provides support and protection to the body. In humans, an internal skeletal system is used as a framework and muscles provide the motive power. Various types of joints allow the human body a wide range of motion.

The immune system is a remarkable and complex system of structures and processes that maintain internal homeostatis and eject or kill foreign invaders such as bacteria, viruses, and parasites.

The endocrine system manufactures special proteins known as hormones. Hormones are carried throughout the body in the bloodstream. While the nervous system controls the body in the short- to medium-term, the endocrine system controls the body in the medium- to long-term.

Practice Test Questions

1. The brain is part of what system?
   A. Musculoskeletal system
   B. Circulatory system
   C. Respiratory system
   D. Nervous system

2. The lungs are part of what system?
   A. Musculoskeletal system
   B. Circulatory system
   C. Respiratory system
   D. Nervous system

Answer Key

1. **D. Nervous system**

   In humans, the nervous system is composed of the central nervous system (e.g., brain and spinal column) and the peripheral nervous systems (the nerves that run throughout the body).

2. **C. Respiratory system**

   All vertebrates, including humans, have lungs as their primary respiratory organ.

How would I use this?

In the military, medical emergency technicians provide medical treatment to injured troops in combat and help care for patients in hospitals. A strong background in chemistry, biology, and general science is a valuable asset for anyone interested in this military career.

CHAPTER 6
MECHANICAL COMPREHENSION

The Mechanical Comprehension subtest of the ASVAB tests your understanding of mechanics and mechanical devices. This chapter covers the principles of mechanics, simple machines, and machine components.

> *The Mechanical Comprehension subtest of the ASVAB tests your understanding of mechanics and mechanical devices.*

Force, Pressure, and Torque

A **FORCE** is a push or pull that causes an object to move or stops its motion. For example, you can apply a force on a book and make it slide across a tabletop. You can apply another force to stop it before it slides off and falls on the floor. If you and I both exert equal forces on the book so it stays in place without moving, we would say that the forces are balancing each other and are in **EQUILIBRIUM**.

> **FORCE:** a push or pull that causes an object to move or stops its motion

> **EQUILIBRIUM:** a state in which two forces are balancing each other

Example

Why does a book stay still on a tabletop even when the force of gravity is pulling down on it?

The tabletop exerts an equal and opposite upward force on the book to keep it in equilibrium.

What a weighty notion...

Did you know that weight is a force? *Mass* is the amount of matter in an object. *Weight* is the force that gravity exerts on a mass.

The terms load and resistance both refer to forces in the context of machines. The term load might refer to a weight that must be lifted by a machine. The term resistance is often used to describe an obstructing force, such as friction, that must be overcome in order to perform some task. Both terms could be used to refer to the same force; there is no hard and fast rule for the use of these terms.

PRESSURE is the force exerted on unit area of a surface. It is given by the formula $P = \frac{F}{A}$, where F is the force exerted and A is the total area on which the force is exerted. If the force is measured in pounds and the area is measured in square inches, the pressure is expressed in the units pounds per square inch (psi).

> **PRESSURE:** the force exerted on unit area of a surface

Flashing formulas!

Don't use flashcards just for vocabulary words—create a flashcard for each new formula, too. Put the name of the formula on the front of an index card and put the formula on the back. You can then shuffle the flashcards and quiz yourself every few days.

Example

The pressure inside a car tire is typically around 30 psi. This means that the air inflating the tire is applying a force of 30 lbs on each square inch of the inside of the tire.

A TORQUE is a turning or rotating force applied at a distance from a pivot point.

TORQUE: a turning or rotating force applied at a distance from a pivot point

Example

A torque is the kind of force you apply to a doorknob to turn it and open a door. You also apply a torque when you push a door or gate to open it. Notice in the diagram below that it is easier to open a gate if you push it farther away from the hinge.

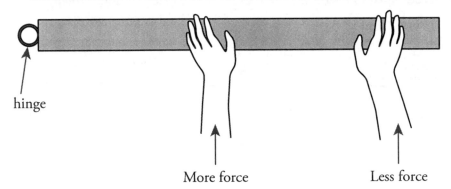

hinge

More force　　　Less force

Top view of a gate being pushed open.

Practice Test Question

1. If you push down on a table with a force of 10 lbs and the area of your palm is 15 square inches, how much pressure are you exerting on the table?

   A. 10 psi

   B. 15 psi

   C. 1.5 psi

   D. 0.667 psi

Work and Power

WORK, in mechanics, is measured by the distance a certain object is moved by a given force.

$$\text{Work} = \text{Force} \times \text{Distance}$$

POWER is the rate of doing work.

$$\text{Power} = \frac{\text{Work}}{\text{Time}}$$

WORK: the distance a certain object is moved by a given force

POWER: the rate of doing work

Example

If you are standing in a checkout line at the grocery store holding a heavy bag of groceries, are you doing work?

In mechanics terms, not at all, even though you are exerting a force on the bag. Since the distance moved by the bag is zero, the work done is zero as well.

Practice Test Question

1. A pulley lifts a box weighing 150 lbs 300 feet off the floor. How much work is done?

   A. 45,000 ft-lb

   B. 150 ft-lb

   C. 0.5 ft-lb

   D. 450 ft-lb

2. A pulley lifts a box weighing 150 lbs 300 feet from the floor. If the pulley lifts the box in 3 minutes, how much power does it use?

   A. 45,000 ft-lb/min

   B. 135,000 ft-lb/min

   C. 3,000 ft-lb/min

   D. 15,000 ft-lb/min

Answer Key

1. **A. 45,000 ft-lb**

   Since the pulley has to overcome gravity to lift the box, the force it applies to the box is equal to force gravity exerts on the box, which is the weight of the box.

   Since work = force × distance, the work done by the pulley = 150 lbs × 300 ft = 45,000 ft-lb.

2. **D. 15,000 ft-lb/min**

   The work done by the pulley was calculated in the previous problem. The work done was 45,000 ft-lb. Since power is the rate of doing work, the power expended by the pulley $= \frac{\text{Work}}{\text{Time}}$ $= \frac{45,000 \text{ ft-lb}}{3 \text{ min.}} = 15,000$ ft-lb/min.

ASVAB tip!
On the CAT-ASVAB, the Mechanical Comprehension subtest is 20 minutes long and has 16 questions.

Simple Machines

Machines help us do work more easily. They do this by increasing the magnitude of a force or by changing its direction, by increasing the speed of a component, or transferring a force to a different place.

Machines help us do work more easily. They do this by increasing the magnitude of a force or by changing its direction, by increasing the speed of a component, or transferring a force to a different place. Many of the machines we use are made up of combinations of six basic simple machines: lever, pulley, inclined plane, wheel and axle, wedge, and screw.

Mechanical advantage

MECHANICAL ADVANTAGE: the ratio of the output force (load) to the input force (effort)

How effective is a machine? One way to measure this is to calculate its MECHANICAL ADVANTAGE. This is the ratio of the output force (load) to the input force (effort).

$$\text{Mechanical advantage} = \frac{\text{Output force}}{\text{Input force}} = \frac{\text{Load}}{\text{Effort}}$$

If you can put in a small effort and lift a big load, the machine has a large mechanical advantage.

Ideal mechanical advantage (IMA) is the mechanical advantage of a system assuming there is no energy loss to friction or any other dissipative force. In the real world there is always friction, air resistance, or some other force that steals part of the energy. Therefore, the actual mechanical advantage (AMA) is typically smaller than the IMA.

Does mechanical advantage sound too good to be true? What's the tradeoff? It's usually distance in place of force. You may have to put in less effort, but you will have to do it over a greater distance. So you still expend the same amount of energy you would have without the machine.

Levers

A LEVER is a setup like the ones shown in the example below. It has a lever arm placed on a fulcrum, around which it pivots. The load and effort are applied at different points of the lever arm. In a FIRST CLASS LEVER, the fulcrum is between the input (effort) and the output (load). In a SECOND CLASS LEVER, the load is between the fulcrum and the effort. In a THIRD CLASS LEVER, the effort is between the fulcrum and the load.

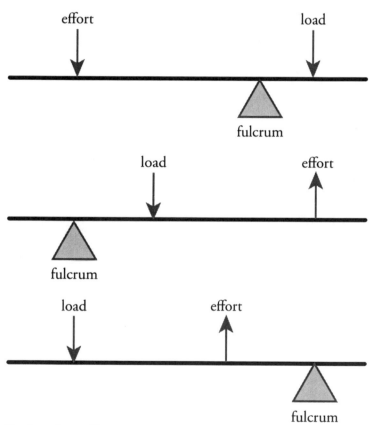

The three classes of levers.

> **LEVER:** a machine with a lever arm placed on a fulcrum, around which it pivots

> **FIRST CLASS LEVER:** a lever in which the fulcrum is between the input (effort) and the output (load)

> **SECOND CLASS LEVER:** a lever in which the load is between the fulcrum and the effort

> **THIRD CLASS LEVER:** a lever in which the effort is between the fulcrum and the load

Looking at the diagram above, you might make an intuitive guess that putting the fulcrum nearer the load would make it possible to lift a heavier load with less effort. You would be perfectly right!

Ideal mechanical advantage of a lever =

$$\frac{\textbf{Length of effort arm (distance from fulcrum to effort point)}}{\textbf{Length of load arm (distance from fulcrum to load point)}}$$

Example

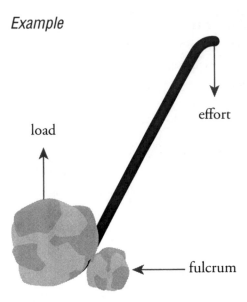

A crowbar is a first class lever.

Example

A wheelbarrow is an example of a second class lever since the fulcrum is at one end, the handle where the effort is placed is at the other end, and the load is in the middle.

Example

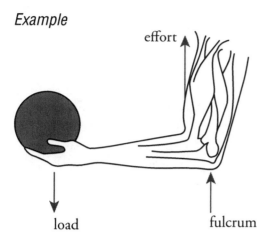

A human arm is a third class lever.

As you can see, for a third class lever, the effort is always closer to the fulcrum than to the load. Therefore, the mechanical advantage is always less than one—you have to put in a lot of effort to lift a light load. Then why use a third-class lever? Because it moves the load over a greater distance. This can be an advantage in some situations.

> **Fun science fact!**
> It is thought that the ancient Greek mathematician Archimedes said, "Give me a lever long enough and a fulcrum on which to place it, and I shall move the world." That would be a lever with some mechanical advantage!

Practice Test Questions

1. The pair of tongs below is:

   A. Not a lever

   B. A first class lever

   C. A second class lever

   D. A third class lever

2. A first class lever has the load placed 2 inches from the fulcrum and effort applied 6 inches from the fulcrum. Its ideal mechanical advantage is:

   A. 6

   B. 3.5

   C. 3

   D. 2.5

3. A first class lever has the load placed 2 inches from the fulcrum and effort applied 6 inches from the fulcrum. It has a rusty fulcrum with a lot of resistance. It can lift a load of only 5 pounds when an effort of 2 pounds is applied. Its actual mechanical advantage is:

   A. 6

   B. 3.5

   C. 3

   D. 2.5

Answer Key

1. **D. A third class lever**

   A pair of tongs is a third class lever because the effort (the pressure you apply to it) is between the fulcrum (the folded end) and the load (the object you are picking up). Since a pair of tongs has two arms, you can think of it technically as a pair of third class levers.

2. **C. 3**

   Ideal mechanical advantage of a lever

   $$= \frac{\text{Length of effort arm}}{\text{Length of load arm}} = \frac{6 \text{ in}}{2 \text{ in}}$$

   $$= 3.$$

3. **D. 2.5**

   Actual mechanical advantage of a lever (or any machine)

   $$= \frac{\text{Output force (load lifted)}}{\text{Input force (effort put in)}} = \frac{5 \text{ lb}}{2 \text{ lb}}$$

   $$= 2.5.$$

Pulleys

PULLEY: a simple machine that consists of a rope routed over a wheel with a grooved rim

A **PULLEY** is a simple machine that consists of a rope routed over a wheel with a grooved rim. For a fixed pulley, the wheel is attached to the ceiling or some other rigid surface. In the case of a moveable pulley, one end of the rope is attached to a fixed surface while the wheel itself is free to move.

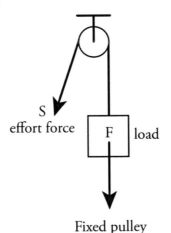

S
effort force

F load

Fixed pulley

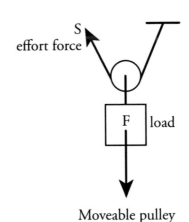

S
effort force

F load

Moveable pulley

A pulley can be fixed or moveable.

A fixed pulley does not reduce the effort needed to pull a load across it. The effort is equal to the load; hence, the mechanical advantage is 1. The function of a fixed pulley is to reverse the direction of the force, which in many cases lets the user take advantage of the force of gravity.

The ideal mechanical advantage of a moveable pulley is equal to the number of ropes holding it up. For the moveable pulley shown above, both ends of the rope are holding the pulley up while the load pulls it down. So each end of the rope is taking half the load. As a result, the effort applied to the rope needs to be only half the magnitude of the load.

$$\text{Mechanical advantage} = \frac{\text{Load}}{\text{Effort}} = \frac{\text{Load}}{\frac{1}{2} \text{ of Load}} = 2$$

> *The ideal mechanical advantage of a moveable pulley is equal to the number of ropes holding it up.*

Example

Pulleys are often used in combination, as in the example shown below.

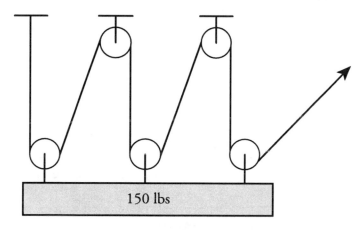

A compound set of pulleys multiplies the mechanical advantage.

Although the setup shown here is quite complicated and involves many pulleys, to find the mechanical advantage of the system, simply count the number of ropes holding up the weight. In this case, it is 6. The force pulling the weight down is 150 lbs. Each section of rope supporting the weight takes up one-sixth of the load. Therefore, the effort applied to the end of the rope (equal to the tension or force in each section of the rope) is 25 lbs.

$$\text{Mechanical advantage of the system} = \frac{\text{Load}}{\text{Effort}} = \frac{150 \text{ lbs}}{25 \text{ lbs}} = 6.$$

Example

A block and tackle combines two or more pulleys into a system where one block of pulleys is fixed while the other remains moveable. It is technically identical to the system described in the previous example.

A block and tackle is commonly used on ships to move a heavy load.

As in the previous example, the ideal mechanical advantage of a block and tackle system is equal to the number of ropes holding up the moveable block. The mechanical advantage of the system shown above is 4. This means that it can be used to lift a weight of 100 lbs with an effort force of 25 lbs, assuming there isn't much friction loss in the system.

Practice Test Questions

1. What is the mechanical advantage of a one-pulley system?

   A. 1

   B. 2

   C. 3

   D. It depends on the type of system

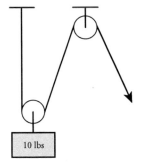

2.

   How much effort must be applied to the rope to lift the 10 lb weight?

   A. 3.3 lbs

   B. 5 lbs

   C. 10 lbs

   D. 20 lbs

Answer Key

1. **D. It depends on the type of system**

   If the pulley is fixed, the mechanical advantage is 1. If the pulley is moveable, the mechanical advantage is 2.

2. **B. 5 lbs**

   Note that 2 ropes are holding up the moveable pulley to the left. This gives a system a mechanical advantage of 2. Since $\frac{\text{Load}}{\text{Effort}} = 2$, Effort $= \frac{\text{Load}}{2}$ $= \frac{10}{2} = 5$ lbs. The fixed pulley to the right does not give any mechanical advantage. Its function is to change the direction of the effort so that one can pull down instead of having to pull up.

Inclined planes

An **INCLINED PLANE** is one of the simplest and oldest machines. To push an object up an incline requires less force than hauling it straight up against the full force of gravity. The tradeoff is that one has to push the object a longer distance.

> **INCLINED PLANE:** one of the simples and oldest machines, it allows an object to be pushed up an incline with less force than hauling the object straight up

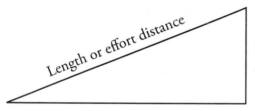

Height or load distance

Inclined planes trade larger force for longer distance.

For an inclined plane, the ideal mechanical advantage (IMA) is:

$$\frac{\text{Length of incline}}{\text{Height of topmost point}}.$$

> **Example**
>
> Inclined planes are routinely used for moving heavy objects. They are a familiar sight in any neighborhood where you can see people loading furniture into a moving van or a lawnmower onto a landscaping truck using a ramp.

Inclined planes make it easy to move heavy furniture.

Practice Test Question

1. Which of the two inclined planes shown below has the higher ideal mechanical advantage?

   A. A

   B. B

   C. Both are equal

   D. It is not possible to find the ideal mechanical advantage

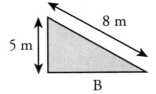

Answer Key

1. **A**

    For an inclined plane, the ideal mechanical advantage (IMA) is:

    $$\frac{\text{Length of incline}}{\text{Height of topmost point}}.$$

    For A, IMA $= \frac{10 \text{ m}}{5 \text{ m}} = 2$.

    For B, IMA $= \frac{8 \text{ m}}{5 \text{ m}} = 1.6$.

Wedges

A **WEDGE** is essentially a double incline. Like the inclined plane, when you use a wedge you trade a larger force applied over a smaller distance for a smaller force applied over a larger distance. A wedge is used to force material apart. For example, the blade of an axe is a wedge.

> **WEDGE:** a simple machine that is essentially a double incline

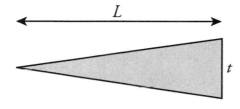

Similar to an inclined plane, the ideal mechanical advantage (IMA) of a wedge is:

$$\frac{\text{Length of wedge (L)}}{\text{Thickness at widest point(t)}}.$$

Example

A wedge converts some of the downward force of the hammer in the diagram below to a sideways force that pries the material apart.

A wedge can be used with a hammer to split a block.

Wheel and axle

The **WHEEL AND AXLE** is another simple machine where you trade force for distance. A smaller turning force applied over a larger distance on the wheel is translated to a stronger force over a shorter distance at the axle.

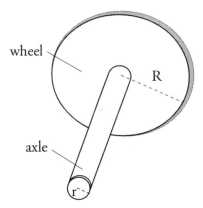

The ideal mechanical advantage of a wheel and axle is:

$$\frac{\text{Radius of wheel}}{\text{Radius of axle}} = \frac{R}{r}.$$

Example

A faucet is a good example of a wheel and axle system. You turn it using a wide grip, which requires less force.

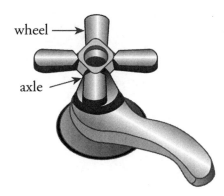

wheel →

axle →

Practice Test Question

1. The top of a faucet has a radius of 2 inches. If the neck of the faucet has a half-inch radius, what is the mechanical advantage of this system?

   A. 4

   B. 0.25

   C. 2

   D. 2.5

Answer Key

1. **A. 4**

The faucet is a wheel and axle system where the top is the wheel with radius = 2 in and the neck is the axle with radius = 0.5 in. The mechanical advantage is:

$$\frac{\text{Radius of wheel}}{\text{Radius of axle}} = \frac{2 \text{ in}}{0.5 \text{ in}} = 4.$$

Screws

A **SCREW** is essentially an inclined plane wrapped around a cylinder. It converts a turning force into a straight line force. It is typically used to raise or lower things and to hold objects together. The lead of a screw thread is the linear distance it moves while the screw goes through one full rotation.

SCREW: a simple machine that is essentially an inclined plane wrapped around a cylinder

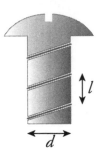

A screw is a modified inclined plane.

The ideal mechanical advantage of a screw is:

$$\frac{\text{circumference of rotation}}{\text{lead of screw thread}} = \frac{\pi d}{l}$$

where d is the diameter of the screw and l is the lead of the thread.

> **Example**
>
> A jackscrew can be used to lift heavy weights. The long handle increases the effective diameter of rotation and reduces the effort needed.

Jackscrew.

Machine Components

Gears

GEAR: a wheel with teeth on it, the job of which is to change the size of a force, the speed of rotation, or the direction of rotation

A **GEAR** is a wheel with teeth on it. These teeth can mesh with teeth on other gears so that when one gear moves, the other one moves as well. The job of a gear is to change the size of a force, the speed of rotation, or the direction of rotation.

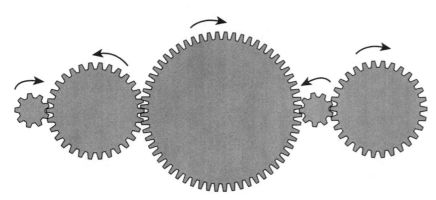

The teeth on meshed gears must be the same size.

Many gears are often linked together in what is called a GEAR TRAIN. The gear to which force is applied is called the DRIVER. The last gear in the train is called the DRIVEN GEAR. The ones in between are called IDLERS. Since each gear turns a distance equal to the same number of teeth in the same amount of time, the smaller gears with fewer teeth turn many more times than the larger gears.

Sink your teeth into this
Each gear in a gear train turns in the direction opposite to the one next to it. The smaller gears turn more quickly.

The gear ratio of a set of meshed gears is:

$$\frac{\text{number of teeth on driven gear}}{\text{number of teeth on driver}}$$

$$= \frac{\text{radius of driven gear}}{\text{radius of driver}}$$

$$= \frac{\text{rotational speed of driver}}{\text{rotational speed of driven gear}}$$

$$= \frac{\text{output torque}}{\text{input torque}} .$$

The GEAR RATIO is a measure of the mechanical advantage of a gear system.

Example
In the diagram below, the larger driven gear has twice the number of teeth as the smaller driver. So the gear ratio is 2. Since the number of teeth is proportional to the circumference of a gear, the larger gear has twice the circumference and twice the radius of the smaller gear. The larger gear turns at half the speed of the smaller gear but provides twice the torque.

GEAR TRAIN: many gears linked together

DRIVER: the gear in a gear train to which force is applied

DRIVEN GEAR: the last gear in a gear chain

IDLERS: the gears in a gear chain between the driver and the driven gear

GEAR RATIO: a measure of the mechanical advantage of a gear system

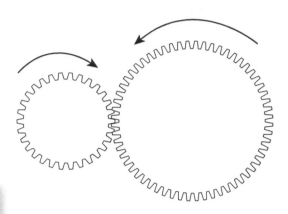

The four basic types of gears are spur gears, bevel gears, worm gears, and rack and pinion gears.

SPUR GEARS: gears in which the wheels are in the same plane and their axles are parallel

HELICAL SPUR GEAR: a kind of spur gear in which the teeth are set at an angle; it is much quieter and smoother than a regular spur gear

The four basic types of gears are spur gears, bevel gears, worm gears, and rack and pinion gears.

The gears discussed above are **SPUR GEARS**. They are the most familiar kind. The wheels are in the same plane and their axles are parallel. They are typically used to transmit rotary motion and to reduce or increase rotation speed. A **HELICAL SPUR GEAR** is a kind of spur gear in which the teeth are set at an angle. Since the teeth don't make contact along their whole length all at once as the gear turns, a helical gear is a lot quieter and smoother than a regular spur gear. These gears are often used in cars.

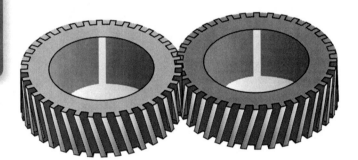

Helical spur gears.

BEVEL GEARS: gears that have teeth that are cut on the same slant of a cone, and are typically meshed at right angles to each other; they change the direction of rotation

BEVEL GEARS have teeth that are cut on the slant of a cone. They are typically meshed at right angles to each other, but can also be meshed at other angles. The direction of rotation is therefore changed when a bevel gear is used. The speed may also change depending on the size of the wheels. Bevel gears can also be made with spiral teeth, like the helical spur gears.

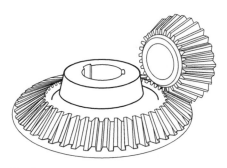

Bevel gears.

A **WORM GEAR** consists of a worm and a worm wheel. A single-thread worm has one tooth that is in the form of a screw thread. You can think of it as a screw and spur gear put together. The worm always drives the worm wheel. It transmits rotational motion at right angles like a bevel gear. These gears are typically used in situations where a high speed reduction is needed.

> **WORM GEAR:** a gear that consists of a worm and a worm wheel; it transmits rotational motion at right angles like a bevel gear

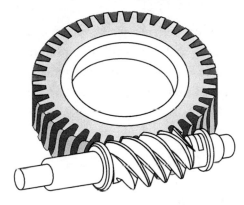

Worm gears.

RACK AND PINION GEARS are gears in which one toothed wheel (pinion) is meshed with a flat, toothed surface (rack). They convert the rotational motion of the pinion into the linear motion of the rack.

> **RACK AND PINION GEARS:** gears in which one toothed wheel (pinion) is meshed with a flat, toothed surface (rack); they convert rotational motion to linear motion

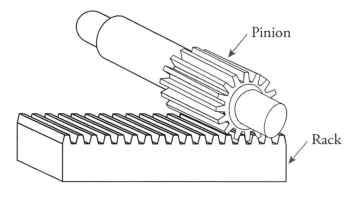

Pinion

Rack

Rack and pinion gears.

Example

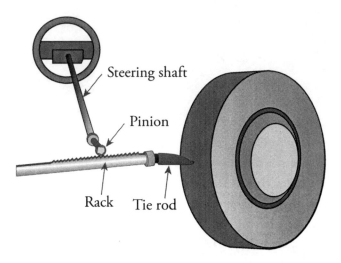

Steering shaft

Pinion

Rack   Tie rod

Can you tell what kind of gear is being used in the car steering arrangement shown? If you look at the bottom end of the steering shaft, you will see a pinion on a flat, toothed rod. When the driver turns the steering wheel, this rack and pinion arrangement is used to change this rotational motion into a linear motion needed to move the car wheel.

Practice Test Questions

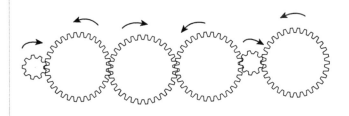

1. **Four spur gears are linked together in a train as shown. The driven gear turns:**

    A. In the same direction as the driver

    B. In a direction opposite that of the driver

    C. First in the same direction, then in the opposite direction

    D. First in the opposite direction, then the same direction

2. **What type of gears is shown below?**

    A. Spur

    B. Bevel

    C. Rack and pinion

    D. Worm

Practice Test Questions (cont.)

3. A system of gears reduces the output speed by one-third in relation to the input speed. The gear ratio is:

   A. $\frac{1}{3}$

   B. 3

   C. 9

   D. 300

4. In the system of gears described in the previous question, the output torque is:

   A. Equal to the input torque

   B. Three times the input torque

   C. One-third the input torque

   D. Not related to the input torque

Answer Key

1. **B. In a direction opposite that of the driver**

   Note that each gear in the train reverses direction. Therefore, there will be three direction changes in a four-gear train. This will make the fourth, or the driven, gear turn in a direction opposite that of the driver.

2. **B. Bevel**

   Notice that the two meshed gears turn at right angles to each other and that the teeth are cut on the slant of a cone.

3. **B. 3**

   Gear ratio is:

   $$\frac{\text{rotational speed of driver}}{\text{rotational speed of driven gear}}$$

   Since the output speed (the rotational speed of the driven gear) is one-third the input speed (the rotational speed of the driver), the driver turns three times as fast as the driven gear. So the gear ratio is 3.

4. **B. Three times the input torque**

   $$\text{Gear ratio} = \frac{\text{output torque}}{\text{input torque}}$$

   Since the gear ratio in the previous question is 3, the output torque must be three times the input torque.

Cams

A **CAM** is a wheel that turns on an axis that is off-center. It turns rotating motion into up-and-down motion. Cams can be of different shapes. In the diagram below, you can see how a circular cam turning around an off-center axis pushes a rod, called a follower, up and down. When the bulk of the cam is down, the

CAM: a wheel that turns on an axis that is off-center; it turns rotating motion into up-and-down motion

follower rod is at its lowest point. As the cam turns, it pushes the rod up until it reaches its highest point.

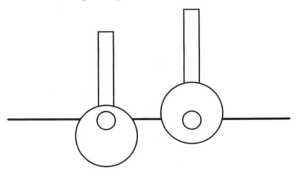

Example

The camshaft of a car turns the rotary motion of the engine to linear motion used to open and close valves. As the camshaft rotates, the lobes (cams) push against the valves to open them.

Camshaft of a car.

Springs

You can compress or extend a spring to store energy in it. As soon as you let go, the spring jumps out or snaps back, releasing the stored energy. Machines often use springs to store energy for part of a cycle and release it later.

Example

Springs are often used in shock absorbers to cushion the impact of a collision or fall.

Shock absorber.

Valves

A **VALVE** controls fluid flow. A faucet is a simple valve you operate manually to turn the water on or off. Other valves are set up to operate automatically. In a toilet water tank, for example, a fill valve is used to control the flow of water into the tank based on the water level.

A **SHUT-OFF VALVE**, such as a faucet, closes or opens the path of a fluid. An **ANTI-REVERSAL VALVE** allows fluid to flow in one direction only. A **THROTTLING VALVE** controls the amount of fluid flow by widening or narrowing the pathway.

> **VALVE:** a machine component that controls fluid flow.

> **SHUT-OFF VALVE:** a valve that closes or opens the path of a fluid

> **ANTI-REVERSAL VALVE:** a valve that allows fluid to flow in one direction only

> **THROTTLING VALVE:** a valve that controls the amount of fluid flow by widening or narrowing the pathway

Practice Test Question

1. A bicycle pump is equipped with a valve the lets the air go into the tire but not out. What kind of valve is this?

    A. Shut-off valve

    B. Anti-reversal valve

    C. Throttling valve

    D. None of the above

Answer Key

1. **B. Anti-reversal valve**

    An anti-reversal valve allows fluid to flow in one direction only. Since the valve in the bicycle pump lets the air flow into the tire but not out, it is an anti-reversal valve.

Instruments

Micrometer	Used for precise measurements of the dimensions of small objects. Can measure at precisions up to a hundredth or thousandth of a millimeter.
Barometer	Used to measure atmospheric pressure.
Tachometer	Used to measure rotation speed, typically in revolutions per minute (rpm).
Beam balance	Used to find the weight of an object by bringing a lever rotating around a fulcrum into equilibrium.
Spring balance	Used to find the weight of an object by measuring how far a spring is stretched when the object is hung from it.
Pressure gauge	Used to measure pressure in a gas or liquid, typically in pounds per square inch (psi).

Practice Test Question

1. **A man wants to measure the air pressure in his car tire. He will use a:**

   A. Micrometer

   B. Barometer

   C. Pressure gauge

   D. Spring balance

Answer Key

1. **C. Pressure gauge**

   A pressure gauge is used to measure the pressure of an enclosed gas.

   A barometer also measures pressure, but it measures the air pressure in the atmosphere.

How would I use this?

In the military, helicopter pilots transport troops and cargo, participate in combat, and perform search and rescue missions. A solid knowledge of mechanics principles and machine components is essential in order to learn about helicopter engines, flight controls, cockpit control panels, flying techniques, and so much more.

CHAPTER 7
ELECTRONICS INFORMATION

The Electronics Information subtest of the ASVAB tests your knowledge of electrical current, circuits, and devices. This chapter covers the fundamentals of electronics, terminology, basic circuits, electronic components, and motors.

Electricity

As you learned in the chemistry discussion, all materials are made from atoms, and all atoms consist of protons, neutrons, and electronics. When an atom is stable, the positively charged protons and the negatively charged electrons balance each other out. However, electrons can detach from an atom, creating free electrons.

When electrons are freed, they are able to move from atom to atom, creating a flow of electrons. This flow of electrons is called CURRENT. The force that pushes the electrons to flow in a particular direction is called the ELECTROMOTIVE FORCE or VOLTAGE. Anything that inhibits the flow of electrons is called RESISTANCE. These three tightly related properties—current, voltage, and resistance—are the essential building blocks of all electrical circuits.

Circuits

An ELECTRIC CIRCUIT is a path along which electrons flow. A simple circuit can be created using a battery (voltage source), a light bulb (resistance), and a switch. When all components are connected, the electrons flow from the negative terminal of the battery through the wire to the device and back to the positive terminal of the battery.

If there are no breaks in the circuit, current will flow and the device will work; for example, the light bulb will light. A circuit with no breaks is called a closed circuit. If there is a break in the flow of electrons, for example, if the switch is open, the device will not work. A circuit with a break in it is called an open circuit.

The Electronics Information subtest of the ASVAB tests your knowledge of electrical current, circuits, and devices.

CURRENT: the flow of free electrons from atom to atom

ELECTROMOTIVE FORCE OR VOLTAGE: the force that pushes the electrons to flow in a particular direction

RESISTANCE: anything that inhibits the flow of electrons

ELECTRIC CIRCUIT: a path along which electrons flow

Practice Test Question

1. In an open circuit:

    A. Current flows

    B. Current doesn't flow

    C. Current increases

    D. Current decreases

Answer Key

1. **B. Current doesn't flow**

    In an open circuit, there is no path for electrons to travel from one terminal of the voltage source to the other, so current can't flow.

For your convenience, the practice test questions also appear the end of the book, so you can sit down and go through them all at once.

For your convenience, the practice test questions also appear the end of the book, so you can sit down and go through them all at once.

Series and parallel circuits

A **SERIES CIRCUIT** is a circuit in which the electrons have only one path along which they can move. When one component in a series circuit fails, the circuit is open and stops functioning. For example, in some strings of Christmas tree lights, if one bulb is missing, none of the bulbs will work.

A **PARALLEL CIRCUIT** is a circuit in which the electrons have more than one path along which to move. If a component along one path fails, the circuit will continue to work because the electrons can use an alternate path to return to the voltage source.

Voltage

VOLTAGE is the potential energy stored in an electrical supply. Voltage is the force that pushes electrons through a closed circuit. When current flows between any two points in a circuit, some potential energy is lost. The difference in potential energy between two points is called voltage drop. Voltage is measured in volts (v).

SERIES CIRCUIT: a circuit in which the electrons have only one path along which they can move

PARALLEL CIRCUIT: a circuit in which the electrons have more than one path along which to move

VOLTAGE: the potential energy stored in an electrical supply; the force that pushes electrons through a closed circuit

This can be confusing…
Electromotive force and voltage are actually the same thing. In formulas and diagrams, these are denoted as E and V, respectively. They are both measured in volts.

DC and AC voltage

Electrical applications are powered by the movement of electrons. Current flowing through a circuit in one direction is called direct current, or **DC**. Current that periodically reverses direction is called alternating current, or **AC**.

Although the terms DC and AC refer to current, they are also used to specify the type of voltage source. Voltage is the driving force behind the flow of current, so to drive an alternating current, the voltage source must also alternate. An alternating voltage source is usually referred to as VAC or Vrms.

The rate at which the voltage changes direction (one cycle forward and back) is called FREQUENCY. Frequency is measured in a unit called hertz. One hertz is one cycle per second.

FREQUENCY: the rate at which the current changes direction

Practice Test Question

1. **Frequency is measured in a unit called:**

   A. RMS

   B. Amps

   C. Volts

   D. Hertz

Answer Key

1. **D. Hertz**

   Frequency is measured in a unit called hertz. One hertz is one cycle per second.

Root mean square (RMS)

Measuring direct current is straightforward. Direct current is measured in a unit called amperes, or amps. However, because alternating current moves back and forth, measuring AC is less straightforward. Alternating current is measured using a complex calculation similar to an average, called root mean square, or RMS. RMS is also used to measure an AC voltage source.

Practice Test Question

1. **Root mean square can be used to calculate:**

    A. Current in a DC circuit

    B. Resistance in a DC circuit

    C. Current in an AC circuit

    D. Resistance in an AC circuit

Answer Key

1. **C. Current in an AC circuit**

    Current in an AC circuit is measured using a complex calculation similar to an average, called root mean square, or RMS.

Keep looking up new words

Your score on the Word Knowledge subtest is critical, so continue to learn the meanings of new words in every chapter of this study guide. If you see an unfamiliar word, look it up, and then create a flashcard for it. For example, if you look up the word *incandescent*, you'll see that one meaning is *glowing or luminous*.

Current Flow vs. Electron Flow

In a DC circuit, electrons flow from the negative terminal of a voltage source to the positive terminal. This flow from the negative terminal to the positive terminal is called electron flow. However, for historical reasons, circuit diagrams are drawn assuming that current flows from the positive terminal to the negative terminal. This convention is called conventional current flow.

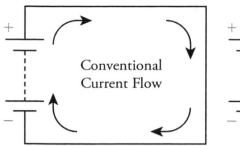
Conventional
Current Flow

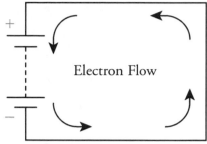
Electron Flow

Resistance

Resistance is the ability to inhibit the flow of current. Resistance is measured in Ohms and denoted as Ω (Omega) or R. As the resistance of a circuit component increases, the voltage drop across that element increases. In order to increase the current flow and decrease the voltage drop, the voltage source would need to be increased.

Ohm's Law

In a DC circuit, current (I) flowing through a resistance (R) is directly proportional to voltage (V) applied across it. In other words, as current increases, voltage increases. Current flowing through a resistance is inversely proportional to the resistance. In other words, as current increases, resistance decreases.

This fundamental relationship is known as Ohm's Law and can be expressed as follows:

$$\text{Current} = \frac{\text{Voltage}}{\text{Resistance}} \text{ or } I = \frac{V}{R}$$

If you know two of the three values in this formula, you can use Ohm's Law to find the third value.

To find voltage: $V = I \times R$

To find current: $I = \frac{V}{R}$

To find resistance: $R = \frac{V}{I}$

Ohm's Law Triangle

To make it easy to remember Ohm's Law, use the Ohm's Law Triangle. The Ohm's Law Triangle below shows how it can be used to find all three formulas. For example, you can see in the third triangle that Resistance (R) is Voltage (V) over Current (I).

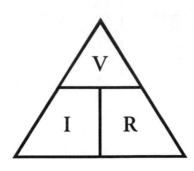

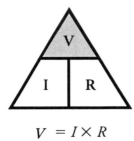

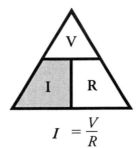

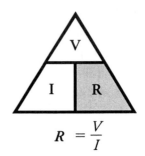

$$V = I \times R$$

$$I = \frac{V}{R}$$

$$R = \frac{V}{I}$$

Practice Test Question

1. **According to Ohm's Law:**

   A. As current increases, voltage decreases

   B. As current increases, resistance increases

   C. As current increases, resistance decreases

   D. As current increases, voltage and resistance decrease

Answer Key

1. **C. As current increases, resistance decreases**

   Current is indirectly proportional to resistance.

Power Law

ELECTRICAL POWER (P) is the rate at which electrical energy is converted to another type of energy (for example, heat) in a circuit. Electrical power is measured in watts (W). To find power, multiply current by voltage.

To find power: $P = I \times V$

To find current: $I = \frac{P}{V}$

To find voltage: $V = \frac{P}{I}$

> **ELECTRICAL POWER (P):** the rate at which electrical energy is converted to another type of energy (for example, heat) in a circuit

Power Law Triangle

To make it easy to remember the Power Law, use the Power Law Triangle. The Power Law Triangle below shows how it can be used to find all three formulas. For example, you can see in the third triangle that Voltage (V) is Power (P) over Current (I).

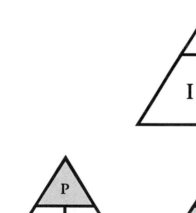

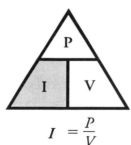

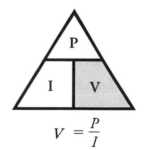

$P = I \times V$ $\qquad$ $I = \frac{P}{V}$ $\qquad$ $V = \frac{P}{I}$

Practice Test Question

1. A 120-volt AC circuit contains a light bulb rated at 60 watts. How much current does the light bulb draw?

   A. 0.5 amps
   B. 2 amps
   C. 60 amps
   D. 120 amps

Answer Key

1. **A. 0.5 amps**

   To find current, use the formula $I = \frac{P}{V}$. Substituting values, you get $I = \frac{60 \text{ watts}}{120 \text{ volts}}$, or $I = 0.5$ amps.

Anxious?

Remember to breathe deep and easy while you're taking the test. We tend to breathe shallow or even hold our breath when life gets stressful. Breathe in for a count of 4, hold for a count of 1, and breathe out for a count of 4. A few breaths like this will help anxiety disappear.

Conductors

CONDUCTOR: a material that contains an abundance of free electrons

An electrical CONDUCTOR is a material that contains an abundance of free electrons. In a closed circuit, the voltage source applies electrical pressure (voltage) to one side of the conductor. This pressure causes electrons to move through the conductor, allowing current to flow freely.

Many metals are excellent conductors. In electrical circuits, metal wires carry current from one component to the next. Wires used in electrical circuits are usually made of copper or silver.

INSULATORS: materials that contain few free electrons, inhibiting the flow of electricity

Insulators

INSULATORS are the opposite of conductors. Insulators contain few free electrons, inhibiting the flow of electricity.

In electrical circuits, insulators are most often used to cover wires. The insulating cover stops electricity from crossing from one wire to another.

> Typical insulators are made from rubber-like materials and plastics.

Practice Test Question

1. **Which of these would be the best insulator?**

   A. Copper
   B. Plastic
   C. Silver
   D. Tin

Answer Key

1. **B. Plastic**

   Insulators contain few free electrons, inhibiting the flow of electricity. Typical insulators are made from rubber-like materials and plastics.

Wires

Wires used as conductors in electrical circuits come in various sizes and configurations. Solid core wires consist of a single thread of metal and are more commonly used in DC circuits. Threaded core wires consist of multiple threads of metal, sometimes twisted together. Threaded core wires are more commonly used in AC circuits.

The diameter of a single wire thread is an important factor in determining the current carrying capacity of a circuit. The diameter of a wire is most often measured using a system called the American Wire Gauge or AWG.

In the AWG system, the larger the gauge number, the smaller the diameter of the wire. Here is a list of common wire gauges.

AWG	Diameter (in inches)
6	0.1620
7	0.1443
8	0.1285
9	0.1144
10	0.1019
11	0.0907
12	0.0808

Practice Test Question

1. Compared to a copper AWG 12 wire, a copper AWG 8 wire:

A. Is more conductive

B. Is less conductive

C. Has a larger diameter

D. Has a smaller diameter

Answer Key

1. **C. Has a larger diameter**

   In the AWG system, the larger the gauge number, the smaller the diameter of the wire.

A history lesson

The AWG numbering system originated from the process for creating wires. Each time a wire is drawn (pulled), its diameter decreases. The gauge number corresponds to the number of times a wire must be drawn.

Voltage Sources

A DC voltage source produces a steady DC current. The most common DC voltage source is a battery. Applications that use DC voltage sources include automobiles, cell phones, and other hand-held electronic devices.

An AC voltage source produces an AC current, which reverses periodically. An example of a common AC voltage source is an outlet in your home. Applications that use AC voltage sources include household appliances, light fixtures, and electric heating.

Symbols are used in schematic diagrams to represent various electronic components. Symbols for DC and AC voltage sources are illustrated below.

> *The most common DC voltage source is a battery.*

> *An example of a common AC voltage source is an outlet in your home.*

DC voltage source   AC voltage source

> **ASVAB tip!**
> Composite scores from all of the subtests of the ASVAB help match new recruits to military occupations.

Cells and batteries

A **BATTERY** is a collection of electrochemical cells. If the cells are connected in series, the voltage of the battery will be the sum of the cell voltages. For example, a 12-volt car battery contains six 2-volt cells connected in series.

If the cells of a battery are connected in parallel, the battery voltage will be the same as the cell voltage, but the current supplied by each cell will be a fraction of the total current. For example, if a battery contains four cells connected in parallel and delivers a current of 1 ampere, the current supplied by each cell will be 0.25 ampere.

Symbols for batteries in schematic diagrams are illustrated here.

> **BATTERY:** a collection of electrochemical cells

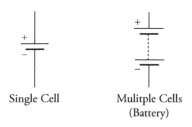

Single Cell   Mulitple Cells
(Battery)

Electronic Components

Resistors

A **RESISTOR** is an electronic component that limits the flow of current by converting it to heat. The total resistance of resistors in series is equal to the sum of their individual resistances.

This is the symbol for a resistor in schematic diagrams.

> **RESISTOR:** an electronic component that limits the flow of current by converting it to heat

Capacitors

A **CAPACITOR** is an electronic component that stores a charge electrostatically. **CAPACITANCE** is a capacitor's ability to hold an electric charge. Capacitance is measured in units called farads (F).

Inside a capacitor, there are two conductors, called plates, separated by an insulator, called a dielectric.

When the capacitor is charging, electrons collect on one of the plates, creating an electrical potential between the two plates. When the capacitor is discharging, electrons flow back in the same direction, depleting the electrical potential. The electrons never actually pass through a capacitor.

> **CAPACITOR:** an electronic component that stores a charge electrostatically

> **CAPACITANCE:** capacitor's ability to hold an electric charge

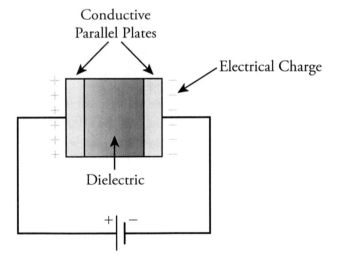

Conductive Parallel Plates

Electrical Charge

Dielectric

Capacitors are typically used in AC circuits where they must quickly charge and discharge. This is the symbol for a capacitor in schematic diagrams.

Practice Test Questions

1. **A typical capacitor contains:**

   A. One charged plate

   B. Two charged plates

   C. Three charged plates

   D. Four charged plates

2. **Capacitance is measured in units called:**

   A. Farads

   B. Hertz

   C. Henries

   D. Ohms

Answer Key

1. **B. Two charged plates**

   A capacitor contains two charged plates. The capacitor stores an electrical potential by collecting more electrons on one plate than on the other plate.

2. **A. Farads**

   Capacitance is the measure of a capacitor's ability to hold an electric charge. Capacitance is measured in units called farads.

Don't be afraid of the spark

An electric spark is a type of electrostatic discharge. A spark occurs when the strength of an electric field becomes so great that air can no longer act as an insulator. Lightning is a dramatic example of an electric spark.

Don't be afraid of the spark. An electric spark is a type of electrostatic discharge. A spark occurs when the strength of an electric field becomes so great that air can no longer act as an insulator. Lightning is a dramatic example of an electric spark.

Inductors

An **INDUCTOR** is an electronic component that stores a charge electromagnetically. **INDUCTANCE** is an inductor's ability to store energy. Inductance is measured in units called henries (H).

Initially, an inductor inhibits the flow of current by building a magnetic field around itself. Once the magnetic field is fully built, the inductor stops acting as an inhibitor and current flows normally. If current stops flowing into the inductor, the magnetic field collapses, releasing a surge of electrical current.

INDUCTOR: an electronic component that stores a charge electromagnetically

INDUCTANCE: an inductor's ability to store energy

A basic inductor is composed of conducting wire coiled around a non-conducting core. The size and shape of the core, type of wire, number of turns, and other factors affect the inductor's ability to store electromagnetic energy.

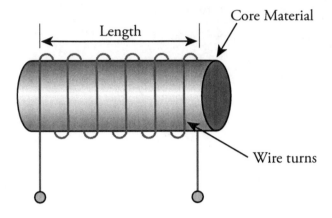

This is the symbol for an inductor in schematic diagrams.

Practice Test Question

1. **An inductor stores an electrical charge:**

   A. Electrochemically

   B. Electrostatically

   C. Electromagnetically

   D. Electromotively

Answer Key

1. **C. Electromagnetically**

   An inductor stores a charge electromagnetically. It stores an electrical charge, or potential, as an electromagnetic field.

Diodes

A DIODE is an electronic component with two terminals. In general, a diode allows current to flow in only one direction. In the conducting direction, a diode presents little or no resistance. However, it does present a fixed voltage drop.

This is the symbol for a diode in a schematic diagram.

Diodes come in many varieties, each of which is designed for a specific purpose. Here are some common diodes.

> **DIODE:** an electronic component with two terminals that generally allows current to flow in only one direction

Type	Typical Voltage Drop	Typical Purpose
Small Signal	0.5V – 0.7V	Low-voltage and high-frequency signal applications
Power	0.5V – 0.7V	High-voltage and high-current rectification
Zener	3.3V, 5V, 9V, 12V	Voltage regulation and over-voltage protection

Practice Test Question

1. **The function of a diode is to:**

   A. Rectify AC current to DC

   B. Rectify DC current to AC

   C. Allow current to flow in one direction

   D. Allow current to flow in two directions

Answer Key

1. **C. Allow current to flow in one direction**

   Although diodes can be used in conjunction with other components to convert AC current to DC, the function of a single diode is to allow current to pass in only one direction.

Switches

ELECTRICAL SWITCH: an electromechanical device used to make, break, or redirect the flow of current in a circuit

An **ELECTRICAL SWITCH** is an electromechanical device used to make, break, or redirect the flow of current in a circuit. There are many different types and configurations of switches. However, the most familiar switch is manually operated and contains one or more sets of contacts. Each set of contacts can be open or closed, allowing the switch to break or make a connection in a circuit.

These are symbols for switches in a schematic diagram.

Open switch   Closed switch

Manual switches are described in terms of poles and throws. The number of poles is the number of sets of contacts. Each pole allows a circuit to be opened or closed. The number of throws is the number of positions that a switch can adopt.

Here are some common types of switches.

Abbreviation	Terminology	Description
SPST	Single pole, single throw	A simple on-off switch that can control one circuit
SPDT	Single pole, double throw	Allows one circuit path to be switched to one or another of two circuit paths
DPST	Double pole, single throw	Allows two circuits to be opened or closed by using one mechanical motion

Practice Test Question

1. What is the simplest switch that will turn a single light bulb on or off?

   A. SPST
   B. DPST
   C. SPDT
   D. DPDT

Answer Key

1. **A. SPST**

   A single light bulb needs only one circuit, so it requires one throw, and it only needs to be turned on and off, so it requires one pole. The simplest switch is a single pole, single throw switch, or SPST.

Measuring Instruments

There are many devices used to help build and diagnose electrical circuits. Here are a few commonly used devices.

Instrument	Purpose
Voltmeter	Used to measure the difference in voltage between two points in a circuit. The difference is the voltage drop
Ammeter	Used to measure the electrical current that flows through a circuit
Ohmmeter	Used to measure the electrical resistance of an electronic component

Ohmmm... Ohmmm...
The first part of the name of a measurement device often matches the unit that it measures. For example, a voltmeter measures volts, and an ohmmeter measures Ohms.

Practice Test Questions

1. To measure the current flow in a circuit, you could use:

    A. An ammeter

    B. A wattmeter

    C. An ohmmeter

    D. A voltmeter

2. The following symbol represents:

    A. A capacitor

    B. An inductor

    C. A resistor

    D. A switch

3. The following symbol represents:

    A. A resistor

    B. A switch

    C. A battery

    D. An inductor

4. The following symbol represents:

    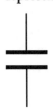

    A. A capacitor

    B. A switch

    C. A resistor

    D. An inductor

Answer Key

1. **A. An ammeter**

    An ammeter is used to measure current, which is measured in amps.

2. **C. A resistor**

    This symbol represents a resistor. It is used in schematic circuit diagrams.

3. **D. An inductor**

    This symbol represents an inductor. It is used in schematic circuit diagrams.

4. **A. A capacitor**

    This symbol represents a capacitor. It is used in schematic circuit diagrams.

Glossary

Here are important electronics terms that you'll need to know.

Alternating current (AC)	An electrical current that flows back and forth in a regular frequency
Battery	An electronic component used for long-term storage of an electrical charge
Capacitor	A component used for very short-term storage of an electrical charge
Conductor	A material, typically metallic, that allows an electrical current to flow freely
Current	The flow of electricity on a closed circuit
Circuit	A system of conductors and components designed to utilize electrical current
Diode	An electronic component that allows current to pass in only one direction
Direct current (DC)	An electrical current that flows in only one direction
Frequency	The number of repetitions of a particular event in a constant period of time, typically expressed in cycles per second (hertz)
Grounding	Removing charge from an object by connecting it to the earth through a conductor
Impedance	The AC equivalent of resistance in a DC circuit, measured in Ohms
Insulator	A material, typically nonmetallic, that inhibits the flow of electrical current
Ohm's Law	A fundamental concept in electronics that defines the relationship between voltage, current, and resistance
Power	The rate at which work is done in an electrical circuit, measured in watts
Rectifier	An electrical circuit that converts AC current to DC

Continued on next page

Resistor	An electronic component that limits the flow of current by converting it to heat
RMS (root mean square)	A measure of AC voltage or current
Switch	A mechanical device used to interrupt or redirect the flow of current through a circuit
Transformer	An electrical device that converts and raises or lowers an AC voltage
Voltage	A source of potential electrical energy, measured in volts

How would I use this?

In the military, radar and sonar operators monitor sophisticated tracking devices and communication systems. They track aircraft, ships, and missiles, and use radar equipment to direct artillery fire, forecast weather, and operate submarine sonar. An aptitude for electronics is essential in this technical career.

CHAPTER 8
SHOP INFORMATION

The Shop Information subtest tests your knowledge of tools and your ability to recognize specific tools. It also covers basic shop practices such as sanding and painting.

The Shop Information subtest tests your knowledge of tools and your ability to recognize specific tools.

Hand Tools

Hand tools allow users either to perform a function they could not with the unaided hand (e.g., drive a nail into concrete) or to perform a task better or more quickly than with the unaided hand (e.g., find horizontal level). Some hand tools are powered by manual force only, while other hand tools use electrical or other motors to provide force.

Hammers, mallets, and sledges

Hammers

HAMMERS are tools used to deliver impact force to an object. Hammers vary widely in form, size, and construction. Most hammers feature a large head area, which adds mass to the tool to aid in the delivery of a forceful impact, and a long handle that works as a force multiplier. Hammers that are intended to drive nails or perform similar functions usually have a large, flat striking surface. Many hammers have an alternative use tool fixed on the head opposite the striking surface—for example, the claw in a claw hammer.

HAMMERS: tools used to deliver impact force to an object

Most hammers feature a large head area, which adds mass to the tool to aid in the delivery of a forceful impact, and a long handle that works as a force multiplier.

Typical claw hammer.

Mallets

MALLETS: hammers that are constructed with relatively large heads of rubber, wood, or soft metals

MALLETS are hammers that are constructed with relatively large heads of rubber, wood, or soft metals. Mallets are typically aused to fit parts or drive assembly pins. Wooden mallets are a common tool in carpentry. Copper, lead, or brass mallets are used when damage to soft parts would be likely with a steel implement.

Typical rubber mallet.

Sledges

SLEDGEHAMMERS, OR SLEDGES: large, heavy hammers usually used with both hands

SLEDGEHAMMERS, OR SLEDGES, are large, heavy hammers usually used with both hands. They are generally constructed with a heavy steel head and a long—perhaps three feet or more—handle. Sledgehammers are often used in demolition. POST SLEDGES are sledges used to drive fence posts into the earth; other specialized sledgehammers are used to drive railroad spikes.

POST SLEDGES: sledges used to drive fence posts into the earth

Typical sledgehammer.

The hammer is probably the oldest tool used by humans, and archaeological samples have been found that are millions of years old. Modified hammers have been used as tools of war for at least thousands of years.

Example

How does handle length affect the force of a hammer? The longer the handle, the greater the force multiplier. The hammer's handle acts as a simple lever to accelerate the hammer's head in an arc that delivers force at the striking surface.

May I use the heel of your shoe?
Any tool can be used as a hammer—so the saying goes—but there is no substitute for a proper hammer. While you might be able to drive a nail with the handle of a screwdriver, the process could damage the screwdriver (and the nail!) and the task would take longer than it should.

Practice Test Question

1. Which striking tool has a relatively large head, which is often made of wood or rubber?

   A. Post sledge

   B. Mallet

   C. Sledge

   D. Claw hammer

Answer Key

1. **B. Mallet**

   Mallets are different from hammers in that they have a relatively large head. Mallet heads are often made from soft materials, such as rubber or wood, to avoid damaging the object struck.

Screwdrivers

SCREWDRIVERS are hand tools used for rotating screws, bolts, or machine elements. Typical screwdrivers comprise a head, or tip, that interfaces with the screw, and an axial shaft affixed to a handle that allows the user to hold the tool without slipping. There are both manual and power screwdrivers, in which the tip is rotated with an electric motor.

Screwdrivers come in many varieties. The most diverse part of the tool is the head, or tip. Here are some common drive heads.

> **SCREWDRIVERS:** hand tools used for rotating screws, bolts, or machine elements

Slot

Phillips

Cross

Frearson

Common drive head types.

The oldest type of screw is the slot head screw. Cross slot screws feature two slots at right angles to each other. An evolved form of the cross slot screw is the Phillips screw, which is designed to cam the screwdriver out of the screw when the screw stalls. This prevents damage to the screw head caused by overdriving. The Frearson screw head improves upon the Phillips by allowing one tip to fit a variety of screw sizes.

Many modern screwdrivers have removable tips that allow a single handle and axial shaft to utilize multiple tips. Some screwdrivers feature a flexible axial shaft to allow driving screws in tight corners or inconvenient places. Many screwdrivers even have magnetic tips, which hold the screws against the tip.

A RATCHETING SCREWDRIVER is a manual screwdriver that allows the user to turn the screwdriver in both directions without removing the tip from the screw. The axial shaft rotates freely in one direction but locks to the handle in the other direction. This lets the user rotate the screwdriver back and forth and continue to drive in the screw.

Numerous newer types of screw head are designed to be tamperproof, or "one way" to allow a screw to be driven in but not removed. Other types are designed to use a proprietary or rare driver head to limit use to authorized individuals. Of course, each type of screw head requires a mating screw driver head or tip.

> **RATCHETING SCREW-DRIVER:** a manual screwdriver that allows the user to turn the screwdriver in both directions without removing the tip from the screw

Practice Test Question

1. **What is the primary advantage of a ratcheting screwdriver?**

   A. The user can rotate the screwdriver in both directions without removing the tip from the screw head

   B. The user can drive in a screw by using a motor

   C. The user can effectively "reach around a corner" to drive a screw in a difficult location

   D. The user can drive in a screw without stripping it

Answer Key

1. **A. The user can rotate the screwdriver in both directions without removing the tip from the screw head**

   A ratcheting screwdriver allows the user to turn the screwdriver in both directions without removing the tip from the screw. It allows the user to rotate the screwdriver back and forth and continue to drive in the screw.

Chisels

CHISELS are tools with a shaped cutting edge on the end. The driving force is supplied manually or by using a mallet. Straight chisel blades have a straight cutting edge; a GOUGE is a type of chisel that has a curved cutting surface, usually appearing as a "U" in profile. Gouges are used in lathes, machines that rotate a piece of wood or other material and shape it.

Typical wood chisel.

In woodworking, chisels are important and come in a variety of styles. BUTT CHISELS are used to cut joints; CARVING CHISELS are used for intricate work. CORNER CHISELS have a blade appearing as an "L" in profile and are used to cut sharp corners. A SKEW CHISEL has an angled cutting blade that is used for finishing work.

There are also stone and masonry chisels. They are used to cut stone, bricks, or concrete, or can be used in carving operations on these substrates. Usually, they are very heavy, with relatively blunt cutting surfaces that wedge and break, rather than cut. Some stone-cutting chisels have toothed cutting edges. Common crowbars feature a chisel end.

CHISELS: tools with a shaped cutting edge on the end

GOUGE: a type of chisel that has a curved cutting surface, usually appearing as a "U" in profile

BUTT CHISELS: chisels that are used to cut joints

CARVING CHISELS: chisels that are used for intricate work

CORNER CHISELS: chisels that are used to cut sharp corners

SKEW CHISEL: a chisel with an angled cutting blade that is used for finishing work

Typical masonry chisel.

Practice Test Questions

1. Which type of chisel is typically used on a wood lathe?

   A. Butt chisel

   B. Gouge

   C. Carving chisel

   D. Corner chisel

2. Which type of chisel is typically used to cut large joints into wood intended for framing?

   A. Butt chisel

   B. Carving chisel

   C. Corner chisel

   D. Skew chisel

Answer Key

1. **B. Gouge**

   The gouge's curved cutting surface works well against the spinning action of a lathe.

2. **A. Butt chisel**

   A butt chisel is used to cut large joints into wooden beams intended for use in framing.

Wrenches

A **WRENCH**, or spanner, is a tool used to provide mechanical advantage while applying torque. They are most often associated with manipulating nuts and bolts. The most common types of wrench are **BOX-END WRENCHES**, which feature a fully enclosed circle that encloses the nut or bolt on all sides; and **OPEN-END WRENCHES**, which look like a "C" and enclose the nut or bolt on about three-quarters of its surface. **COMBINATION WRENCHES** have a box-end and an open-end on opposite ends of the shaft.

Typical combination wrench.

An **ADJUSTABLE-END WRENCH** is an open-ended wrench with an adjustable throw. They are commonly called Crescent wrenches because they were initially developed by the Crescent Tool and Horseshoe Company. A **PIPE WRENCH** is an adjustable wrench for turning a pipe.

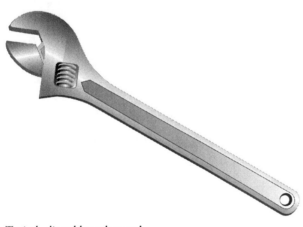

Typical adjustable-end wrench.

WRENCH: a tool used to provide mechanical advantage while applying torque

BOX-END WRENCHES: wrenches that feature a fully enclosed circle that encloses the nut or bolt on all sides

OPEN-END WRENCHES: wrenches that look like a "C" and enclose the nut or bolt on about three-quarters of its surface

COMBINATION WRENCHES: wrenches that have a box-end and an open-end on opposite ends of the shaft

ADJUSTABLE-END WRENCH: open-ended wrench with an adjustable throw

PIPE WRENCH: an adjustable wrench for turning a pipe

SOCKET WRENCHES are ratchet tools with snap-on sockets that fit over bolt heads. They have the advantage of offering good torque ability with which to screw small screws or bolts.

Typical socket wrench and sockets.

Most wrenches are hand operated, but electric and power wrenches are also common, especially in heavier applications. Large, heavy wrenches have industrial uses—for example, fire departments use very large wrenches to uncap fire hydrants. Hand wrenches that are used to torque heavy bolts or bolts that are seized often have very long handles or attachable handles known as breaker bars.

Practice Test Question

1. Which wrench would be the best selection for a job where a number of bolts must be manipulated, but the sizes of the various bolts are not known beforehand?

A. Box-end wrench

B. Combination wrench

C. Adjustable wrench

D. Pipe wrench

Answer Key

1. **C. Adjustable wrench**

   An adjustable wrench, some-times called a Crescent wrench, allows the user to adjust the size of the wrench to fit the bolt head.

Become a test question writer

While you're studying, try *writing* test questions. Then have a friend or relative answer the questions. This is a great learning strategy, because in order to write a good test question, you have to understand the material well.

Saws

SAWS are tools that cut using a wire or, more commonly, a metal blade with a cutting edge. Saws are usually worked by hand, but power saws are also common. Some saws used for lumbering are intended to be used by two people; these saws have serrated edges that cut on both strokes.

SAWS: tools that cut using a wire or, more commonly, a metal blade with a cutting edge

Common types of saws

Crosscut saw	A hand saw that cuts wood perpendicular to the grain
Two-man saw	A hand saw that cuts large logs or trees
Rip saw	A hand saw that cuts wood along the grain
Hacksaw	A hand saw that uses a fine-toothed blade to cut metal and other hard materials
Circular saw	A mechanically powered saw; large circular saws are used in sawmills to cut trees or logs; the same name is given to smaller hand-held saws
Table saw	A mechanically powered saw with a circular blade positioned in a slot in a table; commonly used for woodworking
Jigsaw	A mechanically powered saw that uses a narrow blade to cut irregular shapes

Typical crosscut saw.

Typical hacksaw.

Practice Test Questions

1. Which of the following saws would be best used to cut through timber for firewood?

   A. Crosscut saw

   B. Hacksaw

   C. Table saw

   D. Jigsaw

2. Laurel wants to cut some intricate scrollwork into a piece of mounting wood she is using for an art project. What type of saw should she use for this type of work?

   A. Crosscut saw

   B. Hacksaw

   C. Circular saw

   D. Jigsaw

Answer Key

1. **A. Crosscut saw**

   A crosscut saw is designed for making large cuts perpendicular to the grain and is an excellent choice for cutting timber into firewood. The other saws have specific purposes and wouldn't be good choices for cutting firewood.

2. **D. Jigsaw**

   The crosscut saw, the hacksaw, and the circular saw are all intended to be used to make large and/or straight cuts. They would be particularly unsuitable for fine scrollwork. The only valid choice is a jigsaw, which is also commonly called a scroll saw because of its suitability for this type of work.

ASVAB tip!
On the CAT-ASVAB, the Shop Information subtest is 6 minutes long and has 11 questions.

Levels

LEVELS are measuring instruments that indicate whether a surface is level (horizontal) or plumb (vertical). There are several types of level available, but the most common by far is the **SPIRIT LEVEL**. Spirit levels are used in carpentry, masonry, bricklaying, surveying, and metal work. Spirit levels feature glass or transparent plastic tubes nearly full of liquid. A slight curve in the tube lets a captive bubble rise to the highest point in the curve. This point is marked so that the position of the bubble can be gauged visually to determine if the tube is level.

LEVELS: measuring instruments that indicate whether a surface is level (horizontal) or plumb (vertical)

SPIRIT LEVEL: a level that features a tube nearly full of liquid, in which a bubble indicates whether a surface is level

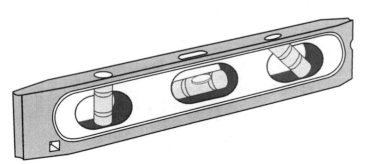

Typical spirit level.

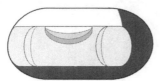

Detail on a spirit level.

Spirit level?
A spirit level got its name from the liquid inside it—alcohol!

Washers, nuts, screws, bolts, and nails

WASHERS are pierced plates, usually round, that are used to distribute the load weight of a fastener. Washers are commonly used with bolts. Washers may also be used as spacers, wearing surfaces, or locking devices. Rubber washers may be used to dampen vibration. However, most washers are made of metal or plastic.

WASHERS: pierced plates, usually round, that are used to distribute the load weight of a fastener

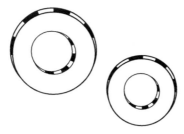

Typical washers.

NUTS: fasteners with a threaded hole that is used with a mating bolt

WING NUTS: nuts with attached finger flanges that are intended to be used in light loading applications

NUTS are fasteners with a threaded hole that is used with a mating bolt. Most modern nuts are hexagonal on their outer surface ("hex nuts"); older nuts were usually square. Some nuts that are intended to be used in light loading applications have finger flanges attached and are called **WING NUTS**. Nuts are measured in either metric or inch pattern and vary by external diameter and shape, internal diameter, thread depth, thread count, and thread pitch. In short, the nut must match the bolt.

Typical hex nut.

Typical wing nut.

SCREWS are threaded fasteners usually used to hold objects together. Most screws have slotted heads that allow them to be driven. The heads of screws vary by application. Wood screws usually have a head designed to sit flush with the wood surface, and metal screws usually have a head that will sit atop the metal surface. Nearly all screws are driven in clockwise rotation and are said to have a right-hand thread.

Typical wood screw.

BOLTS are threaded fasteners usually used to hold objects together. There is no clear distinction between bolts and screws, though one generally true distinction is that screws are capable of self-tapping into wood or another material, while bolts do not have a point at the end and must be inserted through drilled holes.

Typical hex-head bolt.

NAILS are wire-shaped fasteners made of hard metals, usually steel. Nails usually feature one sharp end and one headed end with a flanged head of some type. Nails are driven into wood, concrete, or masonry by hammers. Some specialty nail guns also drive nails by the use of explosive charges or primers.

In the United States, nails are described by penny size, indicated by the abbreviation d (e.g., 12d is a twelve-penny nail). The larger the penny, the longer (and heavier) the nail. Average consumer nails range from about 4d (1.5" long) to about 12d (3.25" long).

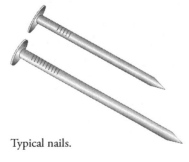

Typical nails.

CALIPER: a measuring device that measures distance, traditionally by using two arms and a mechanical adjustment that drives an indicator along a measuring scale

INSIDE CALIPERS: calipers that are used to measure the internal size of an object

OUTSIDE CALIPERS: calipers that are used to measure the external size of an object

DIVIDER CALIPERS: calipers that are used in metalworking to measure distance and scribe metals surfaces

VERNIER CALIPERS AND DIGITAL CALIPERS: very accurate calipers that use a calibrated scale and one fixed jaw with a pointing jaw that moves along the scale

MICROMETER CALIPERS: very accurate calipers that use a calibrated screw for measurement; usually used to measure very small parts

Practice Test Question

Which of the following is pictured below?

A. Bolt

B. Washer

C. Nut

D. Wing nut

Answer Key

1. **C. Nut**

   A nut is a fastener with a threaded hole. Most modern nuts are hexagonal.

Calipers

A **CALIPER** is a measuring device that measures distance, traditionally by using two arms and a mechanical adjustment that drives an indicator along a measuring scale. Calipers are used in many industries where measurement is important—metalworking, engineering, medicine, carpentry, and more.

Calipers can be divided into two broad types. **INSIDE CALIPERS** are used to measure the internal size of an object (e.g., the inside of a pipe), and **OUTSIDE CALIPERS** are used to measure the external size of an object (e.g., the length of a bolt). In metalworking, **DIVIDER CALIPERS** are used to measure distance and scribe metal surfaces by scratching them. **VERNIER CALIPERS** and **DIGITAL CALIPERS** use a calibrated scale and one fixed jaw with a pointing jaw that moves along the scale. These types of calipers are capable of astounding accuracy. **MICROMETER CALIPERS** use a calibrated screw for measurement and typically are used for highly accurate measurements of very small parts. The tremendous variety of calipers available is a testament to their usefulness in a variety of applications.

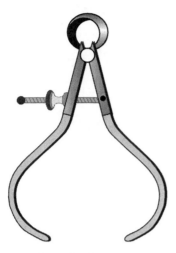

Typical outside caliper.

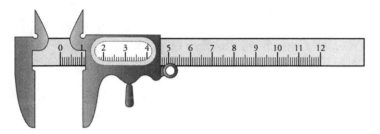

Typical vernier caliper.

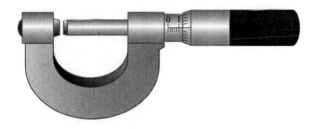

Typical micrometer caliper.

Practice Test Question

1. **Jane needs to measure the thickness of a very small mechanical part. Which type of caliper should she use?**

   A. Vernier caliper

   B. Divider caliper

   C. Micrometer caliper

   D. Inside caliper

Sanding Basics

SANDING is the process of abrading a surface to make it more suitable for a particular application. Sanding most frequently uses sandpaper, a heavy paper bonded on one side to abrasive materials. Sanding can make surfaces smoother (e.g., prior to painting), remove a layer from a surface (e.g., old or damaged paint), or make a surface rougher (e.g., prior to gluing).

> **SANDING:** the process of abrading a surface to make it more suitable for a particular application

Sandpaper backing includes paper, cloth, films, composite polymer fibers, and sometimes rubber. The weight, or durability, of paper backing is often denoted with a letter ranging from A to F; A is the lightest and F is the heaviest. Cloth backings use, from lightest to heaviest, the letters J, X, Y, T, and M.

Sandpaper may be flexible and used with power tools (e.g., belt sanders) or relatively inflexible and fixed upon a surface (e.g., sanding blocks or disc sanders). Sandpaper comes in a variety of sizes and shapes, the most common being a 9" by 11" sheet.

Go with the grain
Wood should be sanded in the direction of the grain.

The abrading surface of sandpaper is often aluminum oxide, but can also be garnet (for woodworking), emery (for metals), silicon carbide (for wet applications), or other specialty abrading materials for specific applications.

> *The most common standard in use in the United States uses a number to denote average grit size; the larger the number, the finer the grit and thus the smoother the finished surface after sanding.*

> **GRIT:** the abrading particles on sandpaper

The abrading material, or **GRIT**, comes in a variety of sizes. Several standards exist to denote grit size and uniformity. The most common standard in use in the United States uses a number to denote average grit size; the larger the number, the finer the grit and thus the smoother the finished surface after sanding.

- Coarse grits, ranging from 24 to 50, remove material very quickly.
- Medium grits range from 60 to 80.

- Fine grits range from 100 to 120.

- Very fine grits range from 150 to 220, and they put a standard finish on materials such as wood.

- Micro grit sizes run from 240 to 1,000; these types of grits will result in polishing of wood or other finished surfaces.

For extra-fine polishing a CROCUS CLOTH can be used, which is a strong and flex-ible type of backing that uses an applied polishing or lapping compound in place of bonded abrading particles.

Sanding applications typically proceed from the initial use of a medium or fine grit paper through the application of very fine or micro grit paper, as needed. Of course, not all applications require such a fine degree of sanding.

> **CROCUS CLOTH:** a strong and flexible type of backing that uses an applied polishing or lapping compound in place of bonded abrading particles

Don't sand it all away

Care should be exercised with coarse grits and especially with power sanders because they can easily remove a large amount of material.

Example

A piece of high-grade wood furniture may go through an initial sanding with 120 grit to remove imperfections; 180 grit is used to finish the wood; 240 grit is used after the first coat of sealer is applied; 320 grit is used between coats of finish sealer; and 600 grit is used on the final coat of sealant to remove some of the shine.

Practice Test Question

1. **Joanne wants to quickly remove old and damaged paint and a thin layer of surface wood from an old hardwood deck. What type of sandpaper should she select?**

   A. 360-600 grit silicon carbide paper

   B. 220-240 grit garnet paper

   C. 150-180 grit emery paper

   D. 40-60 grit aluminum oxide paper

Answer Key

1. **D. 40-60 grit aluminum oxide paper**

   Joanne wants to strip off old, damaged paint and take off the damaged surface layer of an old hardwood deck. For best results, she should select coarse 40-60 grit sandpaper. Aluminum oxide sandpaper is common, inexpensive, and has good durability on wood surfaces.

Painting Basics

Surfaces to be painted must be prepared before the paint is applied. Surfaces in general should be clean, entirely free of oil, grease, and dirt. Holes should be filled with suitable filler that is cured fully before the paint application. A common assumption is that paint will somehow "cover up" surface imperfections—this is not the case.

A common assumption is that paint will somehow "cover up" surface imperfections—this is not the case.

When the surface is clean and dry, the paint or primer can be applied. Many paints work only (or best) if the surface is primed first. PRIMERS are preparatory coatings for paint. They offer adhesion superior to standard paints. Primers also extend the life of most paints. Primers are especially important when painting porous substrates, such as concrete and wood. Primers help seal the surface and prevent mold. If overlaying a dark surface with a light paint, primers will help to fully conceal the darker underlayment.

PRIMERS: preparatory coatings for paint

Once the surface is primed and cured, the paint can be applied. Most commercial painting will use a single application of paint, but often in consumer painting two or more applications, or coats, are required for full coverage.

After painting, brushes, rollers, and other equipment should be cleaned for storage and future use. Most paints can be cleaned by using either water or a specific paint thinner. PAINT THINNERS are solvents used to thin, or wash, oil-based paints. Extreme care must be taken when using solvents because almost all of them are extremely flammable and many of them are dangerous to human health. Always avoid smoking around primers, paints, and paint thinner solvents.

PAINT THINNERS: solvents used to thin, or wash, oil-based paints

Painting tools

Common tools for applying paint are paintbrushes, rollers, and power paint sprayers. Care should be taken when selecting brushes, rollers, and paint to ensure that the tools match the intended application.

Paintbrushes are often constructed by fastening bristles to a handle with a metal ferrule. Commercial grade paintbrushes are intended for multiple uses and will withstand repetitive use and cleaning. Consumer grade paintbrushes include those that are reusable and those intended for one-time use only. In general, a better grade of paintbrush gives a superior paint application and finish.

Typical angle paintbrush.

A good, general, all-purpose paintbrush would perhaps be 2.5" with an angled painting surface. Stiff brushes are generally preferred for exterior applications, while nylon brushes are generally preferred for interior finishes. Brushes with angled cuts or straight cuts are available to suit individual preference. Brushes of about 1.5" work well for touch-up work or trim work. Brushes of about 2.5" work well for baseboard, door, stairs, and other small area jobs. Brushes of about 4" are intended for painting large surfaces, such as walls or ceilings.

Stiff brushes are generally preferred for exterior applications, while nylon brushes are generally preferred for interior finishes.

Paint rollers come in several standard sizes and use a nap, or foam surface, to hold and apply paint. Higher-grade rollers are intended for reuse, but in many cases the roller is used once and then discarded.

Many manufacturers of paint rollers suggest best results can be obtained by prepping the roller before loading the first paint. For water-based paints, the roller can be wetted with water and then spun nearly dry. For oil-based paints, the roller can be dampened with thinner and then spun nearly dry. These pre-treatments help the paint load onto the roller and then coat better when applied.

Paint sprayers range from the common can of spray paint to industrial-quality machines that apply paints in a variety of methods. Common commercial-grade paint sprayers are fairly portable and could be used in home painting.

Practice Test Question

1. **Which of the following is <u>not</u> a benefit of using a primer coat before applying paint?**

   A. Primers offer better surface adhesion

   B. Primers extend the life of paint

   C. Primers reduce the cost of painting

   D. Primers help mask dark underlayment

Answer Key

1. **C. Primers reduce the cost of painting**

   Primers are not free—in fact, good primers are about as expensive as good paint. However, primers mask uneven or dark underlayment, offer better surface adhesion, and extend the life of paint applications. The benefits of using primers far outweigh the costs of using primers.

How would I use this?

In the military, building electricians perform a wide range of jobs, from installing electrical wiring in airplane hangars to wiring circuit breakers to installing lightning rods. This physically demanding career requires the use of wire cutters, insulation strippers, and many other hand tools.

CHAPTER 9
AUTO INFORMATION

The Auto Information subtest of the ASVAB tests your knowledge of automotive technology, maintenance, and repair. This chapter covers engines, transmissions, electrical systems, brakes, and more.

The Auto Information subtest of the ASVAB tests your knowledge of automotive technology, maintenance, and repair.

Basic Principles of an Internal Combustion Engine

The internal combustion engine is the engine in most passenger and commercial road vehicles worldwide, along with many small engines on ATVs, tractors, and lawnmowers. It works by mixing fuel (typically gasoline, kerosene, or compressed natural gas) and air and igniting this mixture in a combustion chamber. Older engines used a carburetor to create this mixture, but carburetors have been replaced on modern vehicles with more efficient and reliable fuel injection systems. Some small engines still use carburetors.

Combustion chamber

The **COMBUSTION CHAMBER** of a typical internal combustion engine is a cylinder (or tube) cast into an engine block. Most car engines have an even number of cylinders, 4, 6, 8, and in some cases 10 or 12. A piston fits into each cylinder.

The **PISTON** is also a cylinder, slightly thinner than the combustion chamber. Flexible metal **PISTON RINGS** fill the gap between the walls of the piston and combustion chamber, creating a tight seal. The bottom of the piston is connected to a crankshaft with a piston rod. As the crankshaft revolves, the piston is drawn down, sucking air or an air/fuel mixture into the combustion chamber through the intake valve or valves. This is the intake stroke.

As piston rings age, the seal in the combustion chamber can be lost, and the cylinder will lose compression. If this happens in just one cylinder, the engine will run roughly, and possibly burn some oil. If this happens in more than one cylinder, the engine may not run at all. This condition can happen more quickly if regular maintenance is not performed.

COMBUSTION CHAMBER: a cylinder (or tube) cast into the engine block of a typical internal combustion engine

PISTON: a cylinder that is slightly thinner than the combustion chamber

PISTON RINGS: flexible metal rings that fill the gap between the walls of the piston and combustion chamber, creating a tight seal

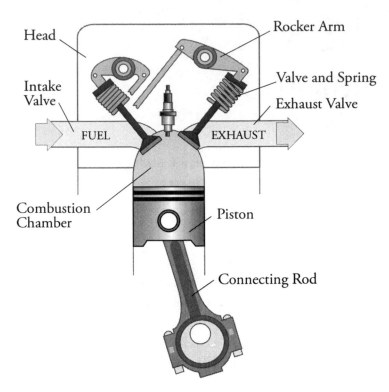

Diagram of a combustion chamber.

Intake and exhaust

The intake and exhaust valves are located in the head, which is attached to the top of the engine block and closes off the top of the combustion chamber. Some cars can have as many as four valves per cylinder: two intake and two exhaust. One or more rotating cam shafts open and close these valves as the engine turns. With age, intake valves can build up deposits and stick. Sometimes the hydraulic lifters that open and close the valves can fail, or the springs that close them can break. These conditions can cause an engine to run roughly.

The intake manifold sits on top of the head, and, as the name implies, takes in the air for the engine through a carburetor or throttle body. In CARBURETED ENGINES, fuel is mixed with air in the carburetor and then sucked into the combustion chamber. FUEL-INJECTED ENGINES use a throttle body with a throttle plate to control the air flow and to spray fuel into the air with fuel injectors.

CARBURETED ENGINES: engines in which fuel is mixed with air in the carburetor and then sucked into the combustion chamber

FUEL-INJECTED ENGINES: engines that use a throttle body with a throttle plate to control the air flow and spray fuel into the air with fuel injectors

Become the teacher

After you've learned about something new in this study guide, teach it to someone. After you read how an engine works, explain it to your mother or your friend. Putting something in your own words helps you understand it and remember it.

Fuel

FUEL INJECTORS are tiny valves that spray a metered amount of fuel into the throttle body, the intake manifold, or directly into the combustion chamber. Once the air/fuel mixture is sucked into the combustion chamber, the valves close and the piston rises and compresses, and squeezes the mixture. This is the compression stroke.

A clogged fuel filter will cause poor engine performance, since the computer calculates the amount of time to open a fuel injector based on a certain pressure in the line. If the pressure is lower than it should be, the injector will not provide enough fuel.

> **FUEL INJECTORS:** tiny valves that spray a metered amount of fuel into the throttle body, the intake manifold, or directly into the combustion chamber

Ignition

The air/fuel mixture is ignited with an electrical spark, and the burning gas expands quickly, forcing the piston down. As the piston moves down, it revolves the crankshaft, providing power to the transmission. The revolution of the crankshaft also drives the other pistons in the engine up and down. This is the power stroke.

A common problem with the ignition system comes from wires that are old and don't provide enough electricity to the spark plugs. Modern electronic ignition systems have far fewer moving parts than older systems, so they have fewer potential points of failure.

After the fuel is burned, the piston rises again and pushes the burnt fuel and air mixture out through the exhaust valve or valves. Pressure from the exhaust pushes it through the exhaust system under the car and out the tailpipe. This is the exhaust stroke.

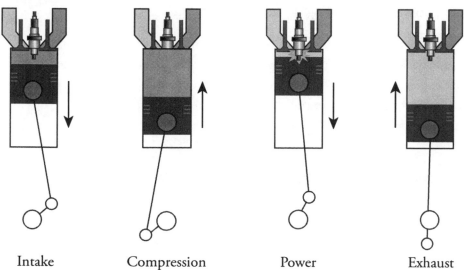

| Intake | Compression | Power | Exhaust |

Diagram showing the four strokes of a four-cylinder engine.

Diesel engines

Diesel engines are similar to gasoline engines, though typically built of heavier and stronger materials because on combustion they produce more power more quickly. Also, they have higher compression, which means that they squeeze the air in the combustion chamber more tightly than gasoline engines do.

The major difference between a diesel engine and a gasoline engine is that diesel engines do not use spark plugs. Instead, they spray the fuel directly into the compressed air, which ignites from the heat and pressure. Diesel engines are much more fuel efficient than gasoline engines, getting 40 or 50 percent of the available power from the fuel. Gasoline-fueled engines typically get 30 percent.

> *The major difference between a diesel engine and a gasoline engine is that diesel engines do not use spark plugs.*

What is RPM?
Engine speed is measured in RPM, or revolutions per minute. All engines have a maximum RPM, which can't be exceeded without damaging the engine.

Two-cycle engines

Two-cycle engines perform the same basic functions as four-cycle engines, but with only two motions of the piston (up/down). They do not use intake and exhaust valves but have ports (or holes) in the cylinder walls.

As the piston moves up to compress the air/fuel mixture, it covers these holes and fresh mixture is drawn in under the piston. As the piston moves down for the power stroke, intake and exhaust ports are exposed in the cylinder wall. The downward motion of the piston pushes the air/fuel mixture from under the piston, through the intake port. The pressure from the incoming mixture pushes the exhaust gas out the exhaust port. The piston rises, sealing off the intake and exhaust ports and compressing the mixture again.

Two-cycle engines are good for small-engine applications, such as lawnmowers and chainsaws, because they have fewer moving parts. This makes it easier to build smaller engines. They are not used for cars in the United States, but some former Soviet countries continued to put them in cars into the 1990s.

ASVAB tip!
On the CAT-ASVAB, the Auto Information subtest is 7 minutes long and has 11 questions.

Other engine types

Another way that engines differ is in piston arrangement. The pistons in many four-cylinder engines are inline, that is, all four pistons sit in one row, from front to back, in the engine. Some older six-cylinder engines were made this way; one famous model was Chrysler's "Slant 6," an inline six-cylinder engine with the pistons tipped 30 degrees to the right. This made the engine lower, and allowed for styling design changes (such as a lowered hood). Inline eight-cylinder engines, or "Straight 8s," were often put in luxury vehicles from the 1920s through the 1940s.

Many modern engines with six or more cylinders use a "V" arrangement, where the cylinders are divided and angled to the right and left. This reduces the overall height, length, and weight of the engine. Some four-cylinder engines (most notably, old VW engines) even have a horizontal layout, so that the pistons are arranged with two lying flat on each side with the crankshaft in the middle.

A WWII relic

An unusual piston arrangement is the radial engine, with the pistons arranged around the crankshaft like spokes on a wheel. These are typically used in aircraft, especially in WWI and WWII military applications, and have never been used in production cars in the United States.

A trend in modern manufacturing is the production of HYBRID VEHICLES, which use batteries powering electric motors as their primary form of propulsion, with a diesel or gasoline engine used to run an electric generator or to supply power to the drive train if the batteries are depleted. The aim of these designs is to reduce pollution and increase gas mileage.

HYBRID VEHICLES: vehicles that use batteries powering electric motors as their primary form of propulsion

Practice Test Question

1. **Which of these is a function of the piston rings?**

   A. They control the flow of fuel into the combustion chamber

   B. They secure the piston to the connecting rod

   C. They keep the piston from tilting in the cylinder as it moves up and down

   D. They form a seal between the cylinder wall and the piston

For your convenience, the practice test questions also appear the end of the book, so you can sit down and go through them all at once.

Answer Key

1. **D. They form a seal between the cylinder wall and the piston**

   Piston rings fill the gap between the piston and the cylinder wall, since the piston must be narrower than the cylinder. This forms a seal in the combustion chamber, but also seals out the oil in the engine, which lubricates the cylinder wall as the piston moves up and down.

Drive Trains: Transmission, Transaxle, and Differential

The transmission takes the power from the engine and sends it to the differential through a combination of gears. The differential takes the power from the transmission and sends it through the axles to the drive wheels. A TRANSAXLE is a unit that combines a transmission and a differential.

TRANSAXLE: a unit that combines a transmission and a differential

There are two major types of transmissions: manual and automatic. (The transmission portion of a transaxle works similarly.) Transmissions allow the engine to move the vehicle at higher speeds or with more power by using gears of different sizes, much like changing gears on a bicycle. When the input gear (the first from the engine) is larger, and the output gear (closest to the wheels) is smaller, the car will go faster while allowing the engine to turn more slowly. When the output gear is larger, the car will go slower, but will be able to do more work.

Remember gear ratios from mechanics?
The gear ratio in a car shows the difference in size between the input gear and the output gear. The larger the gear ratio, the faster the car can go.

Manual transmission

With a manual transmission, the driver selects which gear combination to use. Manual transmissions connect to the engine with a clutch, which is essentially two large, flat plates that press together. One plate is connected to the crankshaft in the engine, while the other is connected to an input shaft in the transmission. Stepping on the clutch pedal separates these two plates, allowing the gears to be changed. Gears can't be changed without using a clutch, because the gears in the transmission are moving at different speeds and the teeth of the gears would grind and break.

Automatic transmission

With an automatic transmission, the vehicle determines which gears are best to use. Older transmissions used a system of hydraulics for this, while newer ones incorporate sensor input and computer commands. The valve body is the part in a transmission that tells the transmission when to shift gears and what gear to use.

There are many different types of automatic transmission designs. Generally speaking, they all use hydraulic pressure to work some kind of clutching system to change gears. Automatic transmissions connect to the engine with a fluid clutch, called a torque converter. A torque converter is permanently connected to both the transmission and the engine.

Inside the torque converter there are two sets of turbine blades and transmission fluid. When the engine spins the first turbine, the turbine spins the fluid, which spins the turbine on the transmission side, sending power to the wheels. When the engine is turning slowly (for example, at a stop light), the fluid pressure isn't enough to move the transmission side of the torque converter. One problem with this is that some power is lost in the fluid motion. Many modern cars also have a plate clutch inside the torque converter to reduce slipping and improve performance when the car is driving at highway speeds.

> **Automotive tip**
> Hydraulic systems are systems that use fluid pressure to provide mechanical force. Most brake systems are hydraulic.

Differential

A differential takes the power coming out of the transmission and splits it between the drive wheels. DRIVE WHEELS are any wheels on a car that have power sent to them.

Most modern passenger cars and minivans are front-wheel drive, meaning that the power is sent to the front wheels only, while most sports cars are rear-wheel drive. Most pickup trucks and SUVs have the capability of being rear-wheel drive or four -wheel drive, meaning that power is sent to all four wheels. Some heavy-duty trucks are four-wheel drive. Rear-wheel drive systems are typically more durable and better suited to abusive use (like police cruisers and snow plows).

DRIVE WHEELS: any wheels on a car that have power sent to them

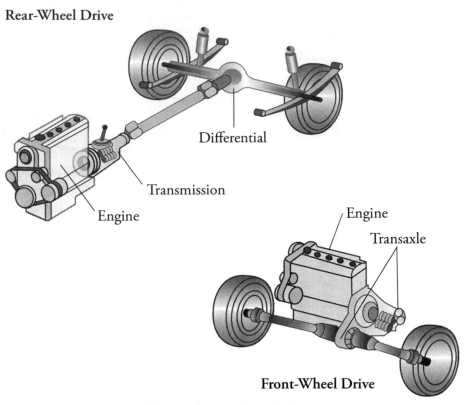

Rear-Wheel Drive

Differential

Transmission

Engine

Engine

Transaxle

Front-Wheel Drive

Diagram showing the general differences between front-wheel drive and rear-wheel drive configurations.

Four-wheel drive vehicles have both a front and rear differential, or a front transaxle and rear differential.

Differentials use a smaller gearbox to take the revolutions from the transmission output shaft and put that revolution into axles, which turn the wheels. Sometimes the direction of the revolution needs to be changed, as with rear-wheel drive cars, since the driveshaft runs the length of the car front to back, but the axles go from side to side. Four-wheel drive vehicles have both a front and rear differential, or a front transaxle and rear differential.

Practice Test Question

1. **What are the three main parts of a manual clutch?**

   A. Pressure plate, clutch plate, throwout bearing

   B. Clutch pedal, main bearing, clutch plate

   C. Torque converter, clutch plate, throwout bearing

   D. Pressure plate, clutch plate, spider gears

Answer Key

1. **A. Pressure plate, clutch plate, throwout bearing**

   The three main parts to a manual clutch are the pressure plate, clutch plate, and throwout bearing. The clutch pedal operates the clutch, but is not considered part of the clutch, so answer B is incorrect. Torque converters are used in automatic transmissions, and replace a clutch, so answer C is incorrect. Spider gears are found in a differential, not a clutch, so answer D is incorrect.

Electrical System

Electrical systems provide power to start the car, fire the spark plugs, run the computer and its sensors, and power the radio, interior lights, and other accessories. The electrical system consists primarily of the battery, the alternator (also called a generator), fuses, and wiring.

When you turn the key, you are turning on an electrical switch, like a light switch, which sends power from the battery through the car. When you turn the key to start the car, some of the unnecessary systems (like the radio) turn off, and power is diverted to the starter motor. The STARTER MOTOR is a large electric motor that spins the engine.

> **STARTER MOTOR:** a large electric motor that spins the engine

The good old days?
When cars were first invented, they didn't have electric starters. You had to crank the engine by hand to start it, which was difficult and could be dangerous.

Fuses protect the car from electrical surges. When wires heat up, electrical problems can start fires. FUSES are thin strips of metal designed to burn out at a certain amperage, which stops the electricity to those wires. A fuse for a radio might be 10 amps, the cigarette lighter might be 20 amps, while the fuse for the starter motor might be 40 amps. Fuses are color coded to indicate their amp rating.

> **FUSES:** thin strips of metal designed to burn out at a certain amperage, which stops the electricity to those wires

Imagine a fire hose...
Amps measure the amount of electricity moving through a circuit. If you think of electricity as water, a fire hose would be high amperage, while a garden hose would be low amperage.

Alternator

ALTERNATOR, OR GENERATOR: a device that produces electricity while a car is running

The ALTERNATOR, also called the GENERATOR, produces electricity while the car is running. The electricity is used for the car's power needs—but it's also used to recharge the battery while the car is running.

Alternators produce AC, or alternating current, but cars use DC, or direct current, so the alternator contains a voltage rectifier. Voltage rectifiers use diodes, which work like one-way electrical valves, changing AC to DC so the car can use the electricity.

Heard of LED lights?
You may be familiar with the word *diode* from the term LED, which is short for *light-emitting diode*.

Battery

The battery stores electricity, which is used to power the starter motor and provide electricity to the car before the engine is running. Most cars have 12-volt batteries.

Car batteries are made with a series of lead plates submerged in a mild acid. Older batteries needed servicing. As the fluid in them evaporated, it needed to be refilled. Modern batteries are sealed, and no longer need servicing.

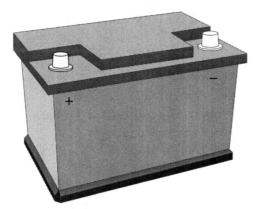

Typical car battery.

Imagine a dam...
Voltage is a measurement of electrical potential. Imagine electricity as water behind two dams. One is 10 feet high, the other is 100 feet high. The higher one has more voltage.

A car battery has a positive (+) terminal and a negative (−) terminal. The positive side is typically marked in red, and the negative side is marked in black or is unmarked. Cars are electrically grounded to the negative side of the battery. This means that the negative side of the battery is connected directly to the metal frame and body of the car, making the frame and body electrically negative. This makes it possible to ground electrical systems in the vehicle directly to the body and chassis instead of having to run each wire to the negative battery terminal.

Red alert!
For safety reasons, when wiring a battery, it is imperative that you do not switch the positive and negative terminals.

One of the most common problems with a car's electrical system is a dead battery. Jump-starting is a procedure where the battery of one car is hooked to the battery of another car and used to start the car with the dead battery. After the jump-start, the alternator of the car with the dead battery will provide power and recharge the battery. When jump-starting cars, it is very important not to cross the positive and negative terminals, as this can damage both batteries and the electrical components in both cars.

When jump-starting cars, it is very important not to cross the positive and negative terminals, as this can damage both batteries and the electrical components in both cars.

Practice Test Questions

1. **The engine does not start. The lights turn on brightly, but the engine will not turn over. Which of these is the most probable cause?**

   A. The battery is dead

   B. The exhaust system is clogged, preventing exhaust gases from exiting the engine

   C. The starter motor is faulty

   D. The fuel lines are clogged, and the engine is not getting fuel

2. **Blown fuses in a car should always be replaced with fuses that have same amp rating or lower. Why?**

   A. Higher amp fuses will not allow enough current to flow, and may stop electronic accessories from working

   B. Higher amp fuses will allow too much current to flow, heating wires and creating a fire hazard

   C. Higher amp fuses will allow too much current to flow, causing headlights and other lights to be too bright and creating a driving hazard

   D. Higher amp fuses will be a different color than the diagram in the car, making future replacement difficult

Answer Key

1. **C. The starter motor is faulty**

    The lights turn on brightly, so you know the battery isn't dead because the battery provides electricity to the car while it's not running, so answer choice A isn't the correct answer. The explanations in answer choices B and D wouldn't cause the engine to not start. Since the function of the starter motor is to turn the engine, it's the most likely cause of the failure, so answer choice C is the correct answer.

2. **B. Higher amp fuses will allow too much current to flow, heating wires and creating a fire hazard**

    When circuits have too much current, the wires heat up. This heating can cause a fire hazard.

Read it aloud
If you're having trouble understanding a new concept, try reading the section aloud. You can read it to someone else, or even to yourself.

Cooling System

The cooling system takes heat away from the engine by running a coolant fluid through a series of tubes cast or drilled into the engine block and head.

Engines produce a great deal of heat. The inside of a combustion chamber can be over 1000 degrees Fahrenheit. The cooling system takes this heat away from the engine by running a coolant fluid through a series of tubes cast or drilled into the engine block and head. A coolant pump circulates this fluid through the engine and the radiator. Cooling systems are pressurized to increase the boiling temperature of the coolant fluid.

Though water would work to cool an engine, antifreeze is used for several reasons. It has a higher boiling point than water. It also has anti-corrosion properties. Older cars used green ethylene glycol, which was more harmful to the environment than antifreeze. Ethylene glycol has a sweet smell and taste, so animals were at risk for drinking it. Propylene glycol has largely replaced ethylene glycol, and newer formulas can be mixed. Ethylene glycol isn't generally sold any more, and should never be used in newer cars, as it will actually tend to corrode the internal parts.

The radiator is used to remove heat from the coolant. Hot coolant is piped into the top of the radiator, which is a series of very thin pipes with thin metal vanes wrapped around them. As the hot coolant runs down through the radiator, a fan blows over it to cool it. The cooling vanes increase the surface area and draw heat out of the coolant. When the engine reaches a certain temperature, a thermostat in the engine block opens to start circulating the coolant through the radiator.

Practice Test Questions

1. Why should you never remove a radiator cap while the engine is running?

   A. The coolant will cool too quickly and damage the engine

   B. Oil and coolant can mix while the engine is running

   C. The cooling system is under pressure, and you could get sprayed with hot fluid

   D. You will introduce air into the system

2. The thermostat controls the flow of coolant through the radiator. Where is it generally located?

   A. In the radiator

   B. On the water pump

   C. As part of the fan circuit

   D. On the engine block

Answer Key

1. **C. The cooling system is under pressure, and you could get sprayed with hot fluid**

   Cooling systems are under pressure and run at temperatures over boiling, so depressurizing the system by taking the cap off may cause the coolant to spontaneously boil or steam, creating a burn hazard.

2. **D. On the engine block**

   Thermostats are bi-metal mechanical valves that work much like a household thermostat. They are typically located on the engine block, near either the inlet or outlet hose on the radiator.

Brake System

Brakes are used to slow and stop the vehicle by applying friction at the wheels. There are two basic types of brakes: drum and disk. Car braking systems are hydraulic, though parking brakes are usually cable operated. Antilock brake systems have been introduced in recent years.

The common part of every braking system is the MASTER CYLINDER. This is a narrow metal tube filled with an oily fluid called hydraulic fluid. When you press on the brake pedal, a plunger applies pressure in the master cylinder. This pressure is transmitted out to the brake cylinders and calipers through thin metal tubes called brake lines.

> **MASTER CYLINDER:** a narrow metal tube filled with hydraulic fluid that is the main component of every braking system

Drum brakes

DRUM BRAKES work by applying pressure outward against the inner walls of a brake drum. Inside the drum there is a brake cylinder, which pushes outward at the top of a pair of brake shoes. The shoes are lined with a friction material, which rubs against the inside of the metal drum.

Disk brakes

DISK BRAKES work by squeezing brake pads together on a brake rotor. A rotor is a flat metal disk that is attached to the wheel. The caliper is a hydraulic piston that squeezes the brake pads together. The pads are lined with a friction material like the brake shoes. Older cars used asbestos for brake linings, but this has been replaced with less toxic materials. Caution should still be taken while working with brakes to prevent inhalation, especially in older cars.

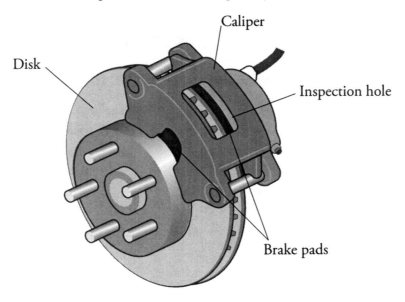

Diagram of a disk brake assembly.

Brake pedal feel is a major indicator of the condition of the braking system. A soft or spongy pedal might be an indication of a small leak, or air in the system. A hard pedal could indicate a caliper that is frozen (not moving properly). Excessive pedal travel, that is, a pedal you have to push a lot before the brakes engage, is an indication of brake wear.

Antilock braking systems have sensors at each wheel that alert the car if a wheel locks up and briefly release the break to the locked wheel, usually by opening a valve.

In an emergency stop, the wheels can lock up, causing the car to enter a skid. This is dangerous, not only because control of the vehicle is lost, but also because the stopping distance is greatly increased. Antilock braking systems have sensors at each wheel that alert the car if a wheel locks up and briefly release the break to the locked wheel, usually by opening a valve. The biggest benefit of this is that steering control is retained.

Practice Test Questions

1. When antilock brakes are active, the brake pedal can sometimes seem to be vibrating or pulsing. Why is this?

   A. The brake rotors are warped and vibrating during hard braking

   B. Valves are opening and closing, causing momentary fluctuations in the fluid pressure in the braking system

   C. The wheels are alternately locking and releasing, sending vibrations to the pedal, which are being transmitted by the hydraulic brake fluid

   D. This is only felt in hybrid vehicles, and is a result of the energy recapturing systems in the brake mechanisms

2. During brake application, the brake pedal is suddenly depressed to the floor. The brakes are still stopping the car, but just barely. What is the most likely problem?

   A. A brake line has failed and the system lost pressure

   B. A leak opened up and sucked air into the system

   C. The brake pads slipped, and holding the brakes down while backing up will correct the problem

   D. The master cylinder has failed

Answer Key

1. **B. Valves are opening and closing, causing momentary fluctuations in the fluid pressure in the braking system**

   Antilock braking systems have sensors at each wheel that alert the car if a wheel locks up, and briefly release the break to the locked wheel, usually by opening a valve. Warped rotors would cause vibrations all the time, not just in emergency situations, so answer A is incorrect. Any vibration or shaking from the wheels would be felt in the steering, not in the brakes, so answer C is incorrect. Answer D is incorrect because this is felt in most antilock systems. Energy recovery systems in hybrids do not produce any vibration.

2. **A. A brake line has failed and the system lost pressure**

   Some braking power may remain if a single brake line fails, since the other three will still have pressure.

ASVAB tip!
On the P&P-ASVAB (the paper-and-pencil version), Shop Information and Auto Information are combined into one subtest.

Exhaust System

Since the late 1960s and early 1970s, exhaust systems have served as the primary means to reduce pollutants produced by internal combustion engines.

EMISSION CONTROLS: the antipollution systems on a car

The primary function of an exhaust system is to take the exhaust fumes away from the passenger compartment. Since the late 1960s and early 1970s, exhaust systems have served as the primary means to reduce pollutants produced by internal combustion engines.

A basic exhaust system consists of an exhaust manifold, a series of exhaust pipes, a muffler, and a tailpipe. The muffler quiets the noise of the exhaust by slowing the exhaust gases through a series of baffles, or metal plates.

The antipollution systems on a car are called **EMISSION CONTROLS**. There are many types, but three that are part of the exhaust system on every car are the EGR system, the catalytic converter, and an O2 sensor. EGR stands for exhaust gas recirculation. This takes some of the exhaust fumes, which still have some unburned fuel in them, and puts them into the intake to get burned again.

The O2 sensor measures the amount of oxygen in the exhaust to see how much unburned fuel is in it. Too much unburned fuel means that the fuel/air mixture is too rich. The computer uses this reading to adjust the mixture.

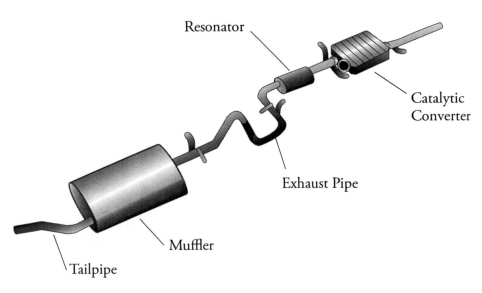

The basic parts of an exhaust system. The exhaust manifold is not shown in this drawing.

For richer or leaner...
Rich and lean are terms used to describe how much air and fuel are being put into the combustion chambers. Rich means more fuel; lean means less fuel. When an engine is cold, you need a richer mixture to help it run.

The catalytic converter uses a metallic catalyst, such as platinum or palladium, to create a chemical reaction that renders some of the pollutants inert. Catalytic converters can be dangerous, because the chemical reaction generates heat.

The car's computer monitors the vehicle's emissions and makes adjustments to the engine operation to keep them as low as possible. When the computer can't compensate or it detects a failure in one of the sensors, it will turn on the Check Engine light. Emissions problems are the most typical reason for turning on the Check Engine light, though other computer problems can also turn it on.

The most common problem with an exhaust system is simply rust. Exhaust pipes are very hot, and often exposed to liquid water. They are underneath the vehicle, and so are constantly exposed to abrasion from road salts and dirt. These are perfect conditions for promoting rust. Modern cars often use stainless steel and other corrosion prevention methods, but this only extends the life of the metal, and cannot prevent rust completely. Replacing worn pipes quickly is important, because exhaust leaks can cause toxic exhaust fumes like carbon monoxide to enter the passenger compartment.

The most common problem with an exhaust system is simply rust.

Practice Test Question

1. **A Check Engine light has come on after fueling. There are no noticeable problems with the running of the engine or transmission. What is the most probable cause?**

   A. The wrong grade of gasoline was put in (lower or higher octane rating than is called for in the owner's manual)

   B. There is excess water in the gas

   C. The fuel cap was not properly tightened

   D. The engine sensor is faulty

Answer Key

1. **C. The fuel cap was not properly tightened**

   Evaporative emission systems on modern cars capture evaporation from the fuel tank. The fuel cap is an integral part of this system, and failure to tighten it can result in a Check Engine light. This is a very common problem, and should be the first thing checked if the light comes on shortly after fueling.

Suspension System

The weight of the vehicle is carried on the suspension system. A basic suspension system is a set of springs at each wheel and some kind of shock absorber. Rear suspensions on larger vehicles use leaf springs, which are long strips of springy metal running from front to back, attached to the frame of the car at either end and to the axle in the middle. Front suspensions are typically coil springs, and many smaller vehicles also use coil springs in the rear.

Shock absorbers are PNEUMATIC (operated by air pressure) or HYDRAULIC (operated by fluid pressure) tubes that dampen the bounce of the springs and the shocks of rough road surfaces. The MacPherson strut was introduced in the early 1950s and incorporated the coil spring and shock absorber in a single unit.

> A basic suspension system is a set of springs at each wheel and some kind of shock absorber.

> **PNEUMATIC:** operated by air pressure

> **HYDRAULIC:** operated by fluid pressure

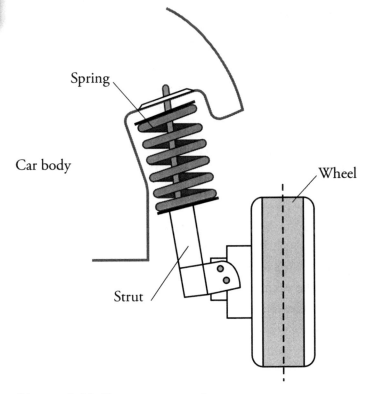

Diagram of a MacPherson strut suspension.

Practice Test Question

1. **Why should suspension components like struts and shock absorbers be replaced in pairs?**

A. Suspension components wear at similar rates, so if one side has failed, the other is probably worn and close to failing as well

B. Replacing just one side may make the vehicle sit at an odd angle, which will affect ride comfort

C. Having a strong suspension on one side and a weak one on the other may create conditions where the vehicle is unstable in emergency situations and lead to an accident

D. All of the above

Answer Key

1. **D. All of the above**

   The entire weight of the vehicle rests on the suspension. Suspension components are designed to optimize vehicle stability and performance.

   Having one corner of the vehicle sag due to worn parts will alter the geometry of the vehicle and impact vehicle performance and safety.

Basic Maintenance

Modern cars require much less maintenance than cars did even 10 or 20 years ago. However, basic maintenance is still important for keeping a car in good running condition and for extending the functional life of the vehicle. All vehicle maintenance should be performed according to the manufacturer's schedule.

Oil change

Oil changes are the most important maintenance procedure to keep your engine running well. As oil circulates through the engine, it picks up deposits from combustion that leak past the piston rings and water from condensation, which helps keep the engine clean.

In the past, oil changes were recommended every three months or 3,000 miles. Newer cars and synthetic oils can go longer between oil changes. Always follow manufacturer's recommendations.

> *Oil changes are the most important maintenance procedure to keep your engine running well.*

The oil is circulated through a filter, which removes some of the deposits. Eventually the filter becomes dirty to the point that it cannot clean the oil properly and needs to be replaced.

Oil changes are done by draining the oil from the oil pan, which is on the bottom of the engine. The oil pan has an oil plug, which is a bolt that is unscrewed to drain the oil. The filter is screwed onto the side of the engine by hand.

You must use the recommended oil viscosity for your engine. Oil viscosity is designated with grades such as 10W30 or 5W30. The higher the number, the thicker the oil.

What does the "W" stand for?
In a motor oil grade, such as 10W30, the "W" stands for *winter*, since oil gets thicker in the cold. Two viscosity ratings are given: a summer number and a winter number.

Other fluids and filters

Automatic transmissions also need to have their oil changed. Models vary, but this is usually done in one of two ways. Typically, an oil pan is unbolted from the bottom of the transmission, granting access to a filter screen. Some transmissions have a screw-on type of filter, like an engine. Transmissions do not need their fluid changed as often as engines, because they are not constantly picking up the kinds of deposits that engines are.

Coolant is another fluid that needs to be changed on a schedule. Over time, antifreeze loses its anticorrosion properties. Coolant is changed by opening a drain on the bottom of the radiator or engine block, and then refilling the system with proper coolant. Some cooling systems need to be bled of air, like a brake system does.

The air filter likewise needs to be replaced regularly. The air filter is located before the intake manifold and, as the name states, filters dirt out of the air before it is sucked into the engine.

The day of your test...
Arrive early, take a short walk, and clear your mind. Take a few deep breaths before the test begins, and remind yourself that you prepared well and are very capable.

Tire pressure should be checked every couple of weeks. Correct tire pressure is listed on the inside of the door frame on the driver's door or in your car owner's manual.

Tires

Tire pressure should be checked every couple of weeks. Correct tire pressure is listed on the inside of the door frame on the driver's door or in your car owner's manual.

Underinflated tires not only reduce gas mileage and make tires wear excessively, but they also reduce vehicle handling and can lead to accidents. When checking tire pressure, also look at tire wear. Uneven wear can be an indication of over- or under-inflation or misalignment. Scalloping and feathering are conditions in which the treads are raised more on one edge than the other.

Tune-ups

Tune-ups include cleaning or replacing spark plugs and checking spark plug wires. Older cars had much more involved maintenance during tune-ups, including steps like checking engine timing and checking points, which sent electricity to the spark plugs.

Many of these steps are not needed anymore, since processes such as timing are monitored and adjusted by the computer, and solid state ignition systems have been replaced by electronic ignition systems. Electronic ignition replaces the physical switches and distributor with computer controls.

Newer systems are much more reliable, since they have fewer moving parts. They also allow for more fuel efficient engines, as the fuel/air mixture and spark timing can be actively adjusted by the computer, depending on driving conditions.

Practice Test Question

1. **In a motor oil grade:**

   A. The lower the number, the thicker the oil

   B. The higher the number, the thicker the oil

   C. The lower the number, the smaller the engine size

   D. The higher the number, the smaller the engine size

Answer Key

1. **B. The higher the number, the thicker the oil**

   Oil viscosity is designated with grades such as 10W30 or 5W30. The higher the number, the thicker the oil.

How would I use this?

In the military, armored assault vehicle crew members operate tanks and other assault vehicles, fire weapons, conduct scouting missions, and support infantry units. Their duties include maintaining and repairing armored vehicles. Therefore, automotive knowledge is a valuable asset in this military career.

CHAPTER 10
ASSEMBLING OBJECTS

The Assembling Objects subtest of the ASVAB tests your ability to connect labeled parts and to assemble parts into objects. In this chapter, you will practice visualizing how pieces fit together to create new objects.

Connecting Labeled Parts

There are two types of questions on the Assembling Objects subtest. One type tests your ability to connect labeled parts. You will be shown two shapes, one with a point labeled "A" and one with a point labeled "B." You will then need to choose how the shapes will look when point A is connected to point B using a connector line.

Here are some important notes and suggestions about these questions:

- Look carefully at the two shapes you are given. Where exactly are points A and B? Those points need to be connected by the connector line.

- The shapes can be moved and rotated in order to connect them. Imagine the shapes lying flat on a table. You can move them and rotate them in order to connect them and find the correct answer.

- The shapes **cannot** be flipped. In other words, the correct answer won't have the mirror image of the original shape. Again, imagine the pieces lying flat on a table. You **cannot** pick a piece up and flip it over.

- Notice what makes points A and B unique. You will need to recognize points A and B as the connected points in the correct answer. For example, point A might be the tip of the longest point on a star, and point B might be the center of a triangle.

Let's try one together.

> **ASVAB tip!**
> On the CAT-ASVAB, the Assembling Objects subtest is 16 minutes long and has 16 questions.

> *The Assembling Objects subtest of the ASVAB tests your ability to connect labeled parts and to assemble parts into objects.*

> *You will be shown two shapes, one with a point labeled "A" and one with a point labeled "B." You will then need to choose how the shapes will look when point A is connected to point B using a connector line.*

Example

Look at the labeled shapes below.

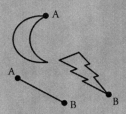

Which figure shows the labeled shapes connected correctly?

A.

B.

Look at points A and B in the shapes you were given. Point A is at one tip of the crescent moon, and point B is at the tip of the lightning bolt. Which figure shows the connector line connecting one tip of the crescent moon to the tip of the lightning bolt? The correct answer is B. Notice that the moon needed to be moved and rotated in order to connect the shapes.

Let's try another.

Test-taking tip

Break down the time for each subtest and make a plan. For example, if a subtest is about 15 minutes long and there are 15 questions, stop at the five-minute mark and make sure you are about five questions into the test. Breaking down the time like this keeps you from getting bogged down on individual questions.

Example

Look at the labeled shapes below.

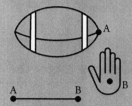

Which figure shows the labeled shapes connected correctly?

A.

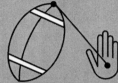

B.

C.

Look at points A and B in the shapes you were given. Point A is at one end of the football. You can tell which end by the curved line on the football. Point B is in the middle of the palm of the hand. Which figure shows the connector line connecting point A to point B? Answer choice A is very close, but notice that the line is connected to the wrong end of the football. In answer choice B, the line is connected to the tip of the finger instead of the palm. The correct answer is C.

Eliminate answer choices

Begin by choosing point A or point B. Look at all of the answer choices and eliminate any that don't connect to that point. This is a quick way to narrow your choices! In the example with the football, you would begin by eliminating any answer choices that don't connect to the center of the palm.

Not so fast...

In the Assembling Objects subtest, don't choose an answer without looking at all of the choices first. One answer choice might be almost correct but not quite. Close isn't close enough.

Now you can try some on your own. For each pair of labeled shapes, choose the figure that shows the shapes connected correctly.

Practice Test Questions

1.

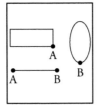

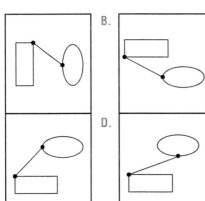

2.

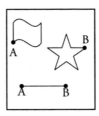

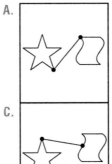

Practice Test Questions

3.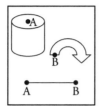

A.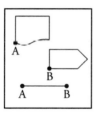

B.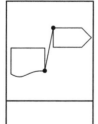

C.

D.

5.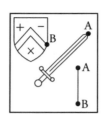

A.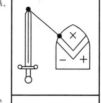

B.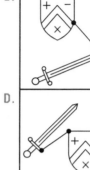

C.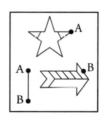

D.

4.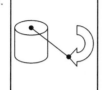

A.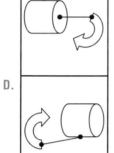

B.

C.

D.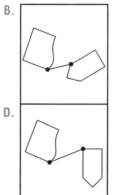

6.

A.

B.

C.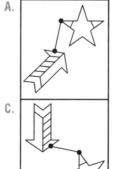

D.

Practice Test Questions

7.

A.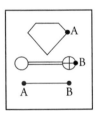

B.

C.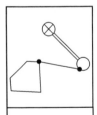

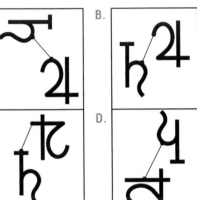

D.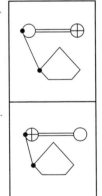

8.

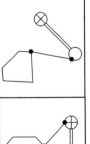

A.

B.

C.

D.

9.

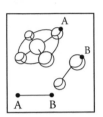

A.

B.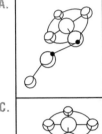

C.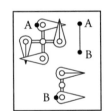

D.

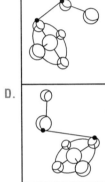

10.

A.

B.

C.

D.

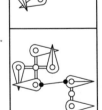

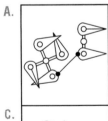

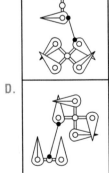

Answer Key

1.	C	6.	C
2.	A	7.	A
3.	B	8.	D
4.	D	9.	D
5.	B	10.	A

Give it a spin
Remember to rotate the shapes in your mind when looking for the correct answer. Some shapes look very different if they've been rotated three-quarters of the way around. If you have trouble picturing this in your mind, cut a simple shape out of a piece of paper, mark a point on the shape, and practice rotating it.

Assembling Puzzle Pieces

The other type of question on the Assembling Objects subtest tests your ability to assemble parts into objects. These questions are very much like putting together jigsaw puzzles. You will be shown several shapes. You will then need to choose how the shapes will look when pieced together.

> You will be shown several shapes. You will then need to choose how the shapes will look when pieced together.

Here are some important notes and suggestions about these questions:

- The "puzzle pieces" can be moved and rotated in order to fit them together. Again, imagine the pieces lying flat on a table. You can move them and rotate them in order to piece them together.

- The puzzle pieces **cannot** be flipped. In other words, the correct answer won't have the mirror image of the original shape. Again, imagine the pieces lying flat on a table. You **cannot** pick a piece up and flip it over.

- Each puzzle piece must be in the correct answer. For example, if one of the pieces is a diamond, there must be a diamond in the assembled object.

- If you're having trouble choosing between two answers, don't look at the entire assembled object. Instead, match the puzzle pieces with the pieces in the object. Isolate each piece, one at a time—is that exact piece in the assembled object?

- Count the number of puzzle pieces. There must be *at least* as many pieces in the assembled object as there are puzzle pieces. There might even be more pieces in the assembled object because when you put pieces together, they can create a shape in the empty space between the pieces.

Tip!
Pick out an unusual puzzle piece, for example, a long, skinny rectangle. Then look at each answer choice. If an answer choice doesn't contain that shape, you can rule it out.

Let's try one together.

Example
Look at the shapes below.

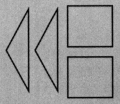

Which figure shows the shapes assembled into an object?

A.
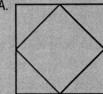

B.
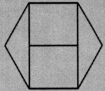

Look at the shapes you were given—two triangles and two squares. Which object contains two triangles and two squares? The correct answer is B. Notice that one of the triangles needed to be rotated in order to create the assembled object.

Let's try another.

Trapezoids and scalene triangles
Knowing the names of shapes can make answering these questions a snap. For example, you could look at the puzzle pieces and think: "one trapezoid and three parallelograms" or "two equilateral triangles and three obtuse triangles." Then just look for the assembled object that contains those shapes. See the Mathematics Knowledge chapter to review the names of two-dimensional shapes and specific types of triangles.

Example

Look at the shapes below.

Which figure shows the shapes assembled into an object?

A.

B.

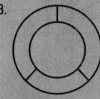

C.

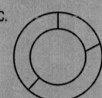

Look at the shapes you were given—three arcs of different sizes. Notice that one is a half circle. Only one answer choice, answer choice A, contains an arc that is a half circle.

Now you can try some on your own. For each set of shapes, choose the figure that shows the shapes assembled into an object.

Practice Test Questions

1.

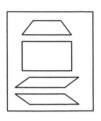

A.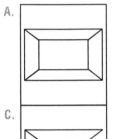

B.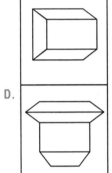

C.

D.

3.

A.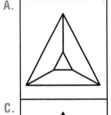

B.

C.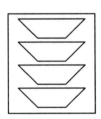

D.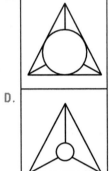

2.

A.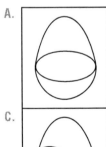

B.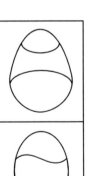

C.

D.

4.

A.

B.

C.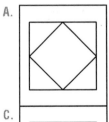

D.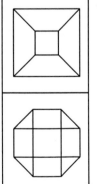

Practice Test Questions

5.

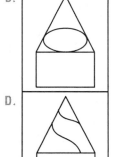

A. B.

C. D.

6.

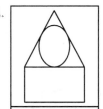

A. B.

C. D.

7.

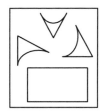

A. B.

C. D.

8.

A. B.

C. D.

Practice Test Questions

9.

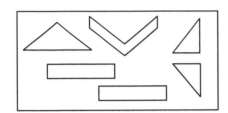

A.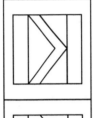

B.

C.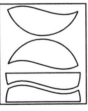

D.

11.

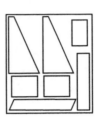

A.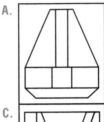

B.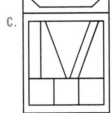

C.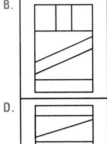

D.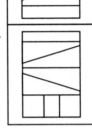

10.

A.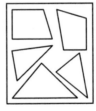

B.

C.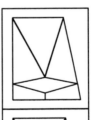

D.

12.

A.

B.

C.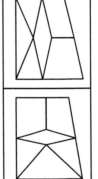

D.

Answer Key

1.	B	7.	A
2.	C	8.	B
3.	C	9.	A
4.	B	10.	D
5.	A	11.	B
6.	B	12.	D

Cut it out!

Cut a large shape out of a piece of construction paper. For example, you might cut out an "L" or the simple outline of a house. Then cut that large shape into four or five basic shapes. Now you can practice taking the pieces apart, moving them around, and then piecing them together to create that shape again. This is great practice for this section of the ASVAB.

How would I use this?

In the military, survival equipment specialists inspect, maintain, and repair parachutes, air-sea rescue equipment, life rafts, and other survival equipment. Attention to detail is a requirement for this job. If parachutes aren't folded, packed, or sewn correctly, they might not work properly. In this military career, the ability to assemble objects accurately could be life saving.

SAMPLE TEST

SAMPLE TEST

Word Knowledge

1. <u>Defeat</u> most nearly means:

   A. Consider

   B. Devote

   C. Overcome

   D. Glare

2. <u>Hazard</u> most nearly means:

   A. Duty

   B. Risk

   C. Occupation

   D. Chamber

3. <u>Meddle</u> most nearly means:

   A. Interfere

   B. Reflect

   C. Merge

   D. Communicate

Choose the word that has nearly the same meaning as the underlined word in questions 4 to 6.

4. Rainy days make me feel <u>languid</u>.

   A. Ill

   B. Lazy

   C. Lonely

   D. Isolated

5. Young children are known for their <u>incessant</u> questions.

   A. Loud

   B. Nosy

   C. Endless

   D. Thoughtful

6. In the end, the accused was <u>vindicated</u>.

   A. Charged

   B. Condemned

   C. Apologetic

   D. Acquitted

7. The word most opposite in meaning to <u>stifle</u> is:

   A. Guide

   B. Adjust

   C. Smother

   D. Encourage

8. The word most opposite in meaning to <u>condone</u> is:

   A. Pardon

   B. Rotate

   C. Disapprove

   D. Prevail

9. The word most opposite in meaning to <u>reprimand</u> is:

   A. Chatter

   B. Praise

   C. Scold

   D. Postpone

10. The word most opposite in meaning to **spontaneous** is:

    A. Deliberate

    B. Impulsive

    C. Magnificent

    D. Confined

11. The word most opposite in meaning to **proponent** is:

    A. Adversary

    B. Witness

    C. Dependent

    D. Supporter

12. **Recede** means:

    A. Carry

    B. Retreat

    C. Seize

    D. Throw

13. **Voracious** means:

    A. Willing

    B. Confused

    C. Hungry

    D. Exhausted

14. **Introspection** means:

    A. Self-examination

    B. Standard

    C. Cumbersome

    D. Go-between

15. **Dysfunctional** means:

    A. Old-fashioned

    B. Extreme

    C. Broken

    D. Appropriate

16. **Genocide** means:

    A. The killing of an entire species of animals

    B. The killing of a cultural, national, or racial group

    C. The killing of an entire group of mammals

    D. The killing of a species of plant

17. **Circumfluent** means:

    A. Examining

    B. Marching

    C. Encompassing

    D. Preventing

18. **Antebellum** means:

    A. Before the war

    B. Afternoon

    C. Within reason

    D. Around midnight

19. **Benevolent** means:

    A. Greedy

    B. Hungry

    C. Confused

    D. Compassionate

Choose the word that has nearly the same meaning as the underlined word in questions 20 to 30.

20. Maggie was hoping to <u>modernize</u> her kitchen.

    A. To make modern

    B. With modern features

    C. Able to be modern

    D. Toward a modern style

21. Looking at the paper, Joe found it quite <u>legible</u>.

    A. To become clear

    B. With understanding

    C. Able to be read

    D. Pertaining to reading

22. Jordan's boss describes him as <u>ambitious</u>.

    A. Without ambition

    B. Like an ambition

    C. Pertaining to ambition

    D. Full of ambition

23. John studied <u>Thatcherism</u> in his government class

    A. The former leader, Margaret Thatcher

    B. The doctrine of Margaret Thatcher

    C. The biography of Margaret Thatcher

    D. The family of Margaret Thatcher

24. A percentage of the budget was <u>appropriated</u> for advertisement costs.

    A. Decreased in volume

    B. Set aside for a specific use

    C. Obtained illegally

    D. Open for public viewing

25. We have to <u>amend</u>, or change, the rules to accommodate the new department.

    A. Alter

    B. Read

    C. Override

    D. Understand

26. The new living quarters are <u>commodious</u>, unlike my current cramped apartment.

    A. Small

    B. Messy

    C. Elegant

    D. Roomy

27. Hospitals are careful not to <u>adulterate</u> the blood supply.

    A. Organize

    B. Reveal

    C. Contaminate

    D. Spread

28. In every major metropolitan area, taxis are <u>ubiquitous</u>.

    A. Everywhere

    B. Mysterious

    C. Urban

    D. Scarce

29. Emma had many cats growing up, so she learned at a young age that cats are <u>tenacious</u> hunters.

    A. Hesitant

    B. Eccentric

    C. Agitated

    D. Persistent

30. When our team scored the home run, my <u>visceral</u> reaction was to jump out of my seat and cheer.

    A. Athletic

    B. Unnatural

    C. Heavy

    D. Instinctive

Paragraph Comprehension

Read the passage below and answer the question that follows.

Time magazine, which typically selects a person of the year, chose Earth as the "planet" of the year in 1988 to underscore the severe problems facing our planet, and therefore us. We hear dismal reports every day about water shortages, ozone depletion, and the obscene volume of trash generated by our society. By choosing Earth as the planet of the year, *Time* was hoping to alert people around the world to these issues and spur solutions to some of these problems.

31. What would a good title be for this passage?

    A. It's Time to Face Earth's Ecological Problems

    B. *Time* Magazine's Person of the Year

    C. Water Shortages, Ozone Depletion, and Trash

    D. Earth's Issues and Solutions

Read the passage below and answer the question that follows.

Every job places different kinds of demands on employees. For example, jobs such as accounting and bookkeeping require mathematical ability, and graphic design requires creative and artistic ability. Medicine requires mainly scientific ability, and engineering requires scientific and mathematical ability. Those studying to be teachers need to be skilled in both psychology and pedagogy, and those wishing to become musicians must have musical and artistic ability.

32. What would a good title for this passage be?

    A. Training for a Job

    B. Different Demands for Different Jobs

    C. What Skills Do You Need to Become an Accountant?

    D. Skills Needed for Success

Read the passage below and answer questions 33 to 35.

Sometimes too much of a good thing can become a very bad thing indeed. In an earnest attempt to consume a healthy diet, dietary supplement enthusiasts have been known to overdose. Vitamin C, for example, long thought to help people ward off cold viruses, is currently being studied for its possible role in warding off cancer and other diseases that cause tissue degeneration. Unfortunately, an overdose of vitamin C— more than 10 mg on a daily basis—can cause nausea and diarrhea. Calcium supplements, commonly taken by women, are helpful in warding off osteoporosis. More than just a few grams a day, however, can lead to stomach upset and even kidney and bladder stones. Niacin, proven useful in reducing cholesterol levels, can be dangerous in large doses to those who suffer from heart problems, asthma, or ulcers.

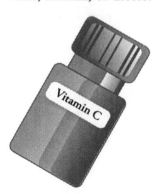

33. **Which of the following statements best states the main idea?**

A. Supplements taken in excess can be a bad thing.

B. Dietary supplement enthusiasts have been known to overdose.

C. Vitamins can cause nausea, diarrhea, and kidney or bladder stones.

D. People who take supplements are preoccupied with their health.

34. **According to this passage:**

A. Vitamin C cannot be taken in excess

B. Too much calcium can cause tissue degeneration

C. Niacin is dangerous for those with diabetes and lupus

D. Vitamin C is being studied for its ability to prevent cancer

35. **What would be the best title for this passage?**

A. A Warning about Calcium

B. Vitamins Can Be Harmful

C. The Benefits of Vitamins

D. Vitamin C and Cancer

Read the passage below and answer the question that follows.

Tim Sullivan had just turned fifteen. As a birthday present, his parents had given him a guitar and a certificate for ten guitar lessons. He had always shown a love of music and a desire to learn an instrument. Tim began his lessons, and before long, he was making up his own songs. At the music studio, Tim met Josh, who played the piano, and Roger, whose instrument was the saxophone. They all shared the same dream, to start a band, and each was praised by his teacher as having real talent.

36. From this passage, the reader can infer that:

    A. Tim, Roger, and Josh are going to start their own band

    B. Tim is going to give up his guitar lessons

    C. Tim, Josh, and Roger will no longer be friends

    D. Josh and Roger are going to start their own band

Read the passage below and answer the question that follows.

The Smith family waited patiently around carousel number 7 for their luggage to arrive. They were exhausted after their five-hour trip and were anxious to get to their hotel. After about an hour, they realized that they no longer recognized any of the other passengers' faces. Mrs. Smith asked the person who appeared to be in charge if they were at the right carousel. The man replied, "Yes, this is it, but we finished unloading that baggage almost half an hour ago."

37. From the man's response, the reader can infer that:

    A. The Smiths were ready to go to their hotel

    B. The Smiths' luggage was lost

    C. The man had their luggage

    D. They were at the wrong carousel

Read the passage below and answer questions 38 and 39.

Student demonstrators lined the streets. They held picket signs and shouted at the cars that drove onto the campus. They were protesting the hiring of a new dean—one who had a record of discrimination against women. Charges had been brought against him, but they had been dropped.

38. Where does this passage take place?

    A. A bank

    B. A police station

    C. A shopping center

    D. A college

39. Based on the passage, the reader can conclude that the:

    A. Students believe it is okay for them to break the law

    B. Students believe that the new dean is guilty of discrimination

    C. Dean is a reasonable man who does not discriminate

    D. Dean is not likely to take the job

Read the passage below and answer the question that follows.

Climbers must endure several barriers on the way to the summit of Mount Everest, including other hikers, steep jagged rocks, and lots of snow. But climbers often find the most grueling part of the trip is their climb back down. They are thoroughly exhausted, and the lack of oxygen often causes problems with judgment. Sometimes climbers feel overconfident because they think that the most difficult part of the trip is over. They might become careless and not take the necessary precautions. Also, weather can become dangerous if a climber waits too long to descend.

40. The author of this passage would agree that:

A. Accidents on Mount Everest are rare but serious

B. Because of the altitude, the weather does not affect climbers

C. Climbers must receive special training on how to descend

D. Climbers should never climb Mount Everest without oxygen

Read the passage below and answer the question that follows.

Someone once said that the two most difficult jobs in the world—voting and being a parent—are given to rank amateurs. The consequences of this inequity are voter apathy and inept parenting leading to, on the one hand, an apparent failure of the democratic process and, on the other hand, misbehaving and misguided children.

41. Based on this passage, the author would be most likely to agree that:

A. Parents should take parenting classes

B. Schools should discipline children

C. Most people should not have children

D. Most children misbehave

Read the passage below and answer questions 42 to 44.

While one day recycling may be mandatory in all states, right now it is voluntary in many communities. Those of us who participate in recycling know just how important it is. By recycling glass, aluminum cans, and plastic bottles, we have reduced the volume of disposable trash by one-third, thereby extending the useful life of local landfills by over a decade. Imagine the difference if those dramatic results were achieved nationwide. The amount of reusable items we thoughtlessly throw away is staggering. For example, Americans dispose of enough steel every day to supply Detroit car manufacturers for three months. Additionally, we dispose of enough aluminum annually to rebuild the nation's air fleet. These statistics, available from the Environmental Protection Agency, should encourage us to watch what we throw away.

42. According to this passage:

A. Through recycling, disposable trash as been reduced by one-half

B. We throw away enough steel each day to supply Detroit car manufacturers for three months

C. Most communities require citizens to recycle glass, aluminum cans, and plastic bottles

D. The United States government has a plan to impose mandatory recycling in every state

43. The author of this passage would agree that recycling

A. Is beneficial

B. Should be mandatory

C. Is only slightly effective

D. Causes several serious problems

44. According to this passage, recycling is:

A. Effortless

B. Time-consuming

C. Mandatory

D. Voluntary

Read the passage below and answer the question that follows.

Rainforests recycle air and clean water. The trees capture and remove a large amount of the carbon dioxide from the air. This decreases the overall temperature of the planet.

45. According to this passage, it's reasonable to assume that:

A. Temperatures will decrease if rainforests are destroyed

B. Carbon dioxide is harmful to plants and animals

C. The rainforests affect people throughout the world

D. The temperature of the rainforests is decreasing

Read the passage below and answer the question that follows.

Countless species of snakes, some more dangerous than others, still lurk on the urban fringes of Florida's towns and cities. They will often invade domestic spaces, frightening people and their pets.

46. According to this passage, it is reasonable to assume that:

A. Snakes are a problem in Florida

B. The people of Florida work to protect their snakes

C. The snakes in Florida are harmless

D. Snakes are more prevalent in Florida than in other states

Read the passage below and answer the question that follows.

The local charity for the homeless is planning to open a new soup kitchen located on Main Street. Its objective is to provide three well-rounded meals to as many as 75 homeless people each day. The kitchen will open at 7:00 in the morning for breakfast and will continue to serve food throughout the day until dinner is over at 6:30 p.m. Local supermarkets have already agreed to supply food to the charity; however, they are still in need of volunteers to help run the food lines. In addition, further donations of money and food are needed to supply the patrons adequately.

47. According to the passage:

A. The soup kitchen will serve up to 75 people each week

B. All volunteers have been lined up

C. People may contribute cash donations

D. Local supermarkets will be providing all the food

Read the passage below and answer questions 48 to 50.

No one really knows how Valentine's Day started. There are several legends, however, which are often told. The first attributes Valentine's Day to a Christian priest who lived in Rome during the third century, under the rule of Emperor Claudius. Rome was at war, and apparently, Claudius felt that married men did not fight as well as bachelors. Consequently, Claudius banned marriage for the duration of the war. However, Valentinus, the priest, risked his life to marry couples secretly in violation of Claudius' law.

The second legend is even more romantic. In this story, Valentinus is a prisoner, having been condemned to death for refusing to worship pagan deities. While in jail, he fell in love with his jailer's daughter, who happened to be blind. He prayed daily for her sight to return, and, miraculously, it did. On February 14, the day that he was condemned to die, he was allowed to write the young woman a note. In this farewell letter, he promised eternal love, and signed at the bottom of the page the now famous words, "Your Valentine."

48. According to this passage:

    A. Emperor Claudius lived during the third century

    B. The legend is believed by all Romans

    C. Emperor Claudius believed in marriage

    D. Only two legends exist about Valentine's Day

49. According to the second legend:

    A. Valentinus was blind

    B. The daughter prayed for her father's sight

    C. Valentinus was condemned to die

    D. Valentinus was freed

50. According to the passage, where does the first legend take place?

    A. France

    B. Germany

    C. Russia

    D. Italy

Arithmetic Reasoning

51. Michael can do 23 pushups, Shin can do 31 pushups, and Dirk can do 17 more pushups than Michael. How many more pushups can Dirk do than Shin?

    A. 6

    B. 8

    C. 9

    D. 14

52. The Rosen family spends $150.00 to have cable television installed. They then spend $39.99 per month for cable television service. What is the total amount that they spend on cable television during the first year?

    A. $189.99

    B. $479.88

    C. $629.88

    D. $2,279.88

53. Ellie buys bottles of water by the gross. One gross costs $72.00. What is the cost of each bottle of water?

    A. $0.50

    B. $0.72

    C. $3.00

    D. $6.00

54. Alicia bought 9 golden delicious apples for $4.23, and Glenn bought 7 red delicious apples for $3.64. Who got the better deal, and what was the difference in price per apple?

    A. Alicia; $0.05

    B. Alicia; $0.59

    C. Glenn; $0.05

    D. Glenn; $0.59

55. Three friends were playing a pickup game of basketball. Julia scored twice as many baskets as Aiden. Samir scored 3 more basket than Aiden. Together, they scored 27 baskets. How many baskets did Julia score?

    A. 6

    B. 8

    C. 9

    D. 12

56. Juan and Niki plow a field. Juan plows $\frac{1}{12}$ of the field, and Niki plows $\frac{1}{3}$ of the field. How much of the field is left unplowed?

    A. $\frac{1}{6}$

    B. $\frac{5}{12}$

    C. $\frac{7}{12}$

    D. $\frac{5}{6}$

57. A farmer has 10 acres of land. He wants to allot $\frac{2}{5}$ of an acre for each kind of vegetable. How many different kinds of vegetables can he plant?

    A. 25

    B. 20

    C. 6

    D. 4

58. Bruno received a score of 80 on his midterm science test. On his final exam, his score increased by 15%. What was the score on his final exam?

    A. 95

    B. 92

    C. 81.5

    D. 12

59. A baseball player got 5% fewer hits in 2010 than he did in 2009. If he got 140 hits in 2009, how many hits did he get in 2010?

    A. 70

    B. 126

    C. 133

    D. 147

60. There are 39 men and 21 women in a softball league. What percent of the players are women?

    A. 35%

    B. 46%

    C. 54%

    D. 65%

61. The cost of an Indian lunch buffet increased from $6.50 to $7.15. What was the percent increase?

    A. 65%

    B. 10%

    C. 6.5%

    D. 0.1%

62. When Vinny moved to Centerville, his car insurance premium increased from $795.00 to $969.90. What was the percent increase?

    A. 0.18%

    B. 0.22%

    C. 18%

    D. 22%

63. Sasha deposits $250.00 into a savings account that earns an annual interest rate of 5.5%. He doesn't withdraw from the account or deposit any additional money in the account. What is the balance after one year?

    A. $13.75

    B. $137.50

    C. $263.75

    D. $387.50

64. Jorge has 78 action DVDs and 26 comedy DVDs. What is the ratio of action DVDs to comedy DVDs?

    A. $\frac{1}{3}$

    B. $\frac{3}{1}$

    C. $\frac{2}{3}$

    D. $\frac{3}{2}$

65. Janine has an annual salary of $22,000 per year. Leonard's annual salary is 25% higher than Janine's. What is the ratio of Janine's salary to Leonard's salary?

    A. $\frac{1}{4}$

    B. $\frac{4}{1}$

    C. $\frac{4}{5}$

    D. $\frac{5}{4}$

66. If Lynn can set up 26 computers in 6 hours, how many computers can she set up in 15 hours?

    A. 65

    B. 62

    C. 60

    D. 52

67. The wingspan on a scale model of an airplane is 1.5 feet. The scale of the model is 1:50. What is the actual wingspan of the plane?

    A. 33 feet

    B. 50 feet

    C. 75 feet

    D. 150 feet

68. A contractor remodeling a kitchen is installing two triangular tiles on the floor. Two triangular pieces of tile are similar. If the shortest sides of the tiles are 4 inches and 6 inches, and the longest side of the larger tile is 15 inches, how long is the longest side of the smaller tile?

    A. 7.5 inches

    B. 10 inches

    C. 12 inches

    D. 13 inches

69. DeShawn reaches into a bag of candy. There are 10 butterscotch candies and 14 chocolate candies in the bag. What is the probability that he will choose a butterscotch candy?

    A. $\frac{5}{7}$

    B. $\frac{14}{24}$

    C. $\frac{5}{12}$

    D. $\frac{1}{10}$

70. Sanjay is playing a board game that has a spinner that is divided into four equal sections of different colors. He spins the spinner twice. What is the probability that the spinner will land on red both times?

    A. $\frac{1}{2}$

    B. $\frac{1}{4}$

    C. $\frac{1}{8}$

    D. $\frac{1}{16}$

71. A window washer is paid 35¢ per window washed. If he can wash 24 windows per hour, how much money can he earn in one hour and 15 minutes?

    A. $10.50

    B. $9.66

    C. $9.24

    D. $8.40

72. Maria works four days a week selling hot dogs from a street cart. She pays $325.00 per week to rent the cart, and she pays $145.00 per week for hot dogs, buns, and other supplies. She sells the hot dogs for $2.50 each. How many hot dogs does she need to sell each week in order to make a profit?

    A. 189

    B. 188

    C. 48

    D. 47

73. Janelle buys 14 pieces of ribbon from a fabric store. Each piece is 18 inches long. If the ribbon costs $3.70 per foot, what is the total cost of the ribbon Janelle buys?

    A. $51.80

    B. $68.11

    C. $77.70

    D. $932.40

74. A medical device manufacturer has a 12-foot piece of plastic tubing. The manufacturer is going to cut it into pieces that are 3 inches long. How many pieces will there be?

    A. 3

    B. 4

    C. 40

    D. 48

75. On Monday, the price of a gallon of gas was $3.25. The price increased 9¢ per gallon Tuesday. The price increased an additional 2¢ per gallon Wednesday. The price then dropped 4¢ per gallon Thursday. By Friday, the price per gallon was $3.33. What was the average price per gallon of gas during the five days?

    A. $3.28

    B. $3.29

    C. $3.32

    D. $4.15

Mathematics Knowledge

76. $5! = ?$

  A. 20

  B. 25

  C. 60

  D. 120

77. $\dfrac{3^{16}}{3^4} = ?$

  A. 3^4

  B. 3^6

  C. 3^{12}

  D. 3^{20}

78. $(x^6)^3 = ?$

  A. x^2

  B. x^3

  C. x^9

  D. x^{18}

79. $\sqrt[3]{216}$

  A. 4

  B. 6

  C. 7

  D. 8

80. $\sqrt{(25 + 36 + y)^2} = ?$

  A. $11 + y$

  B. $11 + y^2$

  C. $61 + y$

  D. $61 + y^2$

81. $5 + 3 \times \sqrt{16} + (11 - 9) \times 6 = ?$

  A. 29

  B. 44

  C. 114

  D. 288

82. $20 - 5(7 + 2) - 8^2 \div 4 = ?$

  A. -41

  B. $17\frac{3}{4}$

  C. 119

  D. 131

83. Solve for x: $2 - 4 \times 10 - 3x = 7x + 3 - 2x - 9$

  A. -16

  B. -4

  C. $-1\frac{3}{4}$

  D. $3\frac{1}{4}$

84. Solve for x: $y^4 + (10 - 2)(7 - 5) = y^2 \times y^3$

  A. 4

  B. 10

  C. 16

  D. 24

85. Solve for x: $12(x - 2) + 7 = 19$.

  A. $\frac{1}{6}$

  B. $1\frac{1}{6}$

  C. 2

  D. 3

86. Solve for d: $100 - 5(d + 8) = 7(d - 3) - 9d$

   A. 23

   B. 27

   C. 37

   D. $53\frac{2}{3}$

87. Evaluate the expression $\frac{m^6}{m^3} \times 4m$, if $m = 5$.

   A. 500

   B. 1,000

   C. 1,500

   D. 2,500

88. Evaluate the expression $9p - 8q \times (p - q) + q^2$, if $p = 8$ and $q = 6$.

   A. 12

   B. 50

   C. 84

   D. 112

89. Solve: $2 + 5(s - 4) > \sqrt{49}$

   A. $s < 1$

   B. $s > 1$

   C. $s < 5$

   D. $s > 5$

90. Solve: $-2t < 2 - (7 - 4)^2 + \sqrt{121}$

   A. $t < -2$

   B. $t > -2$

   C. $t < 2$

   D. $t > 2$

91. What is the name of the shape below?

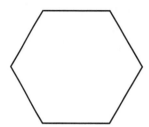

   A. Trapezoid

   B. Parallelogram

   C. Hexagon

   D. Pentagon

92. The angle below is what type of angle?

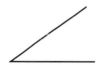

   A. Scalene

   B. Acute

   C. Obtuse

   D. Right

93. The triangle below is what type of triangle?

   A. Equilateral

   B. Isosceles

   C. Obtuse

   D. Right

94. Bernie is going to tile his kitchen floor. One side of his square kitchen is 14 feet long. Tiles that are 1 square foot cost $1.15 each. How much will it cost to tile the floor?

   A. $28.00

   B. $32.20

   C. $196.00

   D. $225.40

95. The perimeter of a rectangle is 42 cm, and the length of one side is 9 cm. What is the area of the rectangle?

   A. 12 cm²

   B. 42 cm²

   C. 108 cm²

   D. 441 cm²

96. Jim installed an above-ground round swimming pool in his backyard. The pool is 12 feet wide. What is the approximate area of the ground that the pool covers?

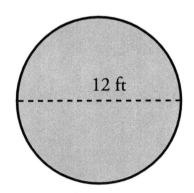

12 ft

   A. 37.68 ft²

   B. 75.36 ft²

   C. 113.04 ft²

   D. 452.16 ft²

97. There is a round fountain in Sawyer Park. The radius of the fountain is 3 meters. Billy walked around the edge of the fountain twice. How far did he walk?

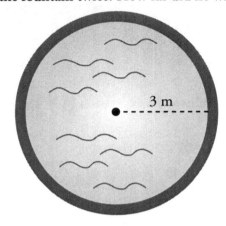

3 m

Fountain shown from above.

   A. 3π m

   B. 6π m

   C. 9π m

   D. 12π m

98. Office Supplies Unlimited sells the small plastic storage cube shown below. What is the volume of the cube?

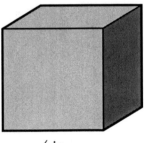

4 in

   A. 8 in³

   B. 12 in³

   C. 16 in³

   D. 64 in³

99. Maria built the storage box below to hold tools. What is the volume of the box?

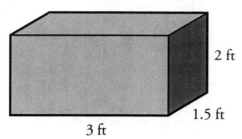

2 ft

1.5 ft

3 ft

A. 4.5 ft³

B. 6 ft³

C. 9 ft³

D. 27 ft³

100. What is the approximate volume of a can that has a diameter of 6 inches and a height of 8 inches?

A. 72 in³

B. 226.08 in³

C. 301.44 in³

D. 904.32 in³

General Science

101. An inflated balloon is left in a refrigerator for a few hours. What do you predict will happen?

A. The balloon will shrink

B. The balloon will expand

C. The balloon volume will remain the same

D. The pressure in the balloon will increase

102. The nucleus of an atom is:

A. Positively charged

B. Negatively charged

C. Neutral

D. Sometimes positively charged, sometimes negatively charged

103. The atomic number of an oxygen atom is 8, and its mass number is 17. This means that the atom of oxygen has:

A. 8 neutrons

B. 9 neutrons

C. 17 neutrons

D. No neutrons

104. The rows of the periodic table are called:

A. Families

B. Elements

C. Groups

D. Periods

105. Which of these is a physical change?

A. Fireworks are set off

B. A nail becomes rusty

C. Ice melts into water

D. An antacid makes you feel better

106. A marble rolls down a smooth curved track. Why does it move more quickly as it goes down?

    A. Some of its potential energy is changed into kinetic energy

    B. Some of its kinetic energy is changed into potential energy

    C. The total energy of the marble increases

    D. The mechanical energy of the marble increases

107. You see a flash of lightning, but the rumble of thunder only gets to you after several seconds. Why is that?

    A. Thunder happens several seconds after the lightning flash

    B. The thunder and lightning are from two different locations

    C. The sound of thunder moves much more slowly than light from the lightning flash

    D. The light from the lightning flash moves much more slowly than the sound of thunder

108. Refraction does not occur in:

    A. Eyeglasses

    B. Rearview mirrors

    C. Rainbows

    D. A lighted fountain

109. You add insulation to your walls to avoid heat loss in winter through:

    A. Conduction

    B. Convection

    C. Radiation

    D. Both convection and radiation

110. The planet that has an atmosphere composed mainly of oxygen and nitrogen is:

    A. Jupiter

    B. Venus

    C. Neptune

    D. Earth

111. The gibbous moon:

    A. Is between the sun and the earth

    B. Is less illuminated than the crescent moon, as seen from the earth

    C. Has more than half of its earth-facing side illuminated

    D. Has exactly half of its earth-facing side illuminated

112. The inner core of the earth is solid because

    A. Otherwise the earth would collapse

    B. It is cooler than the outer core

    C. It is under very high pressure

    D. It is between 5 and 70 km thick

113. The outermost layer of the earth is called the:

    A. Inner core

    B. Outer core

    C. Crust

    D. Mantle

114. Plate movements are not responsible for producing:

    A. Earthquake zones

    B. Tornadoes

    C. Mountain ranges

    D. Volcanoes

115. Thick, fluffy dark rain clouds are called:

    A. Cumulonimbus

    B. Stratonimbus

    C. Stratocumulus

    D. Cirrocumulus

116. Thunderstorms are typically associated with:

    A. Warm fronts

    B. Cold fronts

    C. Occluded fronts

    D. Stationary fronts

117. What structure would not be found in a prokaryotic cell?

    A. Cellular membrane

    B. Nucleus

    C. Cytoplasm

    D. Ribosome

118. Which term describes the entire contents of the cell, including the organelles?

    A. Cytosol

    B. Cytoplasm

    C. Nucleus

    D. Cellular membrane

119. What type of structure would identify a cell as a plant cell?

    A. Chloroplast

    B. Nucleus

    C. Cytoplasm

    D. Ribosome

120. What is the function of the mitochondria in an animal cell?

    A. To transport materials throughout the cell

    B. To produce usable energy

    C. To package molecules made elsewhere in the cell

    D. To protect the genetic material

121. The scientific name for humans is *Homo sapiens*. Choose the proper classification, beginning with kingdom and ending with order.

    A. Animalia, Mammalia, Primate, Hominidae

    B. Animalia, Chordata, *Homo, sapiens*

    C. Animalia, Chordata, Mammalia, Primate

    D. Chordata, Primate, *Homo, sapiens*

122. Which of the following is an example of a producer?

    A. A mouse

    B. A person

    C. A worm

    D. A tree

123. The brain is part of what system?

    A. Musculoskeletal system

    B. Circulatory system

    C. Respiratory system

    D. Nervous system

124. The lungs are part of what system?

A. Musculoskeletal system

B. Circulatory system

C. Respiratory system

D. Nervous system

Mechanical Comprehension

125. If you push down on a table with a force of 10 lbs and the area of your palm is 15 square inches, how much pressure are you exerting on the table?

A. 10 psi

B. 15 psi

C. 1.5 psi

D. 0.667 psi

126. A pulley lifts a box weighing 150 lbs 300 feet off the floor. How much work is done?

A. 45,000 ft-lb

B. 150 ft-lb

C. 0.5 ft-lb

D. 450 ft-lb

127. A pulley lifts a box weighing 150 lbs 300 feet from the floor. If the pulley lifts the box in 3 minutes, how much power does it use?

A. 45,000 ft-lb/min

B. 135,000 ft-lb/min

C. 3,000 ft-lb/min

D. 15,000 ft-lb/min

128. The pair of tongs below is:

A. Not a lever

B. A first class lever

C. A second class lever

D. A third class lever

129. A first class lever has the load placed 2 inches from the fulcrum and effort applied 6 inches from the fulcrum. Its ideal mechanical advantage is:

A. 6

B. 3.5

C. 3

D. 2.5

130. A first class lever has the load placed 2 inches from the fulcrum and effort applied 6 inches from the fulcrum. It has a rusty fulcrum with a lot of resistance. It can only lift a load of 5 pounds when an effort of 2 pounds is applied. Its actual mechanical advantage is:

A. 6

B. 3.5

C. 3

D. 2.5

131. What is the mechanical advantage of a one-pulley system?

    A. 1

    B. 2

    C. 3

    D. It depends on the type of system

132.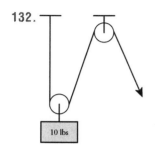

How much effort must be applied to the rope to lift the 10 lb weight?

    A. 3.3 lbs

    B. 5 lbs

    C. 10 lbs

    D. 20 lbs

133. Which of the two inclined planes shown below has the higher ideal mechanical advantage?

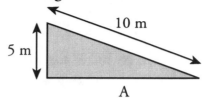

A

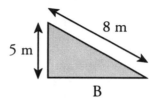

B

    A. A

    B. B

    C. Both are equal

    D. It is not possible to find the ideal mechanical advantage

134. The top of a faucet has a radius of 2 inches. If the neck of the faucet has a half inch radius, what is the mechanical advantage of this system?

    A. 4

    B. 0.25

    C. 2

    D. 2.5

135.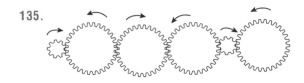

Four spur gears are linked together in a train as shown. The driven gear turns

A. In the same direction as the driver

B. In a direction opposite that of the driver

C. First in the same direction, then in the opposite direction

D. First in the opposite direction, then the same direction

136. What type of gears is shown below?

A. Spur

B. Bevel

C. Rack and pinion

D. Worm

137. A system of gears reduces the output speed by one-third in relation to the input speed. The gear ratio is:

A. $\frac{1}{3}$

B. 3

C. 9

D. 300

138. In the system of gears described in the previous question, the output torque is:

A. Equal to the input torque

B. Three times the input torque

C. One-third the input torque

D. Not related to the input torque

139. A bicycle pump is equipped with a valve the lets the air go into the tire but not out. What kind of valve is this?

A. Shut-off valve

B. Snti-reversal valve

C. Throttling valve

D. None of the above

140. A man wants to measure the air pressure in his car tire. He will use a:

A. Micrometer

B. Barometer

C. Pressure gauge

D. Spring balance

Electronics Information

141. In an open circuit:

A. Current flows

B. Current doesn't flow

C. Current increases

D. Current decreases

142. **Frequency is measured in a unit called:**

   A. RMS

   B. Amps

   C. Volts

   D. Hertz

143. **Root mean square can be used to calculate:**

   A. Current in a DC circuit

   B. Resistance in a DC circuit

   C. Current in an AC circuit

   D. Resistance in an AC circuit

144. **According to Ohm's Law:**

   A. As current increases, voltage decreases.

   B. As current increases, resistance increases.

   C. As current increases, resistance decreases.

   D. As current increases, voltage and resistance decrease.

145. **A 120-volt AC circuit contains a light bulb rated at 60 watts. How much current does the light bulb draw?**

   A. 0.5 amps

   B. 2 amps

   C. 60 amps

   D. 120 amps

146. **Which of these would be the best insulator?**

   A. Copper

   B. Plastic

   C. Silver

   D. Tin

147. **Compared to a copper AWG 12 wire, a copper AWG 8 wire:**

   A. Is more conductive

   B. Is less conductive

   C. Has a larger diameter

   D. Has a smaller diameter

148. **A typical capacitor contains:**

   A. One charged plate

   B. Two charged plates

   C. Three charged plates

   D. Four charged plates

149. **Capacitance is measured in units called:**

   A. Farads

   B. Hertz

   C. Henries

   D. Ohms

150. **An inductor stores an electrical charge:**

   A. Electrochemically

   B. Electrostatically

   C. Electromagnetically

   D. Electromotively

151. The function of a diode is to:

    A. Rectify AC current to DC

    B. Rectify DC current to AC

    C. Allow current to flow in one direction

    D. Allow current to flow in two directions

152. What is the simplest switch that will turn a single light bulb on or off?

    A. SPST

    B. DPST

    C. SPDT

    D. DPDT

153. To measure the current flow in a circuit, you could use:

    A. An ammeter

    B. A wattmeter

    C. An ohmmeter

    D. A voltmeter

154. The following symbol represents:

    A. A capacitor

    B. An inductor

    C. A resistor

    D. A switch

155. The following symbol represents:

    A. A resistor

    B. A switch

    C. A battery

    D. An inductor

156. The following symbol represents:

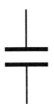

    A. A capacitor

    B. A switch

    C. A resistor

    D. An inductor

Shop Information

157. Which striking tool has a relatively large head, which is often made of wood or rubber?

    A. Post sledge

    B. Mallet

    C. Sledge

    D. Claw hammer

158. **What is the primary advantage of a ratcheting screwdriver?**

    A. The user can rotate the screwdriver in both directions without removing the tip from the screw head

    B. The user can drive in a screw by using a motor

    C. The user can effectively "reach around a corner" to drive a screw in a difficult location

    D. The user can drive in a screw without stripping it

159. **Which type of chisel is typically used on a wood lathe?**

    A. Butt chisel

    B. Gouge

    C. Carving chisel

    D. Corner chisel

160. **Which type of chisel is typically used to cut large joints into wood intended for framing?**

    A. Butt chisel

    B. Carving chisel

    C. Corner chisel

    D. Skew chisel

161. **Which wrench would be the best selection for a job where a number of bolts must be manipulated, but the sizes of the various bolts are not known beforehand?**

    A. Box-end wrench

    B. Combination wrench

    C. Adjustable wrench

    D. Pipe wrench

162. **Which of the following saws would be best used to cut through timber for firewood?**

    A. Crosscut saw

    B. Hacksaw

    C. Table saw

    D. Jigsaw

163. **Laurel wants to cut some intricate scrollwork into a piece of mounting wood she is using for an art project. What type of saw should she use for this type of work?**

    A. Crosscut saw

    B. Hacksaw

    C. Circular saw

    D. Jigsaw

164. **Which of the following is pictured below?**

    A. Bolt

    B. Washer

    C. Nut

    D. Wing nut

165. **Jane needs to measure the thickness of a very small mechanical part. Which type of caliper should she use?**

    A. Vernier caliper

    B. Divider caliper

    C. Micrometer caliper

    D. Inside caliper

166. Joanne wants to quickly remove old and damaged paint and a thin layer of surface wood from an old hardwood deck. What type of sandpaper should she select?

   A. 360-600 grit silicon carbide paper

   B. 220-240 grit garnet paper

   C. 150-180 grit emery paper

   D. 40-60 grit aluminum oxide paper

167. Which of the following is not a benefit of using a primer coat before applying paint?

   A. Primers offer better surface adhesion

   B. Primers extend the life of paint

   C. Primers reduce the cost of painting

   D. Primers help mask dark underlayment

Auto Information

168. Which of these is a function of the piston rings?

   A. They control the flow of fuel into the combustion chamber

   B. They secure the piston to the connecting rod

   C. They keep the piston from tilting in the cylinder as it moves up and down

   D. They form a seal between the cylinder wall and the piston

169. What are the three main parts of a manual clutch?

   A. Pressure plate, clutch plate, throwout bearing

   B. Clutch pedal, main bearing, clutch plate

   C. Torque converter, clutch plate, throwout bearing

   D. Pressure plate, clutch plate, spider gears

170. The engine does not start. The lights turn on brightly, but the engine will not turn over. Which of these is the most probable cause?

   A. The battery is dead

   B. The exhaust system is clogged, preventing exhaust gases from exiting the engine.

   C. The starter motor is faulty

   D. The fuel lines are clogged, and the engine is not getting fuel

171. Blown fuses in a car should always be replaced with fuses that have same amp rating or lower. Why?

   A. Higher amp fuses will not allow enough current to flow, and may stop electronic accessories from working

   B. Higher amp fuses will allow too much current to flow, heating wires and creating a fire hazard

   C. Higher amp fuses will allow too much current to flow, causing headlights and other lights to be too bright and creating a driving hazard

   D. Higher amp fuses will be a different color than the diagram in the car, making future replacement difficult

172. **Why should you never remove a radiator cap while the engine is running?**

    A. The coolant will cool too quickly and damage the engine

    B. Oil and coolant can mix while the engine is running

    C. The cooling system is under pressure, and you could get sprayed with hot fluid

    D. You will introduce air into the system

173. **The thermostat controls the flow of coolant through the radiator. Where is it generally located?**

    A. In the radiator

    B. On the water pump

    C. As part of the fan circuit

    D. On the engine block

174. **When antilock brakes are active, the brake pedal can sometimes seem to be vibrating or pulsing. Why is this?**

    A. The brake rotors are warped and vibrating during hard braking

    B. Valves are opening and closing, causing momentary fluctuations in the fluid pressure in the braking system

    C. The wheels are alternately locking and releasing, sending vibrations to the pedal, which are being transmitted by the hydraulic brake fluid

    D. This is only felt in hybrid vehicles, and is a result of the energy recapturing systems in the brake mechanisms

175. **During brake application, the brake pedal is suddenly depressed to the floor. The brakes are still stopping the car, but just barely. What is the most likely problem?**

    A. A brake line has failed and the system lost pressure

    B. A leak opened up and sucked air into the system

    C. The brake pads slipped, and holding the brakes down while backing up will correct the problem

    D. The master cylinder has failed

176. **A Check Engine light has come on after fueling. There are no noticeable problems with the running of the engine or transmission. What is the most probable cause?**

    A. The wrong grade of gasoline was put in (lower or higher octane rating than is called for in the owner's manual)

    B. There is excess water in the gas

    C. The fuel cap was not properly tightened

    D. The engine sensor is faulty

177. Why should suspension components like struts and shock absorbers be replaced in pairs?

   A. Suspension components wear at similar rates, so if one side has failed, the other is probably worn and close to failing as well

   B. Replacing just one side may make the vehicle sit at an odd angle, which will affect ride comfort

   C. Having a strong suspension on one side and a weak one on the other may create conditions where the vehicle is unstable in emergency situations and lead to an accident

   D. All of the above

178. In a motor oil grade:

   A. The lower the number, the thicker the oil

   B. The higher the number, the thicker the oil

   C. The lower the number, the smaller the engine size

   D. The higher the number, the smaller the engine size

Assembling Objects

For each pair of labeled shapes in questions 179 to 188, choose the figure that shows the shapes connected correctly.

179.

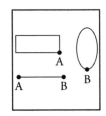

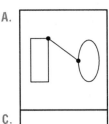

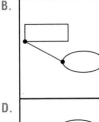

180.

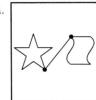

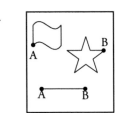

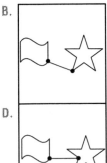

181.

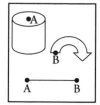

A. 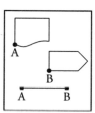 B.

C. D.

182.

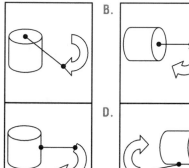

A. 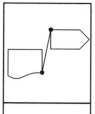 B.

C. 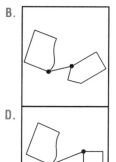 D.

183.

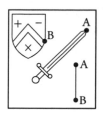

A. 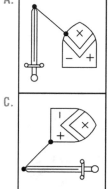 B.

C. D.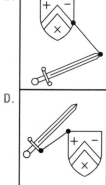

184.

A. 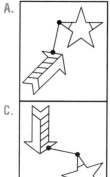 B.

C. D.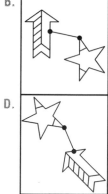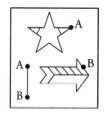

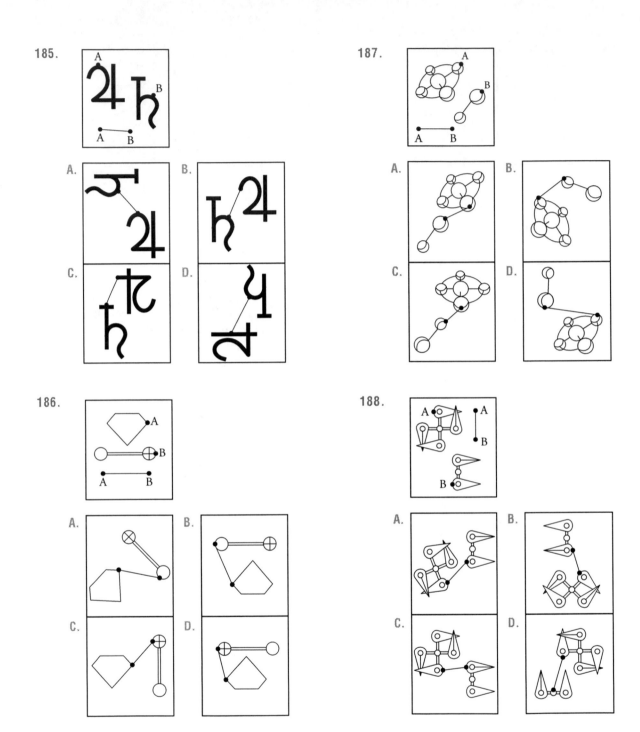

185.

186.

187.

188.

For each set of shapes in questions 189 to 200, choose the figure that shows the shapes assembled into an object.

189.

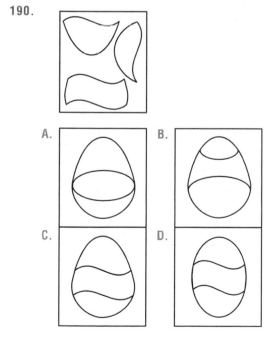

190.

191.

192.

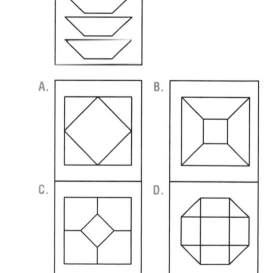

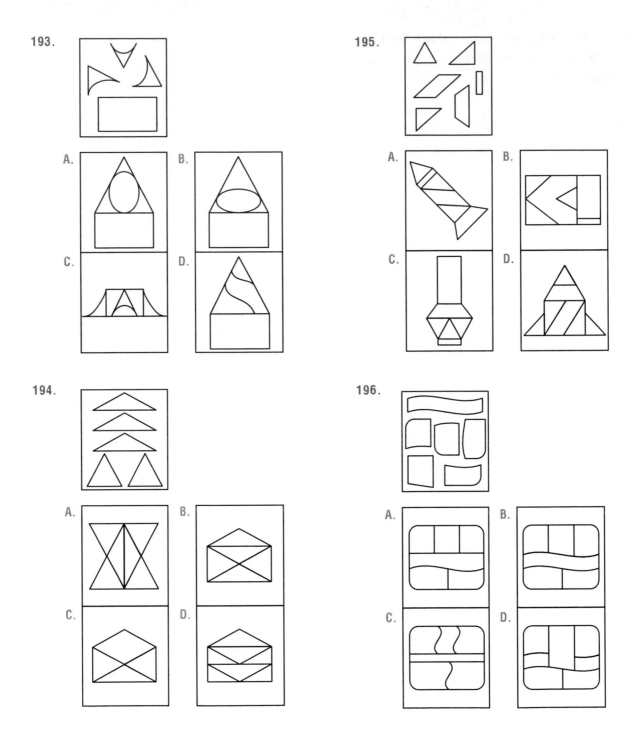

197.

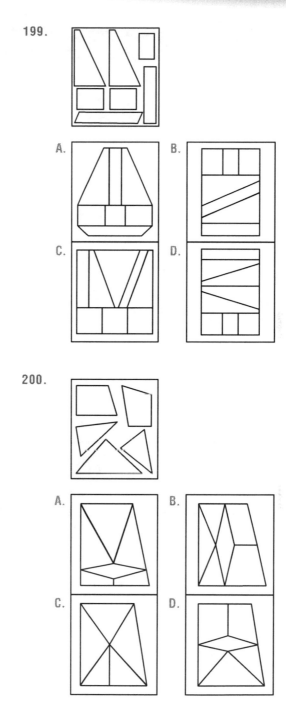

199.

198.

200.

ANSWER KEY

1. C	23. B	45.C	67. C	89. D	111. C	133. A	155. D	177. D	199. B
2. B	24. B	46. A	68. B	90. B	112. C	134. A	156. A	178. B	200. D
3. A	25. A	47. C	69. C	91. C	113. C	135. B	157.B	179. C	
4. B	26. D	48. A	70. D	92. B	114. B	136. B	158. A	180. A	
5. C	27. C	49. C	71. A	93. B	115. A	137. B	159. B	181. B	
6. D	28. A	50. D	72. A	94. D	116. B	138. B	160. A	182. D	
7. D	29. D	51. C	73. B	95. C	117. B	139. B	161. C	183. B	
8. C	30. D	52. C	74. D	96. C	118. B	140. C	162. A	184. C	
9. B	31. A	53. A	75. C	97. D	119. A	141. B	163. D	185. A	
10. A	32. B	54. A	76. D	98. D	120. B	142. D	164. C	186. D	
11. A	33. A	55. D	77. C	99. C	121. C	143. C	165. C	187. D	
12. B	34. D	56. C	78. D	100. B	122. D	144. C	166. D	188. A	
13. C	35. B	57. A	79. B	101. A	123. D	145. A	167. C	189. B	
14. A	36. A	58. B	80. C	102. A	124. C	146. B	168. D	190. C	
15. C	37. B	59. C	81. A	103. B	125. D	147. C	169. A	191. C	
16. B	38. D	60. A	82. A	104. D	126. A	148. B	170. C	192. B	
17. C	39. B	61. B	83. B	105. C	127. D	149. A	171. B	193. A	
18. A	40. C	62. D	84. C	106. A	128. D	150. C	172. C	194. B	
19. D	41. A	63. C	85. D	107. C	129. C	151. C	173. D	195. A	
20. A	42. B	64. B	86. B	108. B	130. D	152. A	174. B	196. B	
21. C	43. A	65. C	87. D	109. A	131. D	153. A	175. A	197. A	
22. D	44. D	66. A	88. A	110. D	132. B	154. C	176. C	198. D	

Sample Test with Rationales:

Word Knowledge

1. <u>Defeat</u> most nearly means:

   A. Consider

   B. Devote

   C. Overcome

   D. Glare

   Answer: C. Overcome

   The word *overcome* has nearly the same meaning as the word *defeat*. They both mean *to win a victory over*.

2. <u>Hazard</u> most nearly means:

   A. Duty

   B. Risk

   C. Occupation

   D. Chamber

   Answer: B. Risk

   The word *risk* has nearly the same meaning to the word *hazard*. They both mean *something that can cause harm*.

3. <u>Meddle</u> most nearly means:

   A. Interfere

   B. Reflect

   C. Merge

   D. Communicate

   Answer: A. Interfere

   The word *interfere* has nearly the same meaning as the word *meddle*. They both mean *to take part in someone's business without being asked*.

Choose the word that has nearly the same meaning as the underlined word in questions 4 to 6.

4. Rainy days make me feel <u>languid</u>.

   A. Ill

   B. Lazy

   C. Lonely

   D. Isolated

   Answer: B. Lazy

   The word *languid* means *sluggish* or *without energy*. The word that has nearly the same meaning as *languid* is *lazy*.

5. Young children are known for their <u>incessant</u> questions.

   A. Loud

   B. Nosy

   C. Endless

   D. Thoughtful

   Answer: C. Endless

   The word *incessant* means *never ending* or *going on for a long time*. The word that has nearly the same meaning as *incessant* is *endless*.

6. In the end, the accused was <u>vindicated</u>.

   A. Charged

   B. Condemned

   C. Apologetic

   D. Acquitted

Answer: D. Acquitted

The word *vindicated* means *to be cleared from accusation or wrongdoing*. The word that has nearly the same meaning as *vindicated* is *acquitted*.

7. **The word most opposite in meaning to stifle is:**

   A. Guide

   B. Adjust

   C. Smother

   D. Encourage

Answer: D. Encourage

To *stifle* means *to quell* or *to end by force; to smother*. The opposite of *stifle* is *encourage*.

8. **The word most opposite in meaning to condone is:**

   A. Pardon

   B. Rotate

   C. Disapprove

   D. Prevail

Answer: C. Disapprove

To *condone* means *to pardon or overlook*. The opposite of *condone* is *disapprove*.

9. **The word most opposite in meaning to reprimand is:**

   A. Chatter

   B. Praise

   C. Scold

   D. Postpone

Answer: B. Praise

To *reprimand* means *to scold or find fault with*. The opposite of *reprimand* is *praise*.

10. **The word most opposite in meaning to spontaneous is:**

    A. Deliberate

    B. Impulsive

    C. Magnificent

    D. Confined

Answer: A. Deliberate

Spontaneous means *not planned or thought out in advance*. The opposite of *spontaneous* is *deliberate*.

11. **The word most opposite in meaning to proponent is:**

    A. Adversary

    B. Witness

    C. Dependent

    D. Supporter

Answer: A. Adversary

A *proponent* is *a person who supports a cause or a belief*. The opposite of *proponent* is *adversary*.

12. **Recede means:**

    A. Carry

    B. Retreat

    C. Seize

    D. Throw

Answer: B. Retreat

Recede contains the root *cede*, meaning *go, give way,* or *yield*. Answer choice B, *retreat*, is another way of saying *to give way* or *to yield*. The root provides a clue to the correct answer. The definition of *recede* is *to move away from; retreat; withdraw*.

13. **Voracious** means:

    A. Willing

    B. Confused

    C. Hungry

    D. Exhausted

Answer: C. Hungry

Voracious contains the root word *vor*, meaning *eat*. Answer choice C, *hungry*, is related to eating. The root word provides a clue to the correct answer. The definition of *voracious* is *craving or consuming large amounts of food* or *exceedingly eager*.

14. **Introspection** means:

    A. Self-examination

    B. Standard

    C. Cumbersome

    D. Go-between

Answer: A. Self-examination

Introspection contains the root word *spec*, meaning *to look or see*. The definition of *introspection* is *the act of looking within oneself*.

15. **Dysfunctional** means:

    A. Old-fashioned

    B. Extreme

    C. Broken

    D. Appropriate

Answer: C. Broken

Dysfunctional contains the root *dys*, meaning *abnormal* or *bad*. The definition of *dysfunctional* is *not working normally or properly*.

16. **Genocide** means:

    A. The killing of an entire species of animals

    B. The killing of a cultural, national, or racial group

    C. The killing of an entire group of mammals

    D. The killing of a species of plant

Answer: B. The killing of a cultural, national, or racial group

The word *genocide* is made up of the root *gen-* which means *birth* or *race*. Answer choice B includes *racial group*. The root is a clue to the correct answer.

17. **Circumfluent** means:

    A. Examining

    B. Marching

    C. Encompassing

    D. Preventing

Answer: C. Encompassing

Circumfluent contains the prefix *circum-*, meaning *around*. Answer choice C, *encompassing*, means *to form a circle around*. This answer choice is related to the prefix meaning *around*. The prefix provides a clue to the correct answer. *Circumfluent* means *flowing around; encompassing*.

18. **Antebellum means:**

   A. Before the war

   B. Afternoon

   C. Within reason

   D. Around midnight

Answer: A. Before the war

Antebellum contains the prefix *ante-*, meaning *before*. Answer choice A, *before the war*, includes the meaning of the prefix. The prefix provides a clue to the correct answer. *Antebellum* means *of or during the period before a war, especially the United States Civil War.*

19. **Benevolent means:**

   A. Greedy

   B. Hungry

   C. Confused

   D. Compassionate

Answer: D. Compassionate

Benevolent contains the prefix *bene-*, meaning *good*. The prefix provides a clue to the correct answer. *Benevolent* must be related to something good, such as the correct answer, *compassionate*.

Choose the word that has nearly the same meaning as the underlined word in questions 20 to 30.

20. **Maggie was hoping to <u>modernize</u> her kitchen.**

   A. To make modern

   B. With modern features

   C. Able to be modern

   D. Toward a modern style

Answer: A. to make modern

The suffix *-ize* means *to become*. When added to the base word *modern*, the definition is *to make or become modern.*

21. **Looking at the paper, Joe found it quite <u>legible</u>.**

   A. To become clear

   B. With understanding

   C. Able to be read

   D. Pertaining to reading

Answer: C. Able to be read

The suffix *-ible* means *able to*. When added to the root word *leg-* (meaning *read*), the definition is *able to be read.*

22. **Jordan's boss describes him as <u>ambitious</u>.**

   A. Without ambition

   B. Like an ambition

   C. Pertaining to ambition

   D. Full of ambition

Answer: D. Full of ambition

The suffix *-ous* means *full of*. When added to the base word *ambition*, the definition is *full of ambition*.

23. John studied <u>Thatcherism</u> in his government class
    A. The former leader, Margaret Thatcher
    B. The doctrine of Margaret Thatcher
    C. The biography of Margaret Thatcher
    D. The family of Margaret Thatcher

Answer: B. the doctrine of Margaret Thatcher

Because the suffix *-ism* means *doctrine of*, we know that the word's meaning is *the doctrine of Margaret Thatcher*.

24. A percentage of the budget was <u>appropriated</u> for advertisement costs.
    A. Decreased in volume
    B. Set aside for a specific use
    C. Obtained illegally
    D. Open for public viewing

Answer: B. Set aside for a specific use

The context of the sentence includes a percentage of the money for advertisement. It makes sense that this money is *set aside for a specific use*.

25. We have to <u>amend</u>, or change, the rules to accommodate the new department.
    A. Alter
    B. Read
    C. Override
    D. Understand

Answer: A. Alter

The word *change* following the underlined word *amend* is the clue that reveals the correct answer, *alter*. *Alter* and *change* are synonyms.

26. The new living quarters are <u>commodious</u>, unlike my current cramped apartment.
    A. Small
    B. Messy
    C. Elegant
    D. Roomy

Answer: D. Roomy

The contrasting phrase, *unlike my current cramped apartment*, reveals that the word *commodious* means *roomy*. *Roomy* is the opposite of *cramped*.

27. Hospitals are careful not to <u>adulterate</u> the blood supply.
    A. Organize
    B. Reveal
    C. Contaminate
    D. Spread

Answer: C. contaminate

It is through our experiences that we understand how important it is to protect the blood supply from contamination. Therefore, *adulterate* must mean *contaminate*.

28. **In every major metropolitan area, taxis are <u>ubiquitous</u>.**

    A. Everywhere

    B. Mysterious

    C. Urban

    D. Scarce

    Answer: A. Everywhere

    Through our experience, we know that there are many taxis in cities. Therefore, *ubiquitous* must mean *everywhere*. You might be tempted to choose answer choice C, but even though metropolitan areas are urban, it doesn't make sense to say that taxis are urban.

29. **Emma had many cats growing up, so she learned at a young age that cats are <u>tenacious</u> hunters.**

    A. Hesitant

    B. Eccentric

    C. Agitated

    D. Persistent

    Answer: D. Persistent

    Anyone who has seen a cat chase a bird or mouse (or even a toy) knows that cats are determined, unrelenting hunters. Therefore, *tenacious* must mean *persistent*.

30. **When our team scored the home run, my <u>visceral</u> reaction was to jump out of my seat and cheer.**

    A. Athletic

    B. Unnatural

    C. Heavy

    D. Instinctive

Answer: D. Instinctive

Anyone who has been to a sporting event or watched one on television has seen the automatic reaction fans have to a touchdown or home run. Therefore, *visceral* must mean *instinctive*.

Paragraph Comprehension

Read the passage below and answer the question that follows.

Time magazine, which typically selects a person of the year, chose Earth as the "planet" of the year in 1988 to underscore the severe problems facing our planet, and therefore us. We hear dismal reports every day about water shortages, ozone depletion, and the obscene volume of trash generated by our society. By choosing Earth as the planet of the year, *Time* was hoping to alert people around the world to these issues and spur solutions to some of these problems.

31. **What would a good title be for this passage?**

    A. It's Time to Face Earth's Ecological Problems

    B. *Time* Magazine's Person of the Year

    C. Water Shortages, Ozone Depletion, and Trash

    D. Earth's Issues and Solutions

Answer: A. It's Time to Face Earth's Ecological Problems

This title includes the topic—*ecological problems*—and the most important idea—*we need to address the problems*. Answer choice B isn't correct because this passage is about *Time* magazine's "planet" of the year. Answer choice C alludes to some of the details in the passage that support the main idea, but they are not the main idea. Answer choice D is too broad to be the main idea.

Read the passage below and answer the question that follows.

Every job places different kinds of demands on employees. For example, jobs such as accounting and bookkeeping require mathematical ability, and graphic design requires creative and artistic ability. Medicine requires mainly scientific ability, and engineering requires scientific and mathematical ability. Those studying to be teachers need to be skilled in both psychology and pedagogy, and those wishing to become musicians must have musical and artistic ability.

32. **What would a good title for this passage be?**

    A. Training for a Job

    B. Different Demands for Different Jobs

    C. What Skills Do You Need to Become an Accountant?

    D. Skills Needed for Success

Answer: B. Different Demands for Different Jobs

This title states the topic and the main idea. People need different skills for different jobs, so different jobs have different demands. Answer choices A and D are too broad. Answer choice C is too specific.

Read the passage below and answer questions 33 to 35.

Sometimes too much of a good thing can become a very bad thing indeed. In an earnest attempt to consume a healthy diet, dietary supplement enthusiasts have been known to overdose. Vitamin C, for example, long thought to help people ward off cold viruses, is currently being studied for its possible role in warding off cancer and other diseases that cause tissue degeneration. Unfortunately, an overdose of vitamin C—more than 10 mg on a daily basis—can cause nausea and diarrhea. Calcium supplements, commonly taken by women, are helpful in warding off osteoporosis. More than just a few grams a day, however, can lead to stomach upset and even kidney and bladder stones. Niacin, proven useful in reducing cholesterol levels, can be dangerous in large doses to those who suffer from heart problems, asthma, or ulcers.

33. **Which of the following statements best states the main idea?**

   A. Supplements taken in excess can be a bad thing.

   B. Dietary supplement enthusiasts have been known to overdose.

   C. Vitamins can cause nausea, diarrhea, and kidney or bladder stones.

   D. People who take supplements are preoccupied with their health.

Answer: A. Supplements taken in excess can be a bad thing.

Answer choice A is a paraphrase of the first sentence and provides a general framework for the rest of the passage—excess supplement intake can be bad. This is the main idea. The rest of the passage discusses the consequences of taking too many supplements.

34. **According to this passage:**

   A. Vitamin C cannot be taken in excess

   B. Too much calcium can cause tissue degeneration

   C. Niacin is dangerous for those with diabetes and lupus

   D. Vitamin C is being studied for its ability to prevent cancer

Answer: D. Vitamin C is being studied for its ability to prevent cancer

The fact that vitamin C is being studied for its ability to prevent cancer is stated directly in the passage.

35. **What would be the best title for this passage?**

   A. A Warning about Calcium

   B. Vitamins Can Be Harmful

   C. The Benefits of Vitamins

   D. Vitamin C and Cancer

Answer: B. Vitamins Can Be Harmful

Answer choice is B, Vitamins Can Be Harmful, is correct because it is the main idea of the passage. The other answer choices all address details in the passage, not the main idea, so they would not make good titles.

Read the passage below and answer the question that follows.

Tim Sullivan had just turned fifteen. As a birthday present, his parents had given him a guitar and a certificate for ten guitar lessons. He had always shown a love of music and a desire to learn an instrument. Tim began his lessons, and before long, he was making up his own songs. At the music studio, Tim met Josh, who played the piano, and Roger, whose instrument was the saxophone. They all shared the same dream, to start a band, and each was praised by his teacher as having real talent.

36. From this passage, the reader can infer that:

    A. Tim, Roger, and Josh are going to start their own band

    B. Tim is going to give up his guitar lessons

    C. Tim, Josh, and Roger will no longer be friends

    D. Josh and Roger are going to start their own band

Answer: A. Tim, Roger, and Josh are going to start their own band

Tim wanted to be a musician and start his own band. After meeting others who shared the same dreams, you can infer that they worked together in an attempt to make their dreams become a reality.

Read the passage below and answer the question that follows.

The Smith family waited patiently around carousel number 7 for their luggage to arrive. They were exhausted after their five-hour trip and were anxious to get to their hotel. After about an hour, they realized that they no longer recognized any of the other passengers' faces. Mrs. Smith asked the person who appeared to be in charge if they were at the right carousel. The man replied, "Yes, this is it, but we finished unloading that baggage almost half an hour ago."

37. From the man's response, the reader can infer that:

    A. The Smiths were ready to go to their hotel

    B. The Smiths' luggage was lost

    C. The man had their luggage

    D. They were at the wrong carousel

Answer: B. The Smiths' luggage was lost

Although not directly stated, it appears that their luggage was lost. All of the baggage had been unloaded at the carousel, but the Smiths' luggage still hadn't arrived. Answer choice A isn't correct, because the Smiths were still waiting for their luggage. Answer choice C isn't correct, because there is no suggestion that the man had their luggage. Answer choice D isn't correct, because the man told them that they were at the right carousel.

Read the passage below and answer questions 38 and 39.

Student demonstrators lined the streets. They held picket signs and shouted at the cars that drove onto the campus. They were protesting the hiring of a new dean—one who had a record of discrimination against women. Charges had been brought against him, but they had been dropped.

38. Where does this passage take place?

    A. A bank

    B. A police station

    C. A shopping center

    D. A college

Answer: D. A college

The passage does not directly state that it takes place at a college, but it uses words such as *student*, *campus*, and *dean*. These allow you to infer where the passage takes place and draw the conclusion that the location is a college campus.

39. Based on the passage, the reader can conclude that the:

A. Students believe it is okay for them to break the law

B. Students believe that the new dean is guilty of discrimination

C. Dean is a reasonable man who does not discriminate

D. Dean is not likely to take the job

Answer: B. Students believe that the new dean is guilty of discrimination

Even though the passage does not state this, you can infer that the students think the dean is guilty because they are demonstrating against his hire. If they believed he was innocent of the charges, they would not likely be demonstrating.

Read the passage below and answer the question that follows.

Climbers must endure several barriers on the way to the summit of Mount Everest, including other hikers, steep jagged rocks, and lots of snow. But climbers often find the most grueling part of the trip is their climb back down. They are thoroughly exhausted, and the lack of oxygen often causes problems with judgment. Sometimes climbers feel overconfident because they think that the most difficult part of the trip is over. They might become careless and not take the necessary precautions. Also, weather can become dangerous if a climber waits too long to descend.

40. The author of this passage would agree that:

A. Accidents on Mount Everest are rare but serious

B. Because of the altitude, the weather does not affect climbers

C. Climbers must receive special training on how to descend

D. Climbers should never climb Mount Everest without oxygen

Answer: C. Climbers must receive special training on how to descend

Because the author stresses the dangers when climbing down the mountain, you can conclude that it is important to have special training on how to descend Mount Everest.

Read the passage below and answer the question that follows.

Someone once said that the two most difficult jobs in the world—voting and being a parent—are given to rank amateurs. The consequences of this inequity are voter apathy and inept parenting leading to, on the one hand, an apparent failure of the democratic process and, on the other hand, misbehaving and misguided children.

41. Based on this passage, the author would be most likely to agree that:

A. Parents should take parenting classes

B. Schools should discipline children

C. Most people should not have children

D. Most children misbehave

Answer: A. Parents should take parenting classes

The author believes parenting is difficult job, and therefore, it is logical to think that the author believes parents should have training.

Read the passage below and answer questions 42 to 44.

While one day recycling may be mandatory in all states, right now it is voluntary in many communities. Those of us who participate in recycling know just how important it is. By recycling glass, aluminum cans, and plastic bottles, we have reduced the volume of disposable trash by one-third, thereby extending the useful life of local landfills by over a decade. Imagine the difference if those dramatic results were achieved nationwide. The amount of reusable items we thoughtlessly throw away is staggering. For example, Americans dispose of enough steel every day to supply Detroit car manufacturers for three months. Additionally, we dispose of enough aluminum annually to rebuild the nation's air fleet. These statistics, available from the Environmental Protection Agency, should encourage us to watch what we throw away.

42. According to this passage:

A. Through recycling, disposable trash as been reduced by one-half

B. We throw away enough steel each day to supply Detroit car manufacturers for three months

C. Most communities require citizens to recycle glass, aluminum cans, and plastic bottles

D. The United States government has a plan to impose mandatory recycling in every state

Answer: B. We throw away enough steel each day to supply Detroit car manufacturers for three months.

Read each answer choice carefully. Answer choice B is the only fact that is stated in the passage.

43. The author of this passage would agree that recycling

A. Is beneficial

B. Should be mandatory

C. Is only slightly effective

D. Causes several serious problems

Answer: A. Is beneficial

The passage states the many benefits of recycling, such as extending the useful life of local landfills. Therefore, it is reasonable to infer that the author would agree that recycling is beneficial.

44. According to this passage, recycling is:

A. Effortless

B. Time-consuming

C. Mandatory

D. Voluntary

Answer: D. Voluntary

The passage states that recycling is voluntary, so answer choice D is the correct answer.

Read the passage below and answer the question that follows.

Rainforests recycle air and clean water. The trees capture and remove a large amount of the carbon dioxide from the air. This decreases the overall temperature of the planet.

45. **According to this passage, it's reasonable to assume that:**

   A. Temperatures will decrease if rainforests are destroyed

   B. Carbon dioxide is harmful to plants and animals

   C. The rainforests affect people throughout the world

   D. The temperature of the rainforests is decreasing

   Answer: C. The rainforests affect people throughout the world.

   The final sentence of the passage is evidence that allows us to infer that the rainforests affect people throughout the world. It might be tempting to choose answer choice A, but be sure to read the passage carefully: According to the passage, it is fair to assume that temperatures would *increase*, not *decrease*.

Read the passage below and answer the question that follows.

Countless species of snakes, some more dangerous than others, still lurk on the urban fringes of Florida's towns and cities. They will often invade domestic spaces, frightening people and their pets.

46. **According to this passage, it is reasonable to assume that:**

   A. Snakes are a problem in Florida

   B. The people of Florida work to protect their snakes

   C. The snakes in Florida are harmless

   D. Snakes are more prevalent in Florida than in other states

   Answer: A. Snakes are a problem in Florida

   The passage states that the snakes scare people and have invaded towns and cities. The reader can therefore infer that the snakes are a problem.

Read the passage below and answer the question that follows.

The local charity for the homeless is planning to open a new soup kitchen located on Main Street. Its objective is to provide three well-rounded meals to as many as 75 homeless people each day. The kitchen will open at 7:00 in the morning for breakfast and will continue to serve food throughout the day until dinner is over at 6:30 p.m. Local supermarkets have already agreed to supply food to the charity; however, they are still in need of volunteers to help run the food lines. In addition, further donations of money and food are needed to supply the patrons adequately.

47. **According to the passage:**

   A. The soup kitchen will serve up to 75 people each week

   B. All volunteers have been lined up

   C. People may contribute cash donations

   D. Local supermarkets will be providing all the food

   Answer: C. People may contribute cash donations

   According to the last sentence, the charity is seeking donations of money and food. Therefore, you know that people may contribute cash donations.

Read the passage below and answer questions 48 to 50.

No one really knows how Valentine's Day started. There are several legends, however, which are often told. The first attributes Valentine's Day to a Christian priest who lived in Rome during the third century, under the rule of Emperor Claudius. Rome was at war, and apparently, Claudius felt that married men did not fight as well as bachelors. Consequently, Claudius banned marriage for the duration of the war. However, Valentinus, the priest, risked his life to marry couples secretly in violation of Claudius' law.

The second legend is even more romantic. In this story, Valentinus is a prisoner, having been condemned to death for refusing to worship pagan deities. While in jail, he fell in love with his jailer's daughter, who happened to be blind. He prayed daily for her sight to return, and, miraculously, it did. On February 14, the day that he was condemned to die, he was allowed to write the young woman a note. In this farewell letter, he promised eternal love, and signed at the bottom of the page the now famous words, "Your Valentine."

48. **According to this passage:**

   A. Emperor Claudius lived during the third century

   B. The legend is believed by all Romans

   C. Emperor Claudius believed in marriage

   D. Only two legends exist about Valentine's Day

Answer: A. Emperor Claudius lived during the third century

The first paragraph states that a priest lived in Rome during the third century, under the rule of Emperor Claudius. Therefore, you know that Emperor Claudius lived during the third century. You might be tempted to choose answer choice D, but be careful: Two legends are discussed in the passage, but the first paragraph states that there are several legends, not just the two in this passage.

49. **According to the second legend:**

    A. Valentinus was blind

    B. The daughter prayed for her father's sight

    C. Valentinus was condemned to die

    D. Valentinus was freed

    Answer: C. Valentinus was condemned to die

    The passage states that he had been condemned to death. None of the other answer choices are facts that are in the passage.

50. **According to the passage, where does the first legend take place?**

    A. France

    B. Germany

    C. Russia

    D. Italy

    Answer: D. Italy

    The legend takes place in Rome, which is in Italy

Arithmetic Reasoning

51. **Michael can do 23 pushups, Shin can do 31 pushups, and Dirk can do 17 more pushups than Michael. How many more pushups can Dirk do than Shin?**

    A. 6

    B. 8

    C. 9

    D. 14

    Answer: C. 9

    You have been asked *how many more* pushups Dirk can do than Shin. You need to subtract the number than Shin can do from the number that Dirk can do. Dirk can do 17 more than Michael (23 + 17), which equals 40. Subtract the number Shin can do, 31, from the number Dirk can do, 40. The answer is 9.

52. **The Rosen family spends $150.00 to have cable television installed. They then spend $39.99 per month for cable television service. What is the total amount that they spend on cable television during the first year?**

    A. $189.99

    B. $479.88

    C. $629.88

    D. $2,279.88

Answer: C. $629.88

They spend $39.99 per month for cable television service, so for an entire year, they would spend $39.99 × 12, or $479.88. They also spend $150.00 to have cable television installed, so add $479.88 and $150.00. The answer is $629.88.

53. Ellie buys bottles of water by the gross. One gross costs $72.00. What is the cost of each bottle of water?

A. $0.50

B. $0.72

C. $3.00

D. $6.00

Answer: A. $0.50

A gross is a dozen dozens, or 144. 144 bottles cost $72.00. To find the cost of each bottle, divide $72.00 by 144. The answer is $0.50.

54. Alicia bought 9 golden delicious apples for $4.23, and Glenn bought 7 red delicious apples for $3.64. Who got the better deal, and what was the difference in price per apple?

A. Alicia; $0.05

B. Alicia; $0.59

C. Glenn; $0.05

D. Glenn; $0.59

Answer: A. Alicia; $0.05

To find out who got the better deal, you need to find the price per apple. $4.23 ÷ 9 is $0.47, and $3.64 ÷ 7 is $0.52, so Alicia got the better deal. The difference between $0.47 and $0.52 is $0.52 − $0.47, or $0.05.

55. Three friends were playing a pickup game of basketball. Julia scored twice as many baskets as Aiden. Samir scored 3 more basket than Aiden. Together, they scored 27 baskets. How many baskets did Julia score?

A. 6

B. 8

C. 9

D. 12

Answer: D. 12

Let x = the number of baskets Aiden scored. Then $2x$ = the number of baskets Julia scored, and $x + 3$ = the number of baskets Samir scored. The sum of these is 27. When you solve for x, the result is 6, but be careful: The variable, x, is the number of baskets Aiden scored. You were asked for the number of baskets Julia scored. She scored twice as many as Aiden, so the correct answer is 12.

56. Juan and Niki plow a field. Juan plows $\frac{1}{12}$ of the field, and Niki plows $\frac{1}{3}$ of the field. How much of the field is left unplowed?

A. $\frac{1}{6}$

B. $\frac{5}{12}$

C. $\frac{7}{12}$

D. $\frac{5}{6}$

Answer: C. $\frac{7}{12}$

First, add the fractional parts that are plowed. To add the fractions, they need to have a common denominator. If you multiply $\frac{1}{3}$ by $\frac{4}{4}$, the common denominator will be 12. Now add the fractions. Be careful: The result, $\frac{5}{12}$, is the amount of the field that has been *plowed*. You are asked how much is left *unplowed*. If $\frac{5}{12}$ of the field has been plowed, $\frac{12}{12} - \frac{5}{12}$, or $\frac{7}{12}$, is unplowed.

57. **A farmer has 10 acres of land. He wants to allot $\frac{2}{5}$ of an acre for each kind of vegetable. How many different kinds of vegetables can he plant?**

A. 25

B. 20

C. 6

D. 4

Answer: A. 25

He's going to *divide* 10 acres into plots that are $\frac{2}{5}$ of an acre, so you need to divide 10 by $\frac{2}{5}$. To divide by $\frac{2}{5}$, "flip" the fraction, and then multiply. $10 \times \frac{5}{2} = 25$.

58. **Bruno received a score of 80 on his midterm science test. On his final exam, his score increased by 15%. What was the score on his final exam?**

A. 95

B. 92

C. 81.5

D. 12

Answer: B. 92

To find 15% of 80, multiply 0.15 by 80. The result, 12, is the increase from his midterm to his final exam. To find the score on the final exam, add 12 to 80.

59. **A baseball player got 5% fewer hits in 2010 than he did in 2009. If he got 140 hits in 2009, how many hits did he get in 2010?**

A. 70

B. 126

C. 133

D. 147

Answer: C. 133

To find 5% of 140, multiply 0.05 by 140. The result, 7, is the decrease. Be careful: The player got fewer hits in 2010, not more. To find the number of hits in 2010, subtract 7 from 140.

60. **There are 39 men and 21 women in a softball league. What percent of the players are women?**

A. 35%

B. 46%

C. 54%

D. 65%

Answer: A. 35%

To find what percent one number is of another, divide the first number by the second. You want to find out what percent of the players are women; in other words, what percent 21 is of the total number of players. Be careful not to divide 21 by 39. You need to divide 21 by the total number of players, which is 60.

61. The cost of an Indian lunch buffet increased from $6.50 to $7.15. What was the percent increase?

    A. 65%

    B. 10%

    C. 6.5%

    D. 0.1%

    Answer: B. 10%

    First, find the amount that the price changed, and then divide that amount by the original price. The price increased by $0.65. Divide $0.65 by $6.50. The result is 0.1, or 10%.

62. When Vinny moved to Centerville, his car insurance premium increased from $795.00 to $969.90. What was the percent increase?

    A. 0.18%

    B. 0.22%

    C. 18%

    D. 22%

    Answer: D. 22%

    First, find the amount that the premium changed, and then divide that amount by the original cost. The premium increased $174.90. Divide $174.90 by $795.00. The result is 0.22, or 22%.

63. Sasha deposits $250.00 into a savings account that earns an annual interest rate of 5.5%. He doesn't withdraw from the account or deposit any additional money in the account. What is the balance after one year?

    A. $13.75

    B. $137.50

    C. $263.75

    D. $387.50

    Answer: C. $263.75

    First, find the interest earned; then add the interest to the amount invested. The interest is 5.5% of $250.00, or 0.055×250, which equals 13.75. To find the balance, add the interest, $13.75, to the amount invested, $250.00. The answer is $263.75.

64. Jorge has 78 action DVDs and 26 comedy DVDs. What is the ratio of action DVDs to comedy DVDs?

    A. $\frac{1}{3}$

    B. $\frac{3}{1}$

    C. $\frac{2}{3}$

    D. $\frac{3}{2}$

    Answer: B. $\frac{3}{1}$

    The ratio of action DVDs to comedy DVDs is $\frac{78}{26}$. A common factor of both 78 and 26 is 26. Divide each number by 26, and the reduced ratio is $\frac{3}{1}$.

65. Janine has an annual salary of $22,000 per year. Leonard's annual salary is 25% higher than Janine's. What is the ratio of Janine's salary to Leonard's salary?

   A. $\frac{1}{4}$

   B. $\frac{4}{1}$

   C. $\frac{4}{5}$

   D. $\frac{5}{4}$

Answer: C. $\frac{4}{5}$

Leonard's annual salary is 25% higher than Janine's. To find Leonard's salary, first find 25% of $22,000. Remember, when you hear the word "of," multiply. 0.25 times $22,000 is $5,500, so Leonard's salary is $5,500 more than Janine's. To find his salary, add her salary, $22,000, to $5,500. His salary is $27,500. The ratio of Janine's salary to Leonard's salary is $\frac{22,000}{27,500}$. This ratio reduces. To reduce the ratio, divide the numerator and denominator by common factors until it can't be reduced anymore. The ratio of her salary to his is $\frac{4}{5}$.

66. If Lynn can set up 26 computers in 6 hours, how many computers can she set up in 15 hours?

   A. 65

   B. 62

   C. 60

   D. 52

Answer: A. 65

The question is asking, "26 computers is to 6 hours, as how many computers is to 15 hours?" Set up the proportion $\frac{26}{6} = \frac{x}{15}$. To solve for x, multiply both sides of the equation by 15. Then do the math. The answer is 65.

67. The wingspan on a scale model of an airplane is 1.5 feet. The scale of the model is 1:50. What is the actual wingspan of the plane?

   A. 33 feet

   B. 50 feet

   C. 75 feet

   D. 150 feet

Answer: C. 75 feet

Set up the proportion $\frac{1.5}{x}$. To solve for x, multiply both sides of the equation by x, and then multiply both sides of the equation by 50. The answer is 75.

68. A contractor remodeling a kitchen is installing two triangular tiles on the floor. Two triangular pieces of tile are similar. If the shortest sides of the tiles are 4 inches and 6 inches, and the longest side of the larger tile is 15 inches, how long is the longest side of the smaller tile?

   A. 7.5 inches

   B. 10 inches

   C. 12 inches

   D. 13 inches

Answer: B. 10 inches

In similar shapes, the ratios of the corresponding sides are equal. Write the ratios and set them equal to each other. The ratio of the shortest sides is $\frac{4}{6}$, and the ratio of the longest sides is $\frac{x}{15}$. Set them equal to each other and write the proportion $\frac{4}{6} = \frac{x}{15}$. To solve for x, multiply both sides of the equation by 15. Then do the math. The answer is 10.

69. DeShawn reaches into a bag of candy. There are 10 butterscotch candies and 14 chocolate candies in the bag. What is the probability that he will choose a butterscotch candy?

    A. $\frac{5}{7}$

    B. $\frac{14}{24}$

    C. $\frac{5}{12}$

    D. $\frac{1}{10}$

Answer: C. $\frac{5}{12}$

To find the probability, divide the number of acceptable outcomes, in this case, the number of butterscotch candies, by the total number of possible outcomes. There are 10 butterscotch candies and a total of 24 candies, so the probability is $\frac{10}{24}$, which reduces to $\frac{5}{12}$.

70. Sanjay is playing a board game that has a spinner that is divided into four equal sections of different colors. He spins the spinner twice. What is the probability that the spinner will land on red both times?

    A. $\frac{1}{2}$

    B. $\frac{1}{4}$

    C. $\frac{1}{8}$

    D. $\frac{1}{16}$

Answer: D. $\frac{1}{16}$

The probability that the spinner will land on red each time he spins is 1 out of 4, or $\frac{1}{4}$. To find the probability of a compound event, multiply the probabilities. In this case, to find the probability that it will land on red twice, multiply $\frac{1}{4}$ by $\frac{1}{4}$. Therefore, the chance that it will land on red both times is $\frac{1}{16}$.

71. A window washer is paid 35¢ per window washed. If he can wash 24 windows per hour, how much money can he earn in one hour and 15 minutes?

    A. $10.50

    B. $9.66

    C. $9.24

    D. $8.40

Answer: A. $10.50

First, find the amount earned in one hour. He can wash 24 windows in one hour. 35¢ (or $0.35) per window × 24 windows is $8.40. To find the amount earned in one hour and 15 minutes (or one and one-quarter hour), multiply $8.40 by 1.25. The answer is $10.50.

72. Maria works four days a week selling hot dogs from a street cart. She pays $325.00 per week to rent the cart, and she pays $145.00 per week for hot dogs, buns, and other supplies. She sells the hot dogs for $2.50 each. How many hot dogs does she need to sell each week in order to make a profit?

A. 189

B. 188

C. 48

D. 47

Answer: A. 189

In order to make a profit, she needs to earn more than she spends. Her expenses are rent ($325.00) plus supplies ($145.00). Her total expenses are $470.00. To make a profit, she needs to make more than $470.00 per week. She sells hot dogs for $2.50 each. $2.50 times what number is more than $470.00? Divide $470.00 by $2.50, and the result is 188. However, be careful: If she sells 188 hot dogs, she'll make exactly $470.00, so she'll break even. In order to make a profit, she needs to sell one more hot dog, so the answer is 189.

73. Janelle buys 14 pieces of ribbon from a fabric store. Each piece is 18 inches long. If the ribbon costs $3.70 per foot, what is the total cost of the ribbon Janelle buys?

A. $51.80

B. $68.11

C. $77.70

D. $932.40

Answer: B. $77.70

The total length of ribbon she bought is 14×18 inches, or 252 inches. The cost of the ribbon is given per foot, not per inch, so you need to convert from inches to feet. Multiply 252 inches by the conversion factor $\frac{1 \text{ foot}}{12 \text{ inches}}$. Therefore, 252 inches is equal to 21 feet. To find the total cost, multiply the number of feet of ribbon, 21, by the cost per foot, $3.70.

74. A medical device manufacturer has a 12-foot piece of plastic tubing. The manufacturer is going to cut it into pieces that are 3 inches long. How many pieces will there be?

A. 3

B. 4

C. 40

D. 48

Answer: D. 48

You need to divide the total length of the tubing into 3-inch pieces, but you're given the total length in feet, so you need to convert units. To convert 12 feet to inches, multiply 12 feet by the conversion factor $\frac{12 \text{ inches}}{1 \text{ foot}}$. Therefore, 12 feet is equal to 144 inches. To divide the 144-inch piece into 3-inch pieces, divide 144 by 3. The answer is 48.

75. On Monday, the price of a gallon of gas was $3.25. The price increased 9¢ per gallon Tuesday. The price increased an additional 2¢ per gallon Wednesday. The price then dropped 4¢ per gallon Thursday. By Friday, the price per gallon was $3.33. What was the average price per gallon of gas during the five days?

    A. $3.28

    B. $3.29

    C. $3.32

    D. $4.15

    Answer: C. $3.32

    First, find the price per gallon each day. The prices were $3.25, $3.34, $3.36, $3.32, and $3.33. Now add all the prices together. The total is $16.60. Divide by the number of values, 5. The answer is $3.32.

Mathematics Knowledge

76. 5! = ?

    A. 20

    B. 25

    C. 60

    D. 120

    Answer: D. 120

    5! is 5 factorial. $5! = 5 \times 4 \times 3 \times 2 \times 1$, which equals 120.

77. $\frac{3^{16}}{3^4} = ?$

    A. 3^4

    B. 3^6

    C. 3^{12}

    D. 3^{20}

    Answer: C. 3^{12}

    The rule is $\frac{n^a}{n^b} = n^{a-b}$, so you need to subtract the exponents. $\frac{3^{16}}{3^4} = 3^{16-4} = 3^{12}$.

78. $(x^6)^3 = ?$

    A. x^2

    B. x^3

    C. x^9

    D. x^{18}

    Answer: D. x^{18}

    The rule is $(n^a)^b = n^{a \times b}$, so you need to multiply the exponents. $(x^6)^3 = x^{6 \times 3} = x^{18}$.

79. $\sqrt[3]{216}$

    A. 4

    B. 6

    C. 7

    D. 8

    Answer: B. 6

    $6 \times 6 \times 6 = 216$. Therefore, $\sqrt[3]{216} = 6$.

80. $\sqrt{(25 + 36 + y)^2} = ?$

A. $11 + y$

B. $11 + y^2$

C. $61 + y$

D. $61 + y^2$

Answer: C. 61 + y

The square root of a number is the number that, when multiplied by itself, produces the number. What number when multiplied by itself produces $(25 + 36 + y)^2$? The answer is $(25 + 36 + y)$, because $(25 + 36 + y)$ times $(25 + 36 + y)$ equals $(25 + 36 + y)^2$. Simplify $(25 + 36 + y)$, and the answer is $61 + y$.

81. $5 + 3 \times \sqrt{16} + (11 - 9) \times 6 = ?$

A. 29

B. 44

C. 114

D. 288

Answer: A. 29

First, perform the operation inside parentheses. Next, find the square root of 16, which is 4. Then multiply from left to right. Finally, add and subtract from left to right.

82. $20 - 5(7 + 2) - 8^2 \div 4 = ?$

A. -41

B. $17\frac{3}{4}$

C. 119

D. 131

Answer: A. −41

First, perform the operation inside parentheses. Next, find 8 squared, which is 64. Then multiply and divide from left to right. Finally, subtract from left to right.

83. Solve for x: $2 - 4 \times 10 - 3x = 7x + 3 - 2x - 9$

A. -16

B. -4

C. $-1\frac{3}{4}$

D. $3\frac{1}{4}$

Answer: B. −4

First, perform the multiplication. Then add and subtract like terms. The result is $-38 - 3x = 5x - 6$. Add $3x$ to both sides of the equation and add 6 to both sides of the equation. The result is $-32 = 8x$. Divide both sides of the equation by 8, and the result is $-4 = x$.

84. Solve for x: $y^4 + (10 - 2)(7 - 5) = y^2 \times y^3$

A. 4

B. 10

C. 16

D. 24

Answer: C. 16

First, perform the operations inside parentheses. The result is $y^4 + 8 \times 2 = y^2 \times y^3$. Then multiply from left to right. Remember: According to the rules of exponents, when you multiply, you add exponents. The result is $y^4 + 16 = y^5$. Subtract y^4 from both sides of the equation, and the answer is 16.

85. Solve for x: $12(x - 2) + 7 = 19$.

   A. $\frac{1}{6}$

   B. $1\frac{1}{6}$

   C. 2

   D. 3

Answer: D. 3

After distributing 12 to the x and the 2, the equation becomes $12x - 24 + 7 = 19$. Add -24 and 7 and you have the equation $12x - 17 = 19$. Add 17 to both sides of the equation, and the equation becomes $12x = 36$. Finally, divide both sides of the equation by 12. The answer is 3.

86. Solve for d: $100 - 5(d + 8) = 7(d - 3) - 9d$

   A. 23

   B. 27

   C. 37

   D. $53\frac{2}{3}$

Answer: B. 27

After distributing on both sides of the equation, the equation becomes $100 - 5d - 40 = 7d - 21 - 9d$. Simplify both sides of the equation, and the equation becomes $60 - 5d = -21 - 2d$. Add 21 to both sides of the equation, and the equation becomes $81 - 5d = -2d$. Add $5d$ to both sides of the equation, and the equation becomes $81 = 3d$. Finally, divide both sides by 3. The answer is 27.

87. Evaluate the expression $\frac{m^6}{m^3} \times 4m$, if $m = 5$.

   A. 500

   B. 1,000

   C. 1,500

   D. 2,500

Answer: D. 2,500

When you substitute 5 for m, the expression becomes $\frac{5^6}{5^3} \times 4 \times 5$. According to the rules of exponents, when you divide, you subtract exponents, so the expression becomes $5^3 \times 4 \times 5$. 5 cubed is 125. Finally, do the multiplication. The answer is 2,500.

88. Evaluate the expression $9p - 8q \times (p - q) + q^2$, if $p = 8$ and $q = 6$.

   A. 12

   B. 50

   C. 84

   D. 112

Answer: A. 12

Substitute 8 for p and 6 for q, and the expression becomes $72 - 48 \times 2 + 36$. Then remember the order of operations: multiply, and then add and subtract. The answer is 12.

89. Solve: $2 + 5(s - 4) > \sqrt{49}$

   A. $s < 1$

   B. $s > 1$

   C. $s < 5$

   D. $s > 5$

Answer: D. $s > 5$

On the left side of the inequality, distribute. The inequality becomes $2 + 5s - 20 > \sqrt{49}$. On the right side of the inequality, take the square root of 49, which is 7. Subtract 20 from 2 and the inequality becomes $5s - 18 > 7$. Add 18 to both sides of the inequality, and then divide both sides by 5. The answer is $s > 5$.

90. **Solve:** $-2t < 2 - (7 - 4)^2 + \sqrt{121}$

   A. $t < -2$

   B. $t > -2$

   C. $t < 2$

   D. $t > 2$

Answer: B. $t > -2$

First, perform the operation inside parentheses. The inequality becomes $-2t < 2 - 3^2 + \sqrt{121}$. Square the 3 and take the square root of 121, and the inequality becomes $-2t < 2 - 9 + 11$. Simplify the right side, and the inequality becomes $-2t < 4$. Finally, divide both sides by -2. Remember: When you divide both sides of an inequality by a negative number, you need to flip the inequality sign. The answer is $t > -2$.

91. **What is the name of the shape below?**

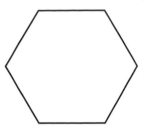

   A. Trapezoid

   B. Parallelogram

   C. Hexagon

   D. Pentagon

Answer: C. Hexagon

A hexagon is a two-dimensional figure with six sides.

92. **The angle below is what type of angle?**

   A. Scalene

   B. Acute

   C. Obtuse

   D. Right

Answer: B. Acute

An acute angle is less than 90°, the angle made by the corner of a piece of paper.

93. The triangle below is what type of triangle?

A. Equilateral

B. Isosceles

C. Obtuse

D. Right

Answer: B. Isosceles

An isosceles triangle has two sides of the same length.

94. Bernie is going to tile his kitchen floor. One side of his square kitchen is 14 feet long. Tiles that are 1 square foot cost $1.15 each. How much will it cost to tile the floor?

A. $28.00

B. $32.20

C. $196.00

D. $225.40

Answer: D. $225.40

You need to find the area of the square kitchen. The formula for area of a square is Area = s^2. Therefore, the area of the square is 196 ft², so he needs 196 square foot tiles. Square foot tiles cost $1.15 each. To find the total cost, multiply 196 by $1.15. The total cost is $225.40.

95. The perimeter of a rectangle is 42 cm, and the length of one side is 9 cm. What is the area of the rectangle?

A. 12 cm²

B. 42 cm²

C. 108 cm²

D. 441 cm²

Answer: C. 108 cm²

The perimeter of the rectangle is 42 cm. Perimeter = $2l + 2w$, and the length of one side is 9 cm. Therefore, $42 = 2 \times 9 + 2w$. When you solve for w, you find that the length of the other side is 12. You are asked for the area of the rectangle. The formula for area of a rectangle is Area = lw. Substitute 9 for length and 12 for width. The answer is 108 cm².

96. Jim installed an above-ground round swimming pool in his backyard. The pool is 12 feet wide. What is the approximate area of the ground that the pool covers?

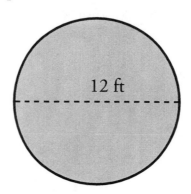

12 ft

A. 37.68 ft²

B. 75.36 ft²

C. 113.04 ft²

D. 452.16 ft²

Answer: C. 113.04 ft²

Area = πr^2. Be careful: You are given the diameter, not the radius. The radius is half the diameter, or 6 ft. Therefore, the area is $\pi \times 6^2$, or $\pi \times 36$. Substitute 3.14 for π, and the answer is 113.04. Therefore the area is approximately 113.04 ft².

97. There is a round fountain in Sawyer Park. The radius of the fountain is 3 meters. Billy walked around the edge of the fountain twice. How far did he walk?

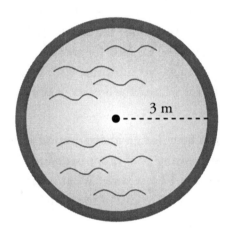

Fountain shown from above.

A. 3π m

B. 6π m

C. 9π m

D. 12π m

Answer: D. 12π m

Billy walked around the edge of the fountain. The distance around the edge of a circle is the circumference, and the formula for circumference = $2\pi r$. You can see that the answer choices are given in terms of pi, so you should *not* substitute 3.14 for π. Substitute 3 for the radius, and the result is 6π. Be careful, though: The question states that he walked around the fountain *twice*. Therefore, the answer is 12π meters.

98. Office Supplies Unlimited sells the small plastic storage cube shown below. What is the volume of the cube?

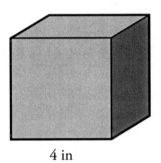

4 in

A. 8 in³

B. 12 in³

C. 16 in³

D. 64 in³

Answer: D. 64 in³

The formula for volume of a cube is Volume = s^3, where s is the length of one side. Substitute 4 for s, and the volume is $4^3 \times 4^3$ is the same as $4 \times 4 \times 4$, which equals 64. Therefore, the volume of the cube is 64 in³.

99. Maria built the storage box below to hold tools. What is the volume of the box?

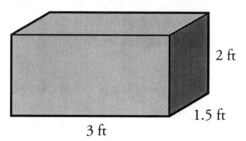

2 ft

1.5 ft

3 ft

A. 4.5 ft³

B. 6 ft³

C. 9 ft³

D. 27 ft³

Answer: C. 9 ft³

The formula for volume of a rectangular prism (or box) is Volume = *lwh*. Substitute the length, width, and height, and the volume is 3 × 1.5 × 2, which equals 9. Therefore, the volume of the box is 9 ft³.

100. What is the approximate volume of a can that has a diameter of 6 inches and a height of 8 inches?

A. 72 in³

B. 226.08 in³

C. 301.44 in³

D. 904.32 in³

Answer: B. 226.08 in³

Volume of a cylinder = $\pi r^2 h$. Be careful: You are given the diameter (6 inches), but you need the radius. Remember that the radius is half the diameter. Substitute the radius and the height, and the volume is $\pi \times 3^2 \times 8$, or 72π. Substitute 3.14 for π, and the result is 226.08. Therefore, the approximate volume is 226.08 in³. The answer is approximate because π is only *approximately* equal to 3.14.

General Science

101. An inflated balloon is left in a refrigerator for a few hours. What do you predict will happen?

A. The balloon will shrink

B. The balloon will expand

C. The balloon volume will remain the same

D. The pressure in the balloon will increase

Answer: A. The balloon will shrink

A balloon is very flexible and will change shape easily. Therefore, the pressure inside the balloon won't decrease—if the pressure decreased inside the balloon, it would simply get smaller. You know that the temperature decreased, and the pressure remained the same. According to the gas laws, at a constant pressure, a decrease in temperature will cause a decrease in volume. In other words, the balloon will shrink.

102. The nucleus of an atom is:

A. Positively charged

B. Negatively charged

C. Neutral

D. Sometimes positively charged, sometimes negatively charged

Answer: A. Positively charged

The nucleus contains only protons, which have a positive charge, and neutrons, which are uncharged. Therefore, the nucleus is positively charged. The atom as a whole is neutral because the negative charge of the electrons equals the positive charge of the protons.

103. The atomic number of an oxygen atom is 8, and its mass number is 17. This means that the atom of oxygen has:

A. 8 neutrons

B. 9 neutrons

C. 17 neutrons

D. No neutrons

Answer: B. 9 neutrons

Since the atomic number is 8, the number of protons is 8. The mass number is the total number of protons and neutrons. Therefore, the number of neutrons is $17 - 8 = 9$.

104. The rows of the periodic table are called:

A. Families

B. Elements

C. Groups

D. Periods

Answer: D. Periods

The periods are the rows numbered down the left side of the periodic table. The columns of the periodic table are called groups or families.

105. Which of these is a physical change?

A. Fireworks are set off

B. A nail becomes rusty

C. Ice melts into water

D. An antacid makes you feel better

Answer: C. Ice melts into water

The melting of ice is a physical change because the water molecules remain unchanged. It is the same substance, water, in two different states—solid and liquid. The other choices involve chemical reactions. There is a rapid release of heat and light energy when fireworks are set off. When a nail becomes rusty, the iron of the nail combines with oxygen to create a red coating. An antacid neutralizes stomach acid in a chemical reaction.

106. A marble rolls down a smooth curved track. Why does it move more quickly as it goes down?

A. Some of its potential energy is changed into kinetic energy

B. Some of its kinetic energy is changed into potential energy

C. The total energy of the marble increases

D. The mechanical energy of the marble increases

Answer: A. Some of its potential energy is changed into kinetic energy

As the marble moves to lower heights, its potential energy is lowered. Since little energy is lost to friction on a smooth track, the total mechanical energy (PE + KE) stays about the same. Therefore, the kinetic energy of the marble increases. In other words, the marble moves more quickly.

107. **You see a flash of lightning, but the rumble of thunder only gets to you after several seconds. Why is that?**

    A. Thunder happens several seconds after the lightning flash

    B. The thunder and lightning are from two different locations

    C. The sound of thunder moves much more slowly than light from the lightning flash

    D. The light from the lightning flash moves much more slowly than the sound of thunder

    Answer: C. The sound of thunder moves much more slowly than light from the lightning flash

    The speed of light is about 300,000,000 meters per second, while the speed of sound is 343 meters per second, so sound is about a million times slower than light. Therefore, even though the thunder and lightning happen at the same place and at the same time, the light gets to you much more quickly than the sound.

108. **Refraction does not occur in:**

    A. Eyeglasses

    B. Rearview mirrors

    C. Rainbows

    D. A lighted fountain

    Answer: B. Rearview mirrors

    Refraction occurs whenever light moves from one medium to another. For choice A, light passes from air to glass and back. For choices C and D, light rays move between air and water. In the case of a rearview mirror, light is reflected and stays in the air. It does not enter another medium.

109. **You add insulation to your walls to avoid heat loss in winter through:**

    A. Conduction

    B. Convection

    C. Radiation

    D. Both convection and radiation

    Answer: A. Conduction

    Since the temperature outside your walls in winter is colder than the temperature on the inside, heat flows from the inside to the outside through conduction. Putting in insulation of material with low heat conductivity helps to reduce this loss.

110. **The planet that has an atmosphere composed mainly of oxygen and nitrogen is:**

    A. Jupiter

    B. Venus

    C. Neptune

    D. Earth

Answer: D. Earth

Earth's atmosphere is about 80% nitrogen and 20% oxygen. It is the only planet that supports life.

111. **The gibbous moon:**

   A. Is between the sun and the earth

   B. Is less illuminated than the crescent moon, as seen from the earth

   C. Has more than half of its earth-facing side illuminated

   D. Has exactly half of its earth-facing side illuminated

Answer: C. Has more than half of its earth-facing side illuminated

The gibbous moon is seen between the first quarter and the full moon during waxing, and between the full moon and the third quarter during waning. So its illumination is between half and full.

112. **The inner core of the earth is solid because**

   A. Otherwise the earth would collapse

   B. It is cooler than the outer core

   C. It is under very high pressure

   D. It is between 5 and 70 km thick

Answer: C. It is under very high pressure

Even though the inner core of the earth is very hot, it is solid because it is under very high pressure and is extremely dense.

113. **The outermost layer of the earth is called the:**

   A. Inner core

   B. Outer core

   C. Crust

   D. Mantle

Answer: C. Crust

The crust is the outermost layer of the earth. It is between 5 and 70 km thick.

114. **Plate movements are <u>not</u> responsible for producing:**

   A. Earthquake zones

   B. Tornadoes

   C. Mountain ranges

   D. Volcanoes

Answer: B. Tornadoes

Plate movements produce many features of the earth's surface, including mountain ranges, volcanoes, and earthquake zones. Tornadoes have no direct link with plate tectonics.

115. **Thick, fluffy dark rain clouds are called:**

   A. Cumulonimbus

   B. Stratonimbus

   C. Stratocumulus

   D. Cirrocumulus

Answer: A. Cumulonimbus

Since "cumulo" refers to thick, fluffy clouds, and "nimbus" refers to dark rain clouds, cumulonimbus clouds combine both of these characteristics.

116. Thunderstorms are typically associated with:

    A. Warm fronts

    B. Cold fronts

    C. Occluded fronts

    D. Stationary fronts

    Answer: B. Cold fronts

    Cold fronts are associated with violent weather more often than other kinds of fronts.

117. What structure would not be found in a prokaryotic cell?

    A. Cellular membrane

    B. Nucleus

    C. Cytoplasm

    D. Ribosome

    Answer: B. Nucleus

    Prokaryotic cells do not have a nucleus; they do have a cellular membrane, cytoplasm, and ribosomes. Any cell with a nucleus is, by definition, a eukaryotic cell.

118. Which term describes the entire contents of the cell, including the organelles?

    A. Cytosol

    B. Cytoplasm

    C. Nucleus

    D. Cellular membrane

    Answer: B. Cytoplasm

    The cellular membrane surrounds and bounds the cell. The cytosol is the fluid inside the cell. The cytosol and the organelles are collectively known as the cytoplasm.

119. What type of structure would identify a cell as a plant cell?

    A. Chloroplast

    B. Nucleus

    C. Cytoplasm

    D. Ribosome

    Answer: A. Chloroplast

    Plant cells contain all of these structures—a nucleus, cytoplasm, ribosomes, and chloroplasts. But *all* eukaryotic cells contain a nucleus, cytoplasm, and ribosomes. Only a chloroplast would definitively identify a cell as a plant cell. Chloroplasts are found in photosynthetic organisms, such as plants.

120. What is the function of the mitochondria in an animal cell?

    A. To transport materials throughout the cell

    B. To produce usable energy

    C. To package molecules made elsewhere in the cell

    D. To protect the genetic material

    Answer: B. To produce usable energy

    Mitochondria are the site of cellular respiration, which converts nutrients in the cell into energy.

121. The scientific name for humans is *Homo sapiens*. Choose the proper classification, beginning with kingdom and ending with order.

   A. Animalia, Mammalia, Primate, Hominidae

   B. Animalia, Chordata, *Homo, sapiens*

   C. Animalia, Chordata, Mammalia, Primate

   D. Chordata, Primate, *Homo, sapiens*

Answer: C. Animalia, Chordata, Mammalia, Primate

The order of classification for humans is as follows: Kingdom, Animalia; Phylum, Chordata; Class, Mammalia; Order, Primate; Family, Hominadae; Genus, *Homo*; Species, *sapiens*.

122. Which of the following is an example of a producer?

   A. A mouse

   B. A person

   C. A worm

   D. A tree

Answer: D. A tree

A producer is an organism that makes its own food, usually through photosynthesis. All plants are producers; therefore, a tree is a producer.

123. The brain is part of what system?

   A. Musculoskeletal system

   B. Circulatory system

   C. Respiratory system

   D. Nervous system

Answer: D. Nervous system

In humans, the nervous system is composed of the central nervous system (e.g., brain and spinal column) and the peripheral nervous systems (the nerves that run throughout the body).

124. The lungs are part of what system?

   A. Musculoskeletal system

   B. Circulatory system

   C. Respiratory system

   D. Nervous system

Answer: C. Respiratory system

All vertebrates, including humans, have lungs as their primary respiratory organ.

Mechanical Comprehension

125. If you push down on a table with a force of 10 lbs and the area of your palm is 15 square inches, how much pressure are you exerting on the table?

   A. 10 psi

   B. 15 psi

   C. 1.5 psi

   D. 0.667 psi

Answer: D. 0.667 psi

Since pressure is the force per unit area, here $P = \dfrac{F}{A} = \dfrac{10 \text{ lbs}}{15 \text{ sq. in.}} = 0.667$ psi.

126. A pulley lifts a box weighing 150 lbs 300 feet off the floor. How much work is done?

    A. 45,000 ft-lb

    B. 150 ft-lb

    C. 0.5 ft-lb

    D. 450 ft-lb

    Answer: A. 45,000 ft-lb

    Since the pulley has to overcome gravity to lift the box, the force it applies to the box is equal to force gravity exerts on the box, which is the weight of the box.

    Since work = force × distance, the work done by the pulley = 150 lbs × 300 ft = 45,000 ft-lb.

127. A pulley lifts a box weighing 150 lbs 300 feet from the floor. If the pulley lifts the box in 3 minutes, how much power does it use?

    A. 45,000 ft-lb/min

    B. 135,000 ft-lb/min

    C. 3,000 ft-lb/min

    D. 15,000 ft-lb/min

    Answer: D. 15,000 ft-lb/min

    The work done by the pulley was calculated in the previous problem. The work done was 45,000 ft-lb. Since power is the rate of doing work, the power expended by the pulley = $\frac{\text{Work}}{\text{Time}}$ = $\frac{45,000 \text{ ft-lb}}{3 \text{ min.}}$ = 15,000 ft-lb/min.

128. The pair of tongs below is:

    A. Not a lever

    B. A first class lever

    C. A second class lever

    D. A third class lever

    Answer: D. A third class lever

    A pair of tongs is a third class lever because the effort (the pressure you apply to it) is between the fulcrum (the folded end) and the load (the object you are picking up). Since a pair of tongs has two arms, you can think of it technically as a pair of third class levers.

129. A first class lever has the load placed 2 inches from the fulcrum and effort applied 6 inches from the fulcrum. Its ideal mechanical advantage is:

    A. 6

    B. 3.5

    C. 3

    D. 2.5

    Answer: C. 3

    Ideal mechanical advantage of a lever = $\frac{\text{Length of effort arm}}{\text{Length of load arm}}$ = $\frac{6 \text{ in.}}{2 \text{ in.}}$ = 3.

130. A first class lever has the load placed 2 inches from the fulcrum and effort applied 6 inches from the fulcrum. It has a rusty fulcrum with a lot of resistance. It can only lift a load of 5 pounds when an effort of 2 pounds is applied. Its actual mechanical advantage is:

A. 6

B. 3.5

C. 3

D. 2.5

Answer: D. 2.5

Actual mechanical advantage of a lever (or any machine) = Output force (load lifted)/Input force (effort put in) = $\frac{5 \text{ lb}}{2 \text{ lb}}$ = 2.5.

131. What is the mechanical advantage of a one-pulley system?

A. 1

B. 2

C. 3

D. It depends on the type of system

Answer: D. It depends on the type of system

If the pulley is fixed, the mechanical advantage is 1. If the pulley is moveable, the mechanical advantage is 2.

132.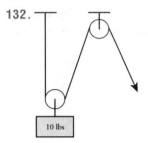

10 lbs

How much effort must be applied to the rope to lift the 10 lb weight?

A. 3.3 lbs

B. 5 lbs

C. 10 lbs

D. 20 lbs

Answer: B. 5 lbs

Note that 2 ropes are holding up the moveable pulley to the left. The gives a system a mechanical advantage of 2. Since, Effort = $\frac{\text{Load}}{2}$ = $\frac{10}{2}$ = 5 lbs. The fixed pulley to the right does not give any mechanical advantage. Its function is to change the direction of the effort so that one can pull down instead of having to pull up.

133. **Which of the two inclined planes shown below has the higher ideal mechanical advantage?**

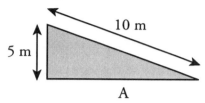

A

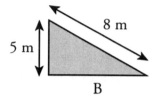

B

A. A

B. B

C. Both are equal

D. It is not possible to find the ideal mechanical advantage

Answer: A

For an inclined plane, the ideal mechanical advantage (IMA) is:

$$\frac{\text{Length of incline}}{\text{Height of topmost point}}.$$

For A, IMA $= \frac{10\text{ m}}{5\text{ m}} = 2.$

For B, IMA $= \frac{8\text{ m}}{5\text{ m}} = 1.6.$

134. **The top of a faucet has a radius of 2 inches. If the neck of the faucet has a half inch radius, what is the mechanical advantage of this system?**

A. 4

B. 0.25

C. 2

D. 2.5

Answer: A. 4

The faucet is a wheel and axle system where the top is the wheel with radius = 2 in and the neck is the axle with radius = 0.5 in. The mechanical advantage is:

$$\frac{\text{Radius of wheel}}{\text{Radius of axle}} = \frac{2\text{ in.}}{0.5\text{ in.}} = 4.$$

135.

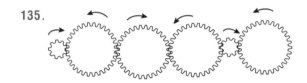

Four spur gears are linked together in a train as shown. The driven gear turns

A. In the same direction as the driver

B. In a direction opposite that of the driver

C. First in the same direction, then in the opposite direction

D. First in the opposite direction, then the same direction

Answer: B. In a direction opposite that of the driver

Note that each gear in the train reverses direction. Therefore, there will be three direction changes in a four gear train. This will make the fourth, or the driven, gear turn in a direction opposite that of the driver.

136. **What type of gears is shown below?**

A. Spur

B. Bevel

C. Rack and pinion

D. Worm

Answer: B. Bevel

Notice that the two meshed gears turn at right angles to each other and that the teeth are cut on the slant of a cone.

137. **A system of gears reduces the output speed by one-third in relation to the input speed. The gear ratio is:**

A. $\frac{1}{3}$

B. 3

C. 9

D. 300

Answer: B. 3

Gear ratio is:

$$\frac{\text{rotational speed of driver}}{\text{rotational speed of driven gear}}$$

Since the output speed (the rotational speed of the driven gear) is one-third the input speed (the rotational speed of the driver), the driver turns three times as fast as the driven gear. So the gear ratio is 3.

138. **In the system of gears described in the previous question, the output torque is:**

A. Equal to the input torque

B. Three times the input torque

C. One-third the input torque

D. Not related to the input torque

Answer: B. Three times the input torque

$$\text{Gear ratio} = \frac{\text{output torque}}{\text{input torque}}$$

Since the gear ratio in the previous question is 3, the output torque must be three times the input torque.

139. **A bicycle pump is equipped with a valve the lets the air go into the tire but not out. What kind of valve is this?**

A. Shut-off valve

B. Snti-reversal valve

C. Throttling valve

D. None of the above

Answer: B. Anti-reversal valve

An anti-reversal valve allows fluid to flow in one direction only. Since the valve in the bicycle pump lets the air flow into the tire but not out, it is an anti-reversal valve.

140. **A man wants to measure the air pressure in his car tire. He will use a:**

A. Micrometer

B. Barometer

C. Pressure gauge

D. Spring balance

Answer: C. Pressure gauge

A pressure gauge is used to measure the pressure of an enclosed gas. A barometer also measures pressure, but it measures the air pressure in the atmosphere.

Electronics Information

141. **In an open circuit:**

    A. Current flows

    B. Current doesn't flow

    C. Current increases

    D. Current decreases

    Answer: B. Current docsn't flow

    In an open circuit, there is no path for electrons to travel from one terminal of the voltage source to the other, so current can't flow.

142. **Frequency is measured in a unit called:**

    A. RMS

    B. Amps

    C. Volts

    D. Hertz

    Answer: D. Hertz

    Frequency is measured in a unit called hertz. One hertz is one cycle per second.

143. **Root mean square can be used to calculate:**

    A. Current in a DC circuit

    B. Resistance in a DC circuit

    C. Current in an AC circuit

    D. Resistance in an AC circuit

Answer: C. Current in an AC circuit

Current in an AC circuit is measured using a complex calculation similar to an average, called root mean square, or RMS.

144. **According to Ohm's Law:**

    A. As current increases, voltage decreases.

    B. As current increases, resistance increases.

    C. As current increases, resistance decreases.

    D. As current increases, voltage and resistance decrease.

    Answer: C. As current increases, resistance decreases

    Current is indirectly proportional to resistance.

145. **A 120-volt AC circuit contains a light bulb rated at 60 watts. How much current does the light bulb draw?**

    A. 0.5 amps

    B. 2 amps

    C. 60 amps

    D. 120 amps

    Answer: A. 0.5 amps

    To find current, use the formula $I = \frac{P}{V}$. Substituting values,

    you get $I = \frac{60 \text{ watts}}{120 \text{ volts}}$, or $I = 0.5$ amps.

146. **Which of these would be the best insulator?**

A. Copper

B. Plastic

C. Silver

D. Tin

Answer: B. Plastic

Insulators contain few free electrons, inhibiting the flow of electricity. Typical insulators are made from rubber-like materials and plastics.

147. **Compared to a copper AWG 12 wire, a copper AWG 8 wire:**

A. Is more conductive

B. Is less conductive

C. Has a larger diameter

D. Has a smaller diameter

Answer: C. Has a larger diameter

In the AWG system, the larger the gauge number, the smaller the diameter of the wire.

148. **A typical capacitor contains:**

A. One charged plate

B. Two charged plates

C. Three charged plates

D. Four charged plates

Answer: B. Two charged plates

A capacitor contains two charged plates. The capacitor stores an electrical potential by collecting more electrons on one plate than on the other plate.

149. **Capacitance is measured in units called:**

A. Farads

B. Hertz

C. Henries

D. Ohms

Answer: A. Farads

Capacitance is the measure of a capacitor's ability to hold an electric charge. Capacitance is measured in units called farads.

150. **An inductor stores an electrical charge:**

A. Electrochemically

B. Electrostatically

C. Electromagnetically

D. Electromotively

Answer: C. Electromagnetically

An inductor stores a charge electromagnetically. It stores an electrical charge, or potential, as an electromagnetic field.

151. **The function of a diode is to:**

A. Rectify AC current to DC

B. Rectify DC current to AC

C. Allow current to flow in one direction

D. Allow current to flow in two directions

Answer: C. Allow current to flow in one direction

Although diodes can be used in conjunction with other components to convert AC current to DC, the function of a single diode is to allow current to pass in only one direction.

152. **What is the simplest switch that will turn a single light bulb on or off?**

    A. SPST

    B. DPST

    C. SPDT

    D. DPDT

    Answer: A. SPST

    A single light bulb only needs one circuit, so it requires one throw, and it only needs to be turned on and off, so it requires one pole. The simplest switch is a single pole, single throw switch, or SPST.

153. **To measure the current flow in a circuit, you could use:**

    A. An ammeter

    B. A wattmeter

    C. An ohmmeter

    D. A voltmeter

    Answer: A. an ammeter

    An ammeter is used to measure current, which is measured in amps.

154. **The following symbol represents:**

    A. A capacitor

    B. An inductor

    C. A resistor

    D. A switch

    Answer: C. A resistor

    This symbol represents a resistor. It is used in schematic circuit diagrams.

155. **The following symbol represents:**

    A. A resistor

    B. A switch

    C. A battery

    D. An inductor

    Answer: D. An inductor

    This symbol represents an inductor. It is used in schematic circuit diagrams.

156. **The following symbol represents:**

    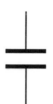

    A. A capacitor

    B. A switch

    C. A resistor

    D. An inductor

    Answer: A. A capacitor

    This symbol represents a capacitor. It is used in schematic circuit diagrams.

Shop Information

157. Which striking tool has a relatively large head, which is often made of wood or rubber?

A. Post sledge

B. Mallet

C. Sledge

D. Claw hammer

Answer: B. Mallet

Mallets are different from hammers in that they have a relatively large head. Mallet heads are often made from soft materials, such as rubber or wood, to avoid damaging the object struck.

158. What is the primary advantage of a ratcheting screwdriver?

A. The user can rotate the screwdriver in both directions without removing the tip from the screw head

B. The user can drive in a screw by using a motor

C. The user can effectively "reach around a corner" to drive a screw in a difficult location

D. The user can drive in a screw without stripping it

Answer: A. The user can rotate the screwdriver in both directions without removing the tip from the screw head

A ratcheting screwdriver allows the user to turn the screwdriver in both directions without removing the tip from the screw. It allows the user to rotate the screwdriver back and forth and continue to drive in the screw.

159. Which type of chisel is typically used on a wood lathe?

A. Butt chisel

B. Gouge

C. Carving chisel

D. Corner chisel

Answer: B. Gouge

The gouge's curved cutting surface works well against the spinning action of a lathe.

160. Which type of chisel is typically used to cut large joints into wood intended for framing?

A. Butt chisel

B. Carving chisel

C. Corner chisel

D. Skew chisel

Answer: A. Butt chisel

A butt chisel is used to cut large joints into wooden beams intended for use in framing.

161. Which wrench would be the best selection for a job where a number of bolts must be manipulated, but the sizes of the various bolts are not known beforehand?

A. Box-end wrench

B. Combination wrench

C. Adjustable wrench

D. Pipe wrench

Answer: C. Adjustable wrench

An adjustable wrench, sometimes called a Crescent wrench, allows the user to adjust the size of the wrench to fit the bolt head.

162. **Which of the following saws would be best used to cut through timber for firewood?**

    A. Crosscut saw

    B. Hacksaw

    C. Table saw

    D. Jigsaw

    Answer: A. Crosscut saw

    A crosscut saw is designed for making large cuts perpendicular to the grain and is an excellent choice for cutting timber into firewood. The other saws have specific purposes and wouldn't be good choices for cutting firewood.

163. **Laurel wants to cut some intricate scroll-work into a piece of mounting wood she is using for an art project. What type of saw should she use for this type of work?**

    A. Crosscut saw

    B. Hacksaw

    C. Circular saw

    D. Jigsaw

    Answer: D. Jigsaw

    The crosscut saw, the hacksaw, and the circular saw are all intended to be used to make large and/or straight cuts. They would be particularly unsuitable for fine scrollwork. The only valid choice is a jigsaw, which is also commonly called a scroll saw because of its suitability for this type of work.

164. **Which of the following is pictured below?**

    A. Bolt

    B. Washer

    C. Nut

    D. Wing nut

    Answer: C. Nut

    A nut is a fastener with a threaded hole. Most modern nuts are hexagonal.

165. **Jane needs to measure the thickness of a very small mechanical part. Which type of caliper should she use?**

    A. Vernier caliper

    B. Divider caliper

    C. Micrometer caliper

    D. Inside caliper

    Answer: C. Micrometer caliper

    A micrometer caliper uses a calibrated screw for measurement. It is used for highly accurate measurements of very small parts.

166. Joanne wants to quickly remove old and damaged paint and a thin layer of surface wood from an old hardwood deck. What type of sandpaper should she select?

    A. 360-600 grit silicon carbide paper

    B. 220-240 grit garnet paper

    C. 150-180 grit emery paper

    D. 40-60 grit aluminum oxide paper

    Answer: D. 40-60 grit aluminum oxide paper

    Joanne wants to strip off old, damaged paint and take off the damaged surface layer of an old hardwood deck. For best results, she should select coarse 40-60 grit sandpaper. Aluminum oxide sandpaper is common, inexpensive, and has good durability on wood surfaces.

167. Which of the following is <u>not</u> a benefit of using a primer coat before applying paint?

    A. Primers offer better surface adhesion

    B. Primers extend the life of paint

    C. Primers reduce the cost of painting

    D. Primers help mask dark underlayment

    Answer: C. Primers reduce the cost of painting

    Primers are not free—in fact, good primers are about as expensive as good paint. However, primers mask uneven or dark underlayment, offer better surface adhesion, and extend the life of paint applications. The benefits of using primers far outweigh the costs of using primers.

Auto Information

168. Which of these is a function of the piston rings?

    A. They control the flow of fuel into the combustion chamber

    B. They secure the piston to the connecting rod

    C. They keep the piston from tilting in the cylinder as it moves up and down

    D. They form a seal between the cylinder wall and the piston

    Answer: D. They form a seal between the cylinder wall and the piston

    Piston rings fill the gap between the piston and the cylinder wall, since the piston must be narrower than the cylinder. This forms a seal in the combustion chamber, but also seals out the oil in the engine, which lubricates the cylinder wall as the piston moves up and down.

169. What are the three main parts of a manual clutch?

    A. Pressure plate, clutch plate, throwout bearing

    B. Clutch pedal, main bearing, clutch plate

    C. Torque converter, clutch plate, throwout bearing

    D. Pressure plate, clutch plate, spider gears

Answer: A. Pressure plate, clutch plate, throwout bearing

The three main parts to a manual clutch are the pressure plate, clutch plate, and throwout bearing. The clutch pedal operates the clutch, but is not considered part of the clutch, so answer B is incorrect. Torque converters are used in automatic transmissions, and replace a clutch, so answer C is incorrect. Spider gears are found in a differential, not a clutch, so answer D is incorrect.

170. **The engine does not start. The lights turn on brightly, but the engine will not turn over. Which of these is the most probable cause?**

    A. The battery is dead

    B. The exhaust system is clogged, preventing exhaust gases from exiting the engine.

    C. The starter motor is faulty

    D. The fuel lines are clogged, and the engine is not getting fuel

Answer: C. The starter motor is faulty

The lights turn on brightly, so you know the battery isn't dead because the battery provides electricity to the car while it's not running, so answer choice A isn't the correct answer. The explanations in answer choices B and D wouldn't cause the engine to not start. Since the function of the starter motor is to turn the engine, it's the most likely cause of the failure, so answer choice C is the correct answer.

171. **Blown fuses in a car should always be replaced with fuses that have same amp rating or lower. Why?**

    A. Higher amp fuses will not allow enough current to flow, and may stop electronic accessories from working

    B. Higher amp fuses will allow too much current to flow, heating wires and creating a fire hazard

    C. Higher amp fuses will allow too much current to flow, causing headlights and other lights to be too bright and creating a driving hazard

    D. Higher amp fuses will be a different color than the diagram in the car, making future replacement difficult

Answer: B. Higher amp fuses will allow too much current to flow, heating wires and creating a fire hazard

When circuits have too much current, the wires heat up. This heating can cause a fire hazard.

172. **Why should you never remove a radiator cap while the engine is running?**

    A. The coolant will cool too quickly and damage the engine

    B. Oil and coolant can mix while the engine is running

    C. The cooling system is under pressure, and you could get sprayed with hot fluid

    D. You will introduce air into the system

Answer: C. The cooling system is under pressure, and you could get sprayed with hot fluid.

Cooling systems are under pressure and run at temperatures over boiling, so depressurizing the system by taking the cap off may cause the coolant to spontaneously boil or steam, creating a burn hazard.

173. The thermostat controls the flow of coolant through the radiator. Where is it generally located?

   A. In the radiator

   B. On the water pump

   C. As part of the fan circuit

   D. On the engine block

Answer: D. On the engine block

Thermostats are bi-metal mechanical valves that work much like a household thermostat. They are typically located on the engine block, near either the inlet or outlet hose on the radiator.

174. When antilock brakes are active, the brake pedal can sometimes seem to be vibrating or pulsing. Why is this?

   A. The brake rotors are warped and vibrating during hard braking

   B. Valves are opening and closing, causing momentary fluctuations in the fluid pressure in the braking system

   C. The wheels are alternately locking and releasing, sending vibrations to the pedal, which are being transmitted by the hydraulic brake fluid

   D. This is only felt in hybrid vehicles, and is a result of the energy recapturing systems in the brake mechanisms

Answer: B. Valves are opening and closing, causing momentary fluctuations in the fluid pressure in the braking system

Antilock braking systems have sensors at each wheel that alert the car if a wheel locks up, and briefly release the break to the locked wheel, usually by opening a valve. Warped rotors would cause vibrations all the time, not just in emergency situations, so answer A is incorrect. Any vibration or shaking from the wheels would be felt in the steering, not in the brakes, so answer C is incorrect. Answer D is incorrect because this is felt in most antilock systems. Energy recovery systems in hybrids do not produce any vibration.

175. During brake application, the brake pedal is suddenly depressed to the floor. The brakes are still stopping the car, but just barely. What is the most likely problem?

   A. A brake line has failed and the system lost pressure

   B. A leak opened up and sucked air into the system

   C. The brake pads slipped, and holding the brakes down while backing up will correct the problem

   D. The master cylinder has failed

Answer: A. A brake line has failed and the system lost pressure

Some braking power may remain if a single brake line fails, since the other three will still have pressure.

176. **A Check Engine light has come on after fueling. There are no noticeable problems with the running of the engine or transmission. What is the most probable cause?**

A. The wrong grade of gasoline was put in (lower or higher octane rating than is called for in the owner's manual)

B. There is excess water in the gas

C. The fuel cap was not properly tightened

D. The engine sensor is faulty

Answer: C. The fuel cap was not properly tightened

Evaporative emission systems on modern cars capture evaporation from the fuel tank. The fuel cap is an integral part of this system, and failure to tighten it can result in a Check Engine light. This is a very common problem, and should be the first thing checked if the light comes on shortly after fueling.

177. **Why should suspension components like struts and shock absorbers be replaced in pairs?**

A. Suspension components wear at similar rates, so if one side has failed, the other is probably worn and close to failing as well

B. Replacing just one side may make the vehicle sit at an odd angle, which will affect ride comfort

C. Having a strong suspension on one side and a weak one on the other may create conditions where the vehicle is unstable in emergency situations and lead to an accident

D. All of the above

Answer: D. All of the above

The entire weight of the vehicle rests on the suspension. Suspension components are designed to optimize vehicle stability and performance. Having one corner of the vehicle sag due to worn parts will alter the geometry of the vehicle and impact vehicle performance and safety.

178. **In a motor oil grade:**

A. The lower the number, the thicker the oil

B. The higher the number, the thicker the oil

C. The lower the number, the smaller the engine size

D. The higher the number, the smaller the engine size

Answer: B. The higher the number, the thicker the oil

Oil viscosity is designated with grades such as 10W30 or 5W30. The higher the number, the thicker the oil.

Assembling Objects

For each pair of labeled shapes in questions 179 to 188, choose the figure that shows the shapes connected correctly.

179.

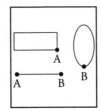

A.

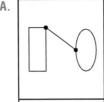

Answer: C

180.

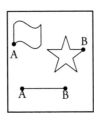

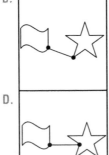

Answer: A

181.

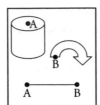

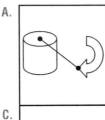

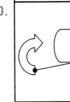

Answer: B

182.

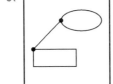

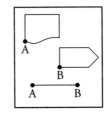

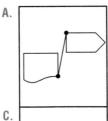

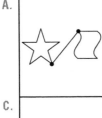

Answer: D

183.

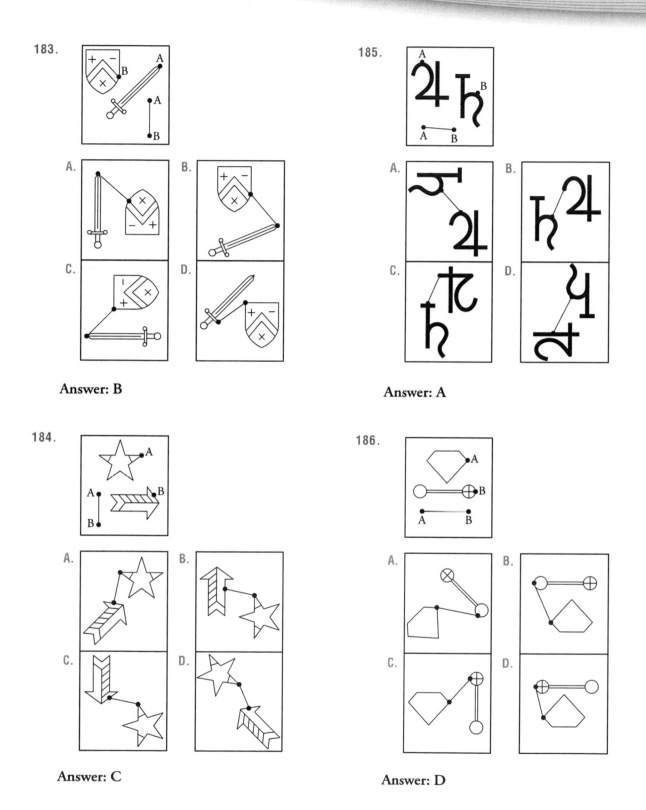

Answer: B

184.

Answer: C

185.

Answer: A

186.

Answer: D

187.

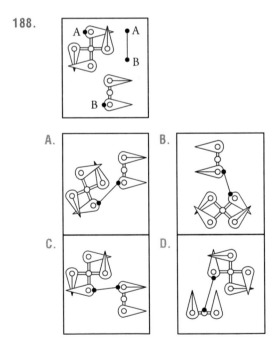

Answer: D

188.

Answer: A

For each set of shapes in questions 189 to 200, choose the figure that shows the shapes assembled into an object.

189.

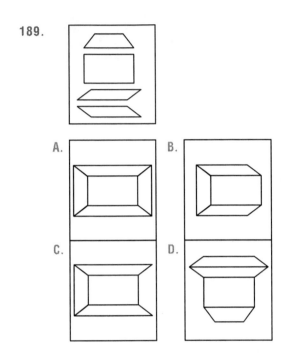

Answer: B

190.

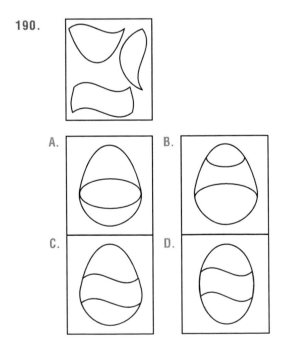

Answer: C

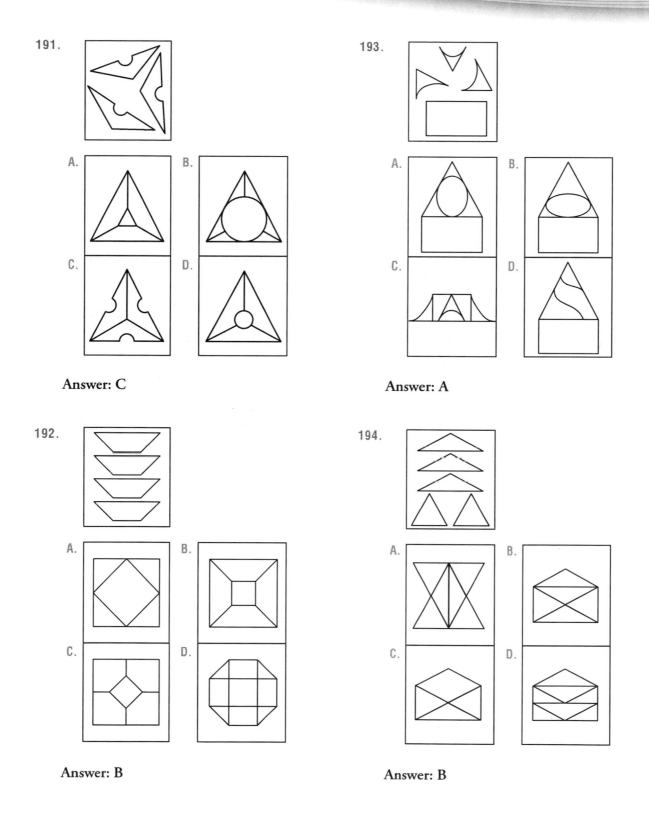

191.

A. B.
C. D.

Answer: C

192.

A. B.
C. D.

Answer: B

193.

A. B.
C. D.

Answer: A

194.

A. B.
C. D.

Answer: B

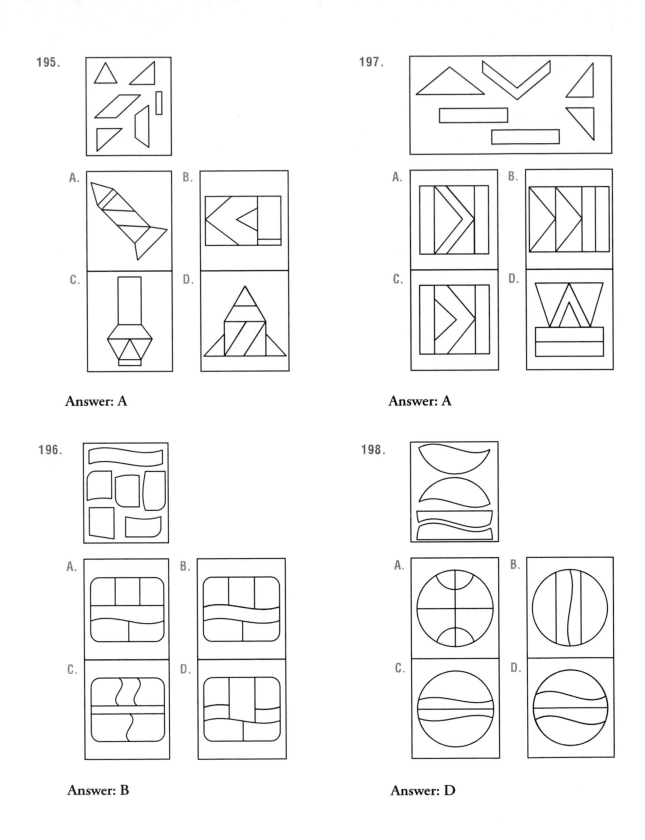

195.

A. B. C. D.

Answer: A

196.

A. B. C. D.

Answer: B

197.

A. B. C. D.

Answer: A

198.

A. B. C. D.

Answer: D

199.

Answer: B

200.

Answer: D

Armed
Services
Vocational
Aptitude
Battery

XAMonline.com

TOTAL PREPARATION
500
Flashcards

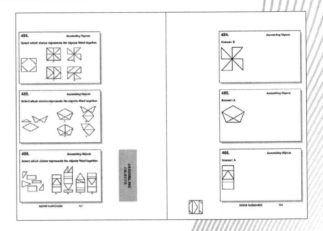

The 500 flashcards can be cut out and carried around as a deck or left in the book as is. One side of each page contains boxed questions and the other side contains boxed answers so you can test yourself and flip quickly to the answers to check your knowledge. These flashcards covers the ten content categories found on the ASVAB exam:

- *Word Knowledge*
- *Paragraph Comprehension*
- *Arithmetic Reasoning*
- *Mathematics Knowledge*
- *General Science*

- *Mechanical Comprehension*
- *Electronics Information*
- *Shop Information*
- *Automotive Information*
- *Assembling Objects*

How to order

ASVABexamStudyGuide.com

Join XAM on

CPSIA information can be obtained at www.ICGtesting.com
Printed in the USA
LVOW031945050612

284783LV00004B/37/P